*The Tragic Tale of Claire Ferchaud
and the Great War*

The Tragic Tale of Claire Ferchaud and the Great War

Raymond Jonas

UNIVERSITY OF CALIFORNIA PRESS

Berkeley   Los Angeles   London

University of California Press
Berkeley and Los Angeles, California

University of California Press, Ltd.
London, England

©2005 by the Regents of the University of California

Unless otherwise noted, photos and illustrations are from the
author's collection.

Library of Congress Cataloging-in-Publication Data

Jonas, Raymond Anthony.
  The tragic tale of Claire Ferchaud and the Great War /
Raymond Jonas.
       p.   cm.
  Includes bibliographical references and index.
    ISBN 0-520-24297-1 (hardcover : alk. paper) —
ISBN 0-520-24299-8 (pbk. : alk. paper)
    1. Ferchaud, Claire, 1896–1972.   2. World War, 1914–1918—
Religious aspects—Catholic Church.   3. Sacred Heart, Devotion
to—France—History of doctrines—20th century.   I. Title.
BX4705.F37J66   2005
D282'.092—dc22   2004006614

Manufactured in the United States of America

13   12   11   10   09   08   07   06   05
10   9   8   7   6   5   4   3   2   1

The paper used in this publication meets the minimum
requirements of ANSI/NISO Z39.48–1992 (R 1997)
(Permanence of Paper).

For Anthony, Elizabeth, and Katherine

I felt my throat gripped by the terrible hand of hysteria; my sight was dazzled by rebellious tears that refused to fall.

Charles Baudelaire, "Le vieux saltimbanque," 1867

The ideal of unmediated reporting is regularly achieved only in fiction, where the writer faithfully reports on what is going on in his imagination.

Janet Malcolm, The Silent Woman, *1995*

CONTENTS

ILLUSTRATIONS

MAPS

FIGURES

ACKNOWLEDGMENTS

The Tragic Tale of Claire Ferchaud has benefited from collegial commentary in a number of congenial settings. I'd like to acknowledge in particular Steven Kaplan and the participants in the French Studies Colloquium at Cornell University, Kathleen Woodward and the Society of Scholars at the Walter Chapin Simpson Center for the Humanities at the University of Washington, and J. P. Daughton and the members of the Stanford French Culture Workshop. I wish that I could acknowledge each participant individually.

Jean-Clément Martin provided critical early support and encouragement over a memorable lunch in Nantes. Nancy Wood, Judith Stone, and Tom Kselman offered valuable insights and suggestions. Patricia Jonas listened patiently as I struggled to get the story right.

Research funding was provided by a Fulbright Senior Scholar award, the Howard and Frances Keller Fund of the Department of History at the University of Washington, and the Center for West European Studies at the University of Washington. Technical support was provided by the staff of CARTAH—the Center for Advanced Research and Teaching in the Arts and Humanities at the University of Washington.

Dore Brown expertly guided this project through completion at the University of California Press. Charles Dibble—copyeditor extraordinaire—untangled prose, flagged errors, and fixed inelegant phrasing. Finally, I'd like to acknowledge my friends at Festyland Productions—Anthony, Elizabeth, and Katherine—visionaries all. This work is dedicated to them.

The Great War in the European Imagination

Claire Ferchaud was born in the west of France at a place called Rinfillières. The date was 5 May 1896. The same day, Claire's parents dressed her in a white christening gown and took her to the church at Le Puy-Saint-Bonnet, where she was christened Claire-Yvonne-Marie-Louise. There was nothing particularly auspicious about Claire's birth or early youth, but her modest origins made her improbable ascent only more spectacular. By the end of 1916, in the midst of the First World War, Claire's admirers compared her to Joan of Arc, the young woman who heard voices, put on men's clothing, fought for France, and crowned a king.

Claire's visions made her a regional—then national—celebrity as she promised speedy victory for France. In December of 1916, Claire was summoned to Poitiers, just as Joan had been in 1429, to account for herself before a learned body of powerful men of the Catholic Church. Although separated by five centuries, both women, Joan and Claire, impressed the men of Poitiers with their confidence and resolve, and both went on to perform prodigious feats. After Poitiers, Joan sought an audience with Charles, the dauphin, the pretender to the throne. She gained Charles's confidence, commanded his armies against an invading occupier, and saw him crowned king of France. As for Claire, after Poitiers her message and her notoriety took her to Paris and the Elysée

1

Palace in March 1917. In a private audience Claire stood face to face with Raymond Poincaré, president of the French Republic. Victory was within reach, she announced. The invading armies could be driven out—provided that he, the president, listen to her and have the courage to risk public ridicule and do as she instructed.

This book is about how Claire Ferchaud came to stand in front of the president of the French Republic at the height of the crisis of the Great War. It is about the forces—people, traditions, memories—that drove her mission, and about Claire's skillful use of those forces. After all, gaining the ear of the president was something for which even powerful and wealthy men had to jockey and jostle. A peasant woman hadn't a chance unless she had a keen sense of purpose and a subtle grasp of how something as improbable as a simple message from an inspired woman could offer a way out of an interminable war.

Claire's is a story of skill and insight. It is also a story of a transcendent vision of how a terrible war might end in victory and salvation. Millenarians, evangelists, visionaries, and revolutionaries talk about transcendence. To transcend means to rise above or move beyond in a qualitative sense; it implies a vision of the future. There was no shortage of transcendent vision during the war and in the years leading up to it, and Claire's was by no means the least compelling. But whose vision of transcendence would prevail? Modern war is often about the past—its defects and failures—but also about the future. War would transform Europe: on this many Europeans could agree; it was the nature of the transformation that left Europeans in disagreement.

For Claire Ferchaud and her supporters, war would bring a kind of millenarian spiritual triumph. But many others also saw war as a passage to a qualitatively different future. In fact, during the years before the outbreak of war in 1914, many Europeans imagined war as a kind of "creative destruction"—a process that would be painful, to be sure, but would ultimately yield a better tomorrow. For partisans of a cultural movement called futurism, the destructive force of war could, paradoxically, have a constructive, bracing effect on civilization. The

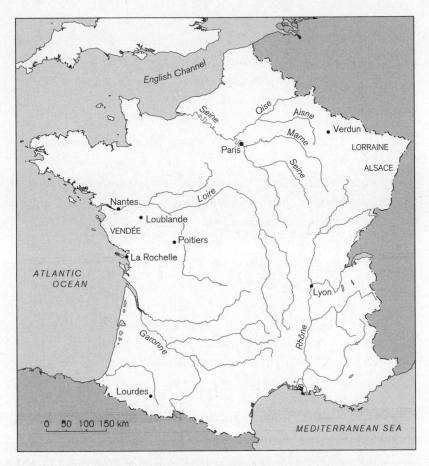

Map 1.   France: Key locations in the stories of Claire Ferchaud and the Great War. (Adapted from original by Anthony Jonas)

new technologies of transportation (the automobile and the airplane) and wireless communication (radio) had accelerated the pace of change. However, the futurists argued, an excessive reverence for the past held progress back, leading to stagnation and the perpetuation of worn-out ideas and ways of thinking. Filippo Marinetti, a leading futurist, compared museums to cemeteries and famously called war "the only hygiene of the world" precisely because of its power to destroy.[1]

Only from the perspective of the gaiety and self-indulgence of the Belle Époque could one think of war as "hygienic." Among other things, futurism was a masculinist worldview that celebrated the "male" virtues of boldness, danger, and violence. Giovanni Boine called war an antidote for "the torpor of the ego." For those convinced that the pleasures of the Belle Époque had yielded an enervated, "feminized" European male, war was a necessary masculinizing tonic. Of course, it was anything but. Four years of war meant death for millions of European men and debilitating mutilation for millions more. War was not the transcendent regenerative experience predicted by futurism; rather, it was a link between the "demasculinized" and "effeminate" Belle Époque imagined by the futurists and the scarred, shattered, and mutilated bodies of male veterans left in its wake.[2]

In the socialist imagination, war could bring transcendence, too. European socialists—for whom politics was, in the final analysis, reducible to class interests—viewed war as the pursuit of capitalist interests by other means. Workers and peasants had no interest in responding to the call to arms, which merely masked class interests with patriotic appeals. Socialists urged them to greet any declaration of war with revolution. In fact, some socialists believed that war just might be the catalyst for the working-class revolution Karl Marx had predicted a half century earlier. War would reveal the political and moral bankruptcy of capitalism. It could even be seen as a symptom of the degenerate state of an exhausted "late capitalism." It would be the passageway by which socialism would transcend the historically circumscribed capitalist moment, leading to a future in which the socialist vision of social and economic equality was made real.

Vladimir Lenin, who would lead a branch of Russian socialists to power in 1917, articulated the most complete analysis of the war in terms of Marxist theory, linking the war with European expansion and empire.[3] One of the characteristic features of the 1880s and 1890s had been the headlong rush of European powers into Africa and Asia in pursuit of empire. For Lenin, European empire was essentially a struggle for resources and markets. Given the finite nature of resources and markets, and capitalism's insatiable appetite, conflict—war—was inevitable. The European scramble for empire had set in motion tensions, conflict, and war, and it would culminate, finally, in socialist revolution. Indeed, Lenin was among the first to argue that what is now called "globalization" was not only a sign of capitalism's triumph but also a signal that capitalism had exhausted the avenues of expansion upon which it depended. What would follow was bankruptcy and collapse—what he called "moribund capitalism." War, therefore, should be understood not as the result of failed diplomacy but as a symptom of systemic and fatal crisis in capitalism. Socialists, he argued, should recognize these symptoms for what they were and prepare for the transcendent socialist revolution that the crisis of war would inevitably bring.

For Kaiser Wilhelm II and the war office of Imperial Germany, victory in war would bring another kind of transcendence. It would mark the arrival of Germany as a Great Power. Unified barely a generation earlier, Imperial Germany was still groping for the boundaries of power that unity had brought. Germany's place in the middle of the European continent had long inspired a sense of vulnerability, notably during the Napoleonic Wars. With the minor states of Germany brought together in a unified Reich in 1870, a sense of vulnerability had given way to a sense of destiny. If Germany possessed the will, the future of Europe could be German.

According to contemporary geostrategic thinking, the future belonged to Great Powers: nations that could organize and control large continental land masses. The United States was a classic example; Japan and China were clear candidates for similar status. Britain, though an island nation of limited territorial extent, nevertheless possessed a strong navy and had amassed an empire to go with it; through these it could justly lay claim to Great Power status.[4]

The situation on the European continent was less clear. At the end of the eighteenth century, at the time of the French Revolution, France had dominated continental Europe, both in ambition and in population. Napoleon triumphed, in part, because the Revolution of 1789 had mobilized the total resources of the nation—utilizing mass conscription, propaganda, requisitioning of food and other essentials—in what may be regarded as the first example of "total war." But French influence had waned over the course of the nineteenth century, as had once-mighty Spain's in the seventeenth century. According to new strategic thinking, Germany's defeat of France in 1870–71 had substantially weakened France's claim to Great Power status, perhaps irretrievably, leaving the field to others. Now, in a new era of total war, the initiative had shifted eastward. Political unity, accompanied by decades of rapid industrial growth, made Germany the power to watch. By sheer demographic weight, however, Russia seemed to possess potential as unlimited as its land and buried resources. No one could say for sure which power, Russia or Germany, would ultimately prevail. The future of continental Europe seemed to depend on whether one trusted in German dynamism or Russian scale.

The very indeterminacy and openness of that future created a sense of urgency, especially within imperial Germany. If Europe's future indeed lay in the dominance of a single power—Germany or Russia—it would be wise for Germany to take action before Russia, the sleeping giant, had the opportunity to mobilize its vast Eurasian resources. The notion of a rapidly closing window of opportunity for Germany had a great deal to do with the outbreak of war in 1914. It was sustained culturally by the popularity of Darwinian ideas adapted to human society, often with racial overtones. If struggle was characteristic of the state of nature, no less for humans than for animals, then nations and races, too, must struggle to seize and actively shape their future; the alternative was to see their future shaped for them by others. Germany, if it was to assure its place among the Great Powers, must seize the moment and establish its vision of *Mitteleuropa*—a German-dominated central Europe—before Russian resources and numbers could affect the strategic outcome. Delay, and Germany would become yet another victim in the unrelenting Darwinian struggle among nations, its hesitation on the threshold of greatness serving as *prima facie* evidence of its unfitness for rule.

Thus when Serbian nationalists assassinated Austrian archduke Francis Ferdinand and his wife at Sarajevo on 28 June 1914, the tragedy was mitigated by some intriguing possibilities. Was this the "showdown" opportunity? Could an assassination be turned into a justification for war? The act brought to a head long-standing tensions between Austria and Serbia concerning Austria's dominant status in southeastern Europe. The assassins were put on trial and convicted, but Austria issued a twelve-point ultimatum to Serbia, a bullying gesture that in effect held the Serbian people collectively responsible for the acts of the assassins. The ultimatum also brought into conflict Russian and German/Austrian interests. Russia had been using pan-Slavism, an ideology that presumed to encompass the interests of all Slavic peoples, to advance Russian interests in the Balkans. Russian support for Slavic Serbia against Austria's intimidation would be a test of pan-Slavism. It was a test the Russians were loath to fail.

For Germany, allied to Austria, the Serbian crisis presented some interesting challenges and opportunities. In choosing to support Austria resolutely against Serbia and its Russian backer, Germany had effectively reconciled itself to either of two outcomes. The first, a Russian backdown, would represent a defeat for pan-Slavism and its Russian patron; it would also be a diplomatic triumph for Germany. The second outcome, of course, was war. This was militarism: the willingness not just to contemplate war but to use it—calmly, deliberately, dispassionately—as an instrument of foreign policy and national ambition. A gross miscalculation about what it might actually cost made war easier to contemplate in August 1914.

The tragic tale of Claire Ferchaud is a tale of transcendence. Claire was a modest person. She didn't have the power of a German chancellor, the eloquence of a socialist orator, or the élan of a futurist intellectual, but she did offer a compelling vision that drew thousands of supporters in France and abroad. In fact, her weakness was part of her strength, part of the persona she projected as a simple girl with a powerful message. That message corresponded to a deeply felt sense of loss at the rupture of an imagined European Christian unity. Schism, pluralism, and secularization—some of the great themes of European history as it moved from medieval to modern times—left Europe in the early twentieth century divided: by faith, by nation, and by disagreements about the proper place of religion in public life. Claire's vision offered reintegration. It responded to nostalgia for an age when for many, "Europe" was synonymous with "Christendom." Unlike the futurists, the socialists, or European geostrategists, Claire's future was embedded in an imagined organic past.

Miracle or "Miracle"?

❧✦❧

The opening of the war of 1914 seemed at first to be startlingly simple. It was common knowledge that if war broke out again between Germany and France, France would seek to recover the territories of Alsace and Lorraine lost in 1871. Accordingly, and predictably, during the first week, French troops entered territory annexed by Germany at the end of the last war. They encountered resistance in Alsace from the German Sixth and Seventh Armies but reached and reoccupied Mulhouse between 8 and 10 August. They then lost the city and retook it on the nineteenth, before losing it again. Similar engagements took place in Lorraine and the Ardennes, with similarly modest yet respectable results. Joseph Joffre, commander in chief of French forces in the northeast, was not yet aware that the main action was elsewhere, near Liège, where twelve corps under the command of Alexander von Kluck and Karl von Bülow were preparing to move into France by way of the Belgian cities of Dinant and Charleroi.[1]

Soon it appeared that the war of 1914 would turn into a replay of the disaster of 1870, with German troops rapidly reaching and encircling the French capital. Unable to halt the German advance pouring in from Belgium, Allied forces retreated, giving up land in order to buy time. In a vast movement hinged at Verdun, British and French troops drew back to the river Marne, which traced a line, roughly, from Verdun in the east to the city of Paris. This movement put the German right flank at Meaux, within a hundred kilometers of Paris. Soldiers bound for a battle *that* close to the city might just as well go by cab—hence, the celebrated "taxis of the Marne" as Parisian taxis shuttled soldiers and munitions to the front.[2] A desperate defense of Paris was to be mounted against the German right flank at the rivers Marne, Ourcq, and Oise.[3]

Parisians, some of whom were old enough to remember the German encirclement and siege of Paris in 1870–71, sought to get out of harm's way. The ability to do so was largely a function of wealth. Taxis being in short supply, a ride to Orléans might cost a thousand francs—Normandy, as much as three times that. Trains were few and jammed.[4] One way or another, half a million Parisians fled the city.[5] So did the government. While some legislators had already departed for the front as soldiers (three of them died in combat in the opening weeks of the war), the National Assembly as a body adjourned as of 4 August and later relocated in the southwest.[6] Matters of state would be directed from Bordeaux. Only when Paris was secure would the government and the assembly return.

On Montmartre, a different kind of assembly was taking place in early September. With the sound of artillery fire audible in the capital, anxious and fearful citizens gathered in prayer. Men, women, and children participated in round-the-clock prayer vigils. Some sought the intercession of the city's patron saint, the shepherdess Geneviève, who had saved Paris from Attila's rampaging Huns in the fifth century.[7] Others made their way to the Basilica of the Sacré-Coeur on Montmartre to invoke the protection of the Sacred Heart. Persuaded that relentless ardent prayer would bend divine will, clusters of volunteers knelt to offer prayers in salvos. While some took their turns at prayer, others gathered provisions, manned kitchens, or served in improvised mess halls. Cots arrayed in nearby buildings allowed volunteers to catch up on sleep between stints of prayerful entreaty. As volunteers shuffled off to these bivouacs—spent after launching volleys of

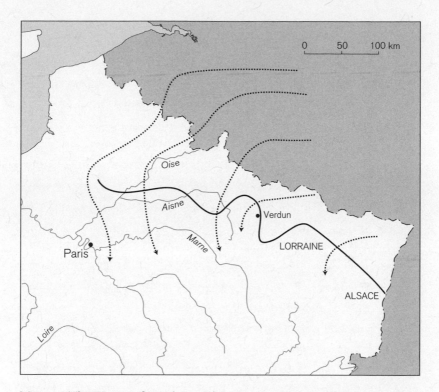

Map 2. The Western front during the opening campaign of the war.
The approximate paths of the German advance are marked with dotted
lines; the approximate location of the Western front after the failure of the
initial German advance is marked with a solid line. (Adapted from original
by Anthony Jonas)

prayer—fresh reserves moved up to take their places on the kneelers in
an uninterrupted cycle of rest, prayer, and patriotic supplication.

As they prayed, the German offensive stalled. On 10 September, von
Kluck's right flank—exhausted and dangerously overextended—
halted just east of Paris. An Allied counterattack to the north behind
von Kluck would threaten the lines of communication of all German
forces involved in the offensive. General Helmuth von Moltke gave the
order to retreat to a more defensible position. The Allies gave weak
pursuit through the seventeenth of the month. Paris, whose capitulation

had seemed imminent, had been spared. For French republicans sensitive to historical precedent, the Marne was like Valmy, where the French Revolution had been saved—surprisingly, "miraculously," fittingly—from an invading army bent on its defeat in 1792.[8] From a resolutely secular republican point of view, the "miracle of the Marne" in September 1914 was a similar, metaphorical "miracle."

For many Catholics, however, the miracle of the Marne was not hyperbole expressed as sacred metaphor. It simply was a miracle. The prayers at Montmartre and elsewhere had not stopped the German advance alone, it was argued, but they *had* made the difference. These prayers, for some, had showed that France still knew how to pray, that France, despite secularization and de-Christianization—despite everything—still merited divine intervention as the "eldest daughter" of the church. The fact that Montmartre had served as the citadel of prayer during the hours of national crisis showed that France's victory and redemption would come under the sign of the Sacred Heart of Jesus. "Sacred Union" no longer meant what it had when Raymond Poincaré first employed the term a month earlier.[9] Instead, the aim of the war became not only victory over Germany but also victory over despair and irreligion—in short, the triumph of Christian France.

By early 1915 the story of the miracle of the Marne and its broader significance for Catholic war aims was already fully integrated with Catholic commentary on the war. In newspapers, prayers, songs, and diocesan bulletins, a consistent and coherent message went out. The miraculous interpretation of the battle of the Marne traveled fastest by sermons and word of mouth. In April 1915, the pastor of Saint-Gervais, a small parish north of Poitiers, wrote of France's divine favor in his journal; he also cited an article in the diocesan bulletin of Poitiers, an article confirming rumors of the direct intervention of the Sacred Heart in the miracle of the Marne.[10] It became the topic of Sunday sermons. A month earlier, Gabriel Blanc, a priest from Digne, had embarked on a lecture tour of provincial cities, speaking on the theme of the Sacred Heart and of transcendent national redemption through war.

The Marne, according to Blanc, showed that God wished not to destroy France but only to test and purify the nation. That is why God allowed the German advance to proceed as far as it did, and that is why God stopped the advance when he wished. France's close call at the Marne meant that now no one was afraid to talk about France's failures and faults. It followed that no one now feared to talk about France's need to invoke divine pardon and divine aid.[11]

By April 1915, the Catholic national press was developing these themes vigorously. *La Croix* drove home its argument about Catholic patriotism as authentic patriotism in an editorial addressed directly to France's political leadership. "We invite you to look heavenward . . . and to remember that God rules the world." After recognizing that soldiers, commanders, and weapons deserved some of the credit, *La Croix* asserted that the difference at the Marne was made by "we Catholics, who, during the critical hours when Paris was fleeing, prayed to the Sacred Heart, Saint Geneviève, and Jeanne d'Arc."[12] The illustrated Catholic weekly *Le Pèlerin* featured an article on heavenly interventions in favor of France. Not wanting misinformation to prevail, *Le Pèlerin* sought to clear up certain misconceptions about what had actually happened at the Marne and in Paris. First of all, it dismissed mere coincidence: 4 September 1915, the turning point in the opening battle of the war, was not just any day; it was a Friday, a First Friday, thus "consecrated to the Sacred Heart."

Second was the decisive role of the crowd in Paris, whose prayerful intervention moved armies on the battlefield. For "while a crowd of worshipers crowded into the Basilica of the National Vow [the Sacré-Coeur de Montmartre], von Kluck's army, which was only a day or two from Paris, moved away and toward the east." This social history of the Parisian population at war continued with a description of public prayers at Montmartre and in the Church of Saint-Étienne du Mont until 8 September, when victory was assured.[13]

Le Pèlerin's reporting of the miracle of the Marne showed how prayer had transformed fear and despair into valor and victory.

And although *Le Pèlerin* was not an official publication of the Catholic Church in France, the story carried a kind of imprimatur. The author of the pamphlet from which the weekly's feature was excerpted was Monsignor Odelin, chief of staff *(vicaire général)* to Cardinal Amette, archbishop of Paris. This left little doubt that this view of the Marne, the war, and its place in French public life had approval and support within the highest reaches of the Catholic hierarchy in France. The pamphlet was vigorously promoted, not only by the major national Catholic daily *(La Croix)* and newsweekly *(Le Pèlerin),* but also in diocesan publications. For the Catholic clergy and hierarchy in France, the miracle of the Marne defined the war as a transcendent moment. The war was about defeating Germany, to be sure, but its deeper meaning was religious; it would initiate France's reconciliation with God. The war would have to be won on the home front, soul by soul, before it could be won in the trenches. In some ways, this was a distinctly modern message: that wars were won in hearts and minds as much as on the battlefield. It was a message that Claire Ferchaud and her visions would carry forward.

Carnal Vision
and Saintly Ambition

❧

The French West, like the American West in the late nineteenth century, was long known for its expanses of land and its scattered population. The area south of the Loire River—comprising the regions of la Vendée, la Vienne, and les Deux-Sèvres—has a distinctive topography of rolling hills, narrow roads, and high hedgerows that fence in fields, livestock, and farms. For some, particularly those who had never lived there, the impenetrability of the landscape and the isolation of its inhabitants described the region's population—insular, backward, and out-of-touch.

In fact, the proximity of the Atlantic seaboard and the great port cities of Nantes and, further south, La Rochelle brought these people and their lands into markets that were global in scope. Nantes and its hinterland prospered from Atlantic trade, including the slave trade, well into the eighteenth century, until the civil wars that followed in the wake of the Revolution of 1789 and the abolition of the slave trade shattered its economy. The people of Cholet, a regional market town some sixty kilometers from Nantes, wove canvas for the sails that caught the wind and pulled ships across the water from Europe to Africa, and the Americas. In short, the French West concealed the global reach of its merchants and markets behind a mask of timelessness and impenetrability.

Figure 1.   The Ferchaud farmhouse at Rinfillières

Claire was born not far from Cholet, at a place called Rinfillières—a property midway between Loublande and Le Puy-Saint-Bonnet, villages that were little more than way stations on the road between Poitiers and Nantes. Farmers in the region cultivated crops for food and feed. Many farmers committed land to pasture for cattle and dairy or, less often, for vineyards. The best was often reserved for cultivating a variety of grape that yielded Muscadet; on soil of lesser quality, vintners might produce Gros Plant (literally, "big plant")—a white wine with a greenish hue and a pronounced bite, hard on the palate and fit only for local consumption.

Like most of their neighbors, Claire's parents were farmers, producing grain and feed for the market. Rinfillières, the farm, did not belong to Claire's parents: it was owned by Baron d'Argenton. As sharecroppers, the Ferchaud family grew wheat and raised sheep to satisfy the terms of the landlord's contract; they also farmed for subsistence, to support themselves. Sharecropping defined an ongoing relationship organized around land owned by one party and farmed by another. The security of sharecroppers can be precarious; a family might be asked to move on at the expiration of its contract. However, the Ferchauds' occupancy of Rinfillières was of such long standing (Claire's grandparents had also farmed it) that the Ferchauds likely felt secure in it.[1] Even so, deference to one's "betters"—defined, in part, by land ownership—was part of the culture of sharecropping. In the arid language of social scientists, sharecropping underpins strong patron/client relationships. Relations of dependency not only determined how the land was used but also shaped a set of less tangible behaviors—politics, religious practice, social and marriage partnerships. As long as the landlord was a present and watchful figure in local life, as was commonly the case throughout the Choletais, remaining in the landowner's good graces was a constant preoccupation.

Family strategies were closely intertwined with economic strategies. Peasant farmers, especially sharecroppers like the Ferchauds, often had large families because they ensured plentiful labor, spread risk, and provided companionship and solace through a lifetime of hard work. Claire had five siblings, two sisters and three brothers. As soon as she was old enough to work, she did. The young girl's main responsibility was to tend the family's sheep and goats. It was an activity that offered few distractions and left plenty of time for meditation and reflection.

TRAUMA AND SPIRITUAL POWER

Claire's visionary powers dated from her earliest recollections. She was little more than a toddler when, at three, she challenged her mother's authority and found solace in a vision of Jesus.

The occasion was a family visit. A young cousin, a boy, arrived at the farm at Rinfillières. Claire's mother called her to greet and kiss her cousin. Claire refused. Madame Ferchaud, seeking to cure her daughter of her indiscipline and willfulness, ordered Claire to kiss the earth. Rather than kiss her cousin, Claire took her mother at her word, dropping to the ground and touching her lips to the earth. Enraged and humiliated by her daughter's insolence, Madame Ferchaud took Claire to the wine cellar, pushed her inside, closed the door, and locked it.

Half an hour later, Madame Ferchaud returned. She unlocked the cellar. Claire was free to go, but her mother wanted proof of Claire's reformed spirit. She brought Claire to her cousin; again she demanded that Claire kiss him. However, Claire had emerged unbroken from her ordeal. She refused.

Madame Ferchaud was now locked with her daughter in an escalating struggle of wills. She whipped Claire in anger and frustration and returned her, sobbing, to the dark and damp cellar. But Claire's investment in her struggle had deepened too. She felt trapped by her stubbornness and pride but she refused to submit to her mother's will. This "violent combat," as she called it, exhausted her. Her gasping sobs quieted. She grew still in the darkness of the wine cellar; then she drifted off to sleep.

Upon awakening, she was no longer alone. Jesus was beside her, rousing her from her sleep. Claire had seen Jesus before; indeed, they were already on familiar terms. So when Claire saw Jesus, she rose and tried to throw her arms around his neck. Jesus rebuffed her.[2] He was in tears. When Claire asked Jesus why he was crying, Jesus expressed surprise. "What?" Jesus asked Claire. "You ask why I cry?" Then Jesus opened his cloak to Claire and showed Claire his heart. Then he scolded her. "You forget, my child, that disobedience wounds me here."[3] The encounter was Claire's first intimation that Jesus felt in his heart the sins of women and men.

Jesus proceeded to turn the day's incident into a parable. The cousin that Claire had refused to kiss was Jesus. Jesus tells Claire that she hurts him when she refuses a kind gesture. Claire objects, "But Jesus, they aren't nice like you." Jesus reproaches her, "So you believe that your niceness attracts me to you? These little ones you scorn, most of them deserve me more than you . . . if I, Jesus, caress you, it is not because you deserve it, but because I love you."[4]

Autobiography carries risks for history. First of all, there is the risk of an artificial coherence, giving events a sense and meaning they may not have possessed at the time. There is also the risk of teleology, defining one's own life as a series of events leading relentlessly to the present, turning history into destiny or the mere record of the guiding hand of providence. Autobiography can function like a script or a screenplay, as artful verisimilitude, in which events are made to unfold in apparently random ways but culminate in the triumph of the author/hero. All the more reason to consider this vision in terms of the trajectory of Claire's life, or how she might have interpreted its significance retrospectively. Because we know that Claire selected the episode for her memoirs, we are invited to ask why.

In a superficial first reading, the incident, as Claire recounts it, reads like a fairly bland and generic testimony of faith: Claire learns to see Jesus in others; she also finds solace in her faith and, quite literally, in Jesus. Beyond that, however, the story highlights a vexed relationship with authority, because Claire's encounter with Jesus followed an act of stubborn disobedience to her mother. Her earliest recorded vision of Jesus involved a contest of power in which she must decide whether to submit to authority, just as her national "mission" during the war set her on a path where she would collide, as a rogue force, with both secular and religious authorities. Moreover, Claire's vision follows a very unpleasant encounter with the real world; it emerges almost as an alternative to it. Meanwhile, the traumatic elements that accompany the clash of wills—the bodily punishment and deprivation, the sullen resistance and sobbing—would reappear in Claire's crises later in life. The choices Claire's mother asked her to mull over in the quiet, damp solitude of the wine cellar were the very ones that haunted her public career.

CLAIRE'S VOCATION

Bernard Shaw called Joan of Arc "one of the first Protestant martyrs"—a remark that emphasized both her independence from the clergy and the lethal consequences of that independence.[5] Like any visionary, Joan didn't need the clergy to sustain her relationship with God. It wasn't that she was anticlerical, but rather that clergy can become irrelevant when a person speaks directly to God and God speaks back.

In this sense, Claire truly was like Joan, and, indeed, they ran similar risks with respect to the institutions and personnel of the Catholic Church. Claire reveled in her access to Jesus, direct and unmediated by clergy. She was untroubled by questions of orthodoxy or concerns about whether her experience of Jesus fit within church-defined boundaries of Christian faith. However, that same privileged access to Jesus implicitly challenged the authority of the Catholic Church and its clergy, who traced their path to God through an array of prayers and sacraments that they themselves controlled. But where did that leave Claire, who didn't need to go to heaven in order to see God? Did it follow that she didn't need clergy to help her get there? In time, Claire would find that although she didn't need clergy to *see* God, she needed clerical validation that what she saw *was* God.

From her earliest days, Claire's approach to the Sacred frequently turned on questions of authority. Claire knew that moral conviction and the pursuit of sanctity could overcome impossible odds. In this regard, Claire placed herself squarely within a long line of holy women who found personal strength and redemption in their search for spiritual perfection. In the fourteenth century, Margery Kempe's quest for sanctity liberated her from convention and the husband by whom she bore fourteen children. Joan of Arc's faith and vision in the fifteenth century allowed her to overcome the weakness and vacillation of those around her, including that of the man she made king of France. In the seventeenth century, Marguerite-Marie Alacoque's communications with Jesus helped her to triumph over her convent enemies at Paray-le-Monial, advance the devotion to the Sacred Heart of Jesus, and pursue her own sanctity.[6] Claire's sense of self, like that of Joan, frequently pitted her heavenly mandate against earthly authority. Claire's mission, like that of Joan and Marguerite-Marie, called upon her to bring her message, despite her lowly origins, to the inner circles of power.

Claire's relations with her parents could be more subtly problematic. Unlike the Catholic clergy, Claire's parents had no independent point of reference, no dogma, no orthodoxy, no hierarchy to which they, as her parents, could appeal. Little wonder, then, that Claire's mother would later express ambivalence about her daughter's notoriety for saintliness. In 1916, as Claire's saintly reputation was taking shape, one of Claire's admirers rushed to congratulate Claire's mother: "Ah! How happy you must be to be the mother of a saint!" Madame Ferchaud responded wearily, "All the same, it's sometimes a nuisance!"[7] She was far less easily impressed by Claire, her visions, and her will to sanctity. Like any mother, she knew too well.

Claire's sense of mission and her stubbornness were balanced and occasionally challenged by a persistent feeling of unworthiness. She sensed that she was not her parents' favorite. In fact, she was convinced that she was not, recalling her feelings of displacement and abandonment upon being told by her father that a new baby would be joining the family. Claire would no longer be the youngest, the darling of the family. Nor could Claire's parents make the kinds of sacrifices necessary to provide outlets for their daughter's spirit, talent, and imagination. Given the expectations that peasant families were likely to have for their daughters, it would have been unusual if Claire's parents had any ambitions for her that would have taken her far from home. Claire's education was brief, largely because her parents needed her labor on the farm.

Claire's parents sent her to a Catholic school at Loublande, a village near her farm. When Claire went to school, she probably took with her a keen sense of herself as a Catholic in the west of France. Such a sensibility was virtually the birthright of anyone born there after 1789, when initial support for the Revolution had given way to religious and political dissent and, ultimately, a civil war known by the name of the region where it was fought—the Vendée. The Vendéen counterrevolution had some early successes and over the next couple of years its armies of adherents grew. The most common symbol of their cause was the

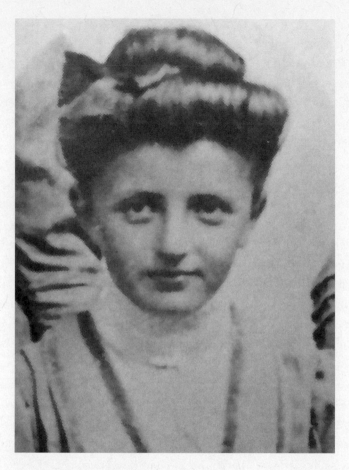

Figure 2.   Claire Ferchaud at fifteen

Sacred Heart emblem, which, when affixed to jacket or lapel, served both as insignia and as protective talisman in battle.

Following the initial success of the counterrevolutionary forces, republican armies struck back in 1793–94, smashing opposition to the Revolution in villages like Loublande across the Vendée.[8] When the armies of the counterrevolution had been destroyed, republican troops went after the population and resources that had sustained them in their treason. By the time the fighting and repression ended, entire villages had been razed and tens of thousands of lives had been lost. Memory of the brutal repression of the counterrevolution would mark the region for generations.

Even at a distance of a hundred years from the events of 1789, Claire's schooling could only have deepened her consciousness of the local tradition of counterrevolutionary politics. The Sisters of the Sacred Heart, a teaching order marked by its clandestine origins in the French Revolution, offered instruction at the girls' school at Loublande. As a teaching order, they took it upon themselves to use their network of convents and schools to shape the minds and values of the Catholic women of France.[9] Claire was thus taught by a religious order whose vision was formed during a period of combat and persecution for the Catholic Church.

Claire's life changed in 1907, and not for the better. She received her first communion and was promptly taken out of school. She had just turned eleven.

Her education was hardly complete, but her parents evidently saw school as a place primarily for religious training, where one learned only the most rudimentary skills. First communion was a religious rite of passage; it appears that Claire's parents saw it as a fitting conclusion to her education, a view not uncommon at the time, particularly with respect to the schooling of girls. When Claire left school, she took with her a lingering doubt about her ability to write; throughout her spiritual career, nuns and spiritual counselors assisted Claire in composing her thoughts in writing. She would remain prey to insecurity about her education throughout her life.

How much Claire resented her abbreviated education is unclear. She would later remark that her parents needed her "poor little arms, although still weak" to assist them in their work. On its face, the remark acknowledges, in a characteristically cloying and self-deprecating way, the parents' needs as paramount—but it also questions how much Claire was truly able to contribute. Did it justify pulling her from school? In any event, for the next nine years, life for Claire consisted of the routine of farm work, mostly the tending of the animals. What she remembered most about these years was that her work left her exposed to the cold of winter, but also that she enjoyed the isolation that her work brought. "I was so happy to find myself alone," she would say.[10] During these years, Claire cultivated her imaginative and visionary gifts. Out in the pasture, among the animals in her care and alone with her thoughts, her spiritual life flourished. The hours of solitude seem to have fostered a profoundly inner sense of self; she discovered a world populated by holy companions. This is where her spiritual dialogues began, in the rolling hills around Rinfillières, where she used the solitude of her days "to speak to Jesus, to the Virgin, to the Angels."[11]

Given Claire's piety and her powerful imagination, her solitude allowed her to develop an uncommonly robust spirituality, where the encounters of her inner life, as she described them, seemed as present and meaningful to her as those of everyday life. She later recalled how she would hide herself in the tall, thick Scotch broom "to speak face to face with God."[12] She found God wherever she could, not only by day, in the fields or in pastures, but also at night, when she waited on her knees in prayer beside her bed.

As Claire's spiritual life became richer and more complex, her attendance at mass in the parish church at Loublande became more frequent. Attendance at weekly or even daily mass has a clear social component. In some communities, especially in regions of scattered farms where social contacts are few, the Sunday ritual is sometimes the only consistent form of social contact beyond the household, particularly for women. Whether this would explain Claire's frequent attendance at church is unclear, but one can well imagine that attendance at mass, which required a walk from the farm at Rinfillières into the village of Loublande, helped Claire break the sense of isolation she felt upon leaving school.

Claire cultivated her relationship with her pastor, Father Audebert. She began attending Audebert's *patronage,* a church group for young girls in the parish. At one meeting, Audebert spoke of how Jesus would choose a certain number of "victims" (persons devoted to penance) from across France. Claire pondered Audebert's remark and approached him afterward. She offered the opinion that she might be among the chosen victims; then she knelt before the altar and offered herself in prayer. It was said that she developed an appetite for suffering ("un grand attrait pour la souffrance sous toutes les formes"). Claire's prayerful routine began to include long stints of prayer that, over time, became the occasion for her visions, as when Jesus asked her to pass several nights on her knees before him, like a "living lamp before the Tabernacle." She sought permission from Audebert to do so for a week, which turned into two weeks, and finally five, at the end of which she emerged strengthened, even though she did not sleep. During this time, she also abandoned her usual responsibilities. She no longer occupied herself with farm work and household duties.[13]

After a time, Claire trusted Audebert enough to describe for him some of her visions and intimate conversations with Jesus. She described one such episode to Audebert in July of 1916. Claire was on her knees in prayer in her room. It was three or four in morning. Jesus appeared out of the darkness. He advanced toward Claire, showing her his wounded heart and speaking of the wounds inflicted by priests unfaithful to their vows and their faith. He showed her another wound, fresh and bleeding. Then, in a gesture of spiritual intimacy, he approached Claire so that she might contemplate his flayed heart.[14]

Audebert listened with rapt attention. He became a believer in Claire's vision of the Sacred Heart wounded by the indifference of men.

Spiritual Patronage
and a Mission to Save France

❧

Claire packed her things for Saint-Laurent-sur-Sèvre in November of 1916. Her spiritual retreat had been in the works for some time. Father Audebert, the pastor at Loublande, had been increasingly impressed with Claire's singular spiritual gifts, but his experience with such persons was limited. After all, how often do parishioners claim to have seen and spoken to Jesus directly? Claire was special, of that he was convinced. At the very least, she must have seemed a promising candidate for a religious vocation, but as a parish priest there were limits to what Audebert could do for Claire; in fact, her spiritual life was taking her beyond his competence and experience. On retreat at Saint-Laurent, Claire would be in the company of women devoted to the religious life, and her qualities could be cultivated, as they could not at Rinfillières. Her talent and her zeal would guide her from there.

Claire's father hesitated. It wasn't the idea of a religious vocation that bothered him; he and Madame Ferchaud already had a daughter in a convent. He undoubtedly recognized Claire's spiritual qualities, but with two sons away at war, he was also keenly aware of the shortage of hands on the farm. Claire's spiritual development had taken place at the expense of her responsibilities to the household and the farm; her retreat would have to wait until autumn labors at the farm were done.

When the time finally came for Claire to leave for Saint-Laurent, the event had accrued a kind of momentousness. Aside from a pilgrimage to Lourdes undertaken with her family in 1913, Claire's travels had taken her no farther from Rinfillières than the parish church of Loublande and the neighboring village of Le Puy-Saint-Bonnet, a distance of two and a half miles at most.[1] Not only was Claire's stay at the retreat house at Saint-Laurent one of her rare sojourns away from Rinfillières, it was the first time in her life that she lived apart from her parents. She was twenty years old.

Saint-Laurent would also serve to extend Claire's renown and support among the Catholic clergy. At Loublande, Claire had won the sympathies of Father Audebert, who was the first to appreciate Claire's gifts and had arranged Claire's retreat. At Saint-Laurent, Claire would find another guide, patron, and vigorous advocate, Father Bourget. Bourget was something of a local celebrity. Middle-aged in 1916 and at the height of his powers, Bourget preached, organized retreats, and offered spiritual guidance for lay and religious at Saint-Laurent and throughout the Châtillon region. The relationship between a spiritually gifted person and an advisee is a very special one, somewhat akin to the relationship between a trainer and a gifted athlete. Their reputations and careers become closely entwined. Bourget's eventual "adoption" of Claire as his spiritual pupil was one of several successful transitions in her career; each such transition gave Claire new confidence, new clerical "authentication," and new fields of endeavor. Each new counselor, however, would hold her to new standards and shape her message. Someone of Claire's age might be excused for feeling giddy with all the attention her exceptional qualities and gifts had earned.

Bourget's acceptance of Claire, however, was nearly compromised by her timidity. In fact, simply talking to Bourget was difficult for Claire. Although Saint-Laurent gave Claire a sense of freedom and the means to develop her prodigious spiritual gifts, she remained deeply private and painfully shy. While mystical reveries gratified her, conversation with strangers pained her, as if an inability to verbalize went in tandem with an extraordinarily rich inner life. At her first encounter with Father Bourget, the twenty-year-old found herself unable to speak—an inauspicious beginning for a woman who would save France. Bourget, a sympathetic man and an experienced spiritual counselor, encouraged her to write down her visions.[2] It was a brilliant suggestion, because the interiority of writing matched perfectly the disposition of a woman whose inner world offered a richer array of possibilities than did the encounters of everyday life.

Claire wrote for herself, but she also wrote to share her visions with Bourget. Literate in only a rudimentary way, Claire struggled with spelling and syntax. Getting subject and predicate to agree required concentration. Infinitives and past participles sounded the same but were spelled differently. The precious quality of her mature writing showed the traces of these earliest struggles and prodigious efforts. Slowly, Claire gained confidence in herself and her powers of expression. First through her writings and eventually through speech, Claire found the words she needed to articulate her feelings with confidence. Gradually she abandoned writing, at least as a crutch, in favor of direct conversation with Father Bourget. She could sit across from him and confide in him her belief in the divine origins of things she saw and heard. As she spoke she described to Bourget "the things I believe I receive from the Good Lord, whose words I hear."

As for Bourget, he had to come to terms with Claire's self-consciousness and her modest origins. Would God speak through a semiliterate young woman? Neither patrician status nor age was a prerequisite for sanctity, and in recent years the heavens had opened up to children and young adults. In 1846, at La Salette, the Virgin Mary spoke to two shepherd children, Maximin Giraud and Melanie Mathieu. At Lourdes in 1858, the Virgin had appeared in a grotto to an impoverished fourteen-year-old named Bernadette Soubirous. In 1871, the Virgin appeared to peasant children in the sky above Pontmain. Bourget listened to Claire and found himself—despite her timidity, despite her origins, perhaps because of her origins—believing.[3]

Figure 3.   The children of Pontmain, young visionaries in a time of war

A DEMAND FOR SIGNS

Despite his favorable inclinations, Bourget wanted confirmation. He wanted signs. That meant that he wanted to draw Claire out of her solipsism, the world only she knew—the world of voices and prodigious visions. He wanted her to enter the world they shared and to manifest her experience of it. He wanted her to show knowledge—empirically verifiable knowledge—of hidden things in the present world that she could not know without divine help, things irrefutably linking her visionary domain to the world they shared. Bourget began to put Claire to the test.

Bourget assembled several photographs of members of the clergy and arrayed them in a virtual line-up. He slipped among them the photograph of one who had "fallen"—that is, a priest who had sinned or undergone a crisis of faith or vocation. Bourget described for Claire the nature of the test and then asked her to pick the fallen priest out of the line-up. Claire scanned the faces, reflected, and chose. She chose correctly.

It was just the sort of sign Bourget had sought—a sign that Claire had access to occult knowledge, to unseen things. At the end of one such session with Claire, Bourget pronounced himself "bowled over"— he had never seen anything like it.[4] Claire could read men's hearts; she seemed to know the personal weaknesses and private doubts of the holy men around her. Later, Bourget would claim for Claire the ability "to read souls."[5] She had won over one of her most powerful advocates.

Claire became Bourget's protégé. Virtually all women who had achieved Catholic sanctity in modern times had done so with the guidance of a spiritual counselor. Typically, this was a man, a priest, who combined the roles of confidant, counselor, and impresario—a person who guided, sponsored, protected, and promoted. Bourget had assumed this role for himself. Under his guidance, Claire's personality turned outward, as did her visionary talents and, ultimately, her message. When Claire met Bourget, she possessed an innocent, almost childlike faith and, of course, prodigious spiritual gifts. With Bourget's tutelage, Claire's message took shape, and she was ready to set out on a path that led to Paris and a national mission to rescue France.

In a sense, Claire's message contained nothing new. The outlines of the message that would emerge from Rinfillières were already known to anyone familiar with the image of France crafted by conservative Catholics in postrevolutionary France. It was an image in which France and the French were essentially Catholic. In it, France had had a Christian mission ever since the conversion of the Frankish king Clovis. On the eve of battle in 496, Clovis had vowed to be baptized if his army should prevail in battle. Following his victory, and urged on by his Christian spouse, Clothilde, Clovis made good on his vow and France, so the story went, was baptized with its monarch. The glories of France were the result.

The Revolution of 1789 brought rupture. France had denied its faith and, in a sense, denied its true nature. Everything that had happened since, from France's relative decline in Europe to the nation's increasingly apparent inability to win a war with Germany now, in late 1916, dragging into its third year, derived from secularization—France's official apostasy.[6] Under Audebert's guidance, Claire's spiritual mission converged with long-standing Catholic preoccupations regarding French decadence and decline. What set Claire apart was that this familiar message was harnessed to her phenomenal visionary power, which both endorsed and amplified it.

Key elements of what would become Claire's worldview had recently been articulated in a powerful pamphlet published in 1915 by Jean-Baptiste Lemius, chaplain at the Basilica of the Sacré-Coeur on Montmartre. Entitled *Les grands desseins du Sacré-Coeur de Jésus et la France,* this pamphlet laid out a transcendent vision of victory in war. France would triumph in the Great War following a national consecration to the Sacred Heart of Jesus.[7] Had Bourget read Lemius's *Les grands desseins?* It is certainly possible; Lemius, quite likely contacted by Bourget, was among the first outside of Loublande to learn of Claire. Soon, Lemius would become one of Claire's most eager supporters; she, in turn, became the living vehicle for his message—a perfect union of message and messenger.

Claire's mission—to lead the fight for the soul of France— was also a mission to reclaim France's status in the twentieth century. Claire's goal would be to lead France back to its divine relationship and its Christian identity. How? In visions that were now much more politically explicit, the Sacred Heart told her. France must renew the baptism of Clovis, the Frankish king whose conversion and baptism some Catholics saw as symbolic of the Christianization of France. It was an event whose fourteen-hundredth anniversary in 1896 coincided with Claire's birth. France must be publicly consecrated to the Sacred Heart, and the emblem of the Sacred Heart must appear on the white band of the tricolor French flag. Under the emblem of the Sacred Heart, France would triumph over its enemies and recover its place at the head of nations. This message had some of the simple qualities of a French children's picture book, the colorful, simple, heroic gestures of an *histoire en images.* It was a message imparted to Marguerite-Marie Alacoque in the seventeenth century. Now Claire, the *fleur champêtre,* the wildflower of the Vendée, was its privileged bearer.

TRANSFIGURATION

As a result of her stay at Saint-Laurent, Claire was no longer merely a visionary, a woman of great spiritual gifts; she was now a woman with a national mission. How had Claire's mission suddenly taken such sharp focus? A lengthy and supportive summary of Claire's career, forwarded to the Vatican by the bishop of Poitiers in 1917, describes in awestruck terms Claire's capacity for guidance. "God always seems to follow the same path with this child. The instructions for her various missions at first seem rather vague. She doesn't always understand them herself; they become clearer and more precise as the time approaches to carry them out."[8]

If Claire's divine instructions lacked emphatic clarity, this could only enhance the role of her spiritual advisers—hence, the critical importance of Father Bourget. He gave Claire's visions a direction and import that extended well beyond the failings of the clergy and the redemption of souls. Bourget shaped her words—he would even correct her spelling—and through him Claire became a voice for Catholic France.[9] When Bourget validated Claire as a visionary, he acquired a vehicle for a powerful message. The timeliness of Claire's message, as it took shape, and her claim to privileged information from heaven helped her to tap into long-standing political animosities, burgeoning national self-doubt, and growing skepticism about political leadership during a time of war.

In effect, Claire's gifts had been nationalized. Her father had doubted whether he could spare his daughter for the Saint-Laurent retreat, especially since the nation had already called two of his sons away to war. Now he found that the war was taking his daughter, too, as Claire became a national figure, pointing the path to France's conse-cration and regeneration.

From pulpits, parish bulletins, and by pathways of rumor, word spread quickly around the west of France. A *voyante,* a visionary, had become the select intermediary between France and God at a time of supreme national peril. From the Choletais and beyond, people flocked to see Claire. They were drawn by the possibility of knowing, or at least seeing, someone marked out for sainthood. They came not because they thought that saintliness was a thing of the past. On the contrary, each generation in recent memory had had its time and place for mirac-ulous intervention and divine solicitude—witness the children of La Salette, Lourdes, and Pontmain, the curé of Ars, and Thérèse of Lisieux.[10] Now, Loublande would have its turn, its prodigy. They came to see saintliness for their own times.

The retreat at Saint-Laurent, thanks to Bourget's guidance, vali-dated Claire's visionary gifts and honed her public message. It also strengthened Claire and prepared her for the challenges to come— local notoriety, Poitiers, Paris eventually, and national celebrity. Although scarcely six kilometers from her home at Rinfillières, Saint-Laurent allowed Claire to transcend her origins. At Saint-Laurent, Claire was free to contemplate her life on her own account and on her own terms. Free of parental demands and the mundane concerns of farm life, she could finally see her way free of the modest expectations and limited horizons normally available to a sharecropper's daughter. At Saint-Laurent, she was no longer simply Claire, the Ferchaud's middle child. At Saint-Laurent she became Claire the *voyante,* the visionary, the child blessed by divine favor, the privileged interlocutor of Jesus.

Claire's retreat was an epiphany and, in a modest way, a liberation. It gave her a critical perspective on herself by allowing her to step outside the tiny world of Loublande, a world where everyone had known her since infancy and there were no secrets, no mysteries. The retreat allowed her to understand how others—that is, those outside her family and village—might see her and how she might present herself to them. Mademoiselle de la Pintière, a local notable who had known Claire before Saint-Laurent, was among those who observed how a mere two weeks had given Claire poise and a new confidence. "When she returned to the village," de la Pintière noted, "one perceived that a change had come over her. To her simplicity was added a distinctiveness of manner that was discernible to all those she encountered."[11] "This child receives you like a young lady of a great house," another remarked. Yet another referred to the new Claire as "transfigured"—a telling remark befitting her new public and spiritual role.[12]

Claire knew it too. "I returned from this retreat animated by a vigor I had not known before. Dare I say it? I was like a priest who had just been ordained." And, in a sense, she had been. As a final step before returning from Saint-Laurent, Claire had celebrated her "mystical marriage" *(noces mystiques)*. Her pastoral mission defined, Claire consecrated her virginity to her Divine Spouse.[13] Her public career was about to begin.

Silent Eruptions

Claire and Her Public

❖

Loublande had a "little visionary."[1] This sobriquet adopted by the press left plenty of room for the imagination. A child? A visionary? What does she see? Would she lead an army and fight like Joan? Crowds of pilgrims descended upon Loublande in search of answers.

Loublande was a village totally unprepared for the crush of visitors. It didn't have a train station. Pilgrims from Angers, like those from Nantes, could get no closer to Loublande than the station at Cholet, a good six or seven miles away. From there the average visitor had to make do with a wagon, while the well-off made the journey in automobiles. From Poitiers it was even more difficult; one could get off the train at Mauléon, but Loublande was still eight miles beyond. Étienne Garnier, a reporter for the *Télégramme de Toulouse*, estimated the number of pilgrims at thirty thousand for the second week in December 1916, an improbable figure that would put the average daily attendance above four thousand.[2] Loublande, a village of a few hundred, was swamped.

Where would they stay? Loublande didn't have a hotel; it didn't even have a café. These visitors—pilgrims, the curious, the skeptical—stayed in extra beds and hastily arranged quarters on nearby farms. Saint-Laurent, with its convent and retreat accommodations, took much of the overflow. During the day, there were few places for visitors to gather. It was probably typical of life in villages like Loublande that the village church was one of the few public spaces that offered protection from the damp Atlantic air.

Loublande's church, the Church of Saint-André as it was known, was where Audebert served as pastor. It was also where the day began for most pilgrims, who rose in the winter darkness to make their way to morning mass, a service that Claire faithfully attended. While Audebert prepared for the ceremony in the sacristy, visitors from throughout the west of France shuffled respectfully through the twin doors of the village church. They took their places among the two narrow banks of pews, hoping to catch a glimpse of the *voyante,* the woman who saw Jesus.

At the far end of the narrow Gothic nave, behind the white marble altar, stained glass nurtured the imagination with scenes of saintly women—a window behind the altar depicted Marguerite-Marie Alacoque on her knees before a vision of the Sacred Heart at Paray-le-Monial. The parish church at Loublande was a shrine to the rich soil of France that had produced so many saintly women. Heads turned to watch for Claire's arrival. When she entered the church, eyes dwelled attentively upon the features of a woman many believed to be the heir apparent in a succession of virginal national saints: Joan, Marguerite-Marie, Bernadette. Claire—plain, composed, unassuming—held the promise of holiness for her times.[3]

For Claire, it was a burden borne uneasily. Many of her visions occurred at night, but morning mass could be a richly visual time for her too. Often her private companions were there to sustain her in the face of her new public notoriety. "Fear nothing," Mary, the mother of Jesus, once told her; "Jesus and your Mother will carry you in their arms." Joan of Arc promised to stand beside her. When Claire invoked Joan at mass one November morning, she sensed a presence near her. Then she heard a voice. "Are you weaker than I when I was a little shepherdess? Submit to God's will. He alone is your strength, and by Jesus and Mary I am with you and will never abandon you."[4] The content of these messages was reassuring, but the voices put Claire in heady company.

Claire not only heard voices; she also saw things—vivid apparitions that revealed the terrifying power of an irrepressible imagination. Morning after morning, in the quiet calm of the crowded Church of Saint-André, the liturgy became a reenactment of bloody sacrifice. Claire's inspired reading of the sacrifice of the mass refused to submit to the routine of ritual; her mind reeled with thoughts of the consecration as redemption through the shedding of blood.

Claire described her visions to Father Audebert in vivid detail. "Three mornings in a row the blood of Jesus ran in torrents," she told him. "When the Host was raised in adoration, I saw the Host in its ordinary form," she recounted, "but then it spurted blood." Blood squirted from the Host, surged over the sides of the chalice, and gushed down onto the altar. Blood flowed everywhere; soon Audebert was bathed in it. "You, my father, were so red with blood!" Transubstantiation became a torrent. Finally, Claire could no longer see the altar, only "a vast expanse of blood." Claire's powerful faith had stimulated her lush imagination; the discharge of grace overwhelmed the symbolic objects of consecration. The displacement of the sacrificial act onto proxies failed. The ritualized performance of the divine gifts of sacrifice and redemption erupted in a climax of blood.[5]

The pilgrims knew nothing of the bloody eruptions shaking Claire. They transposed their tidy world onto hers. They saw her peacefully at prayer, following the ceremony dutifully with gestures and genuflections while Audebert and his acolytes bowed before an altar of crisp, starched, immaculate linens. Only the murmur of the Latin liturgy unsettled the silence.

MANAGING CONTACT

After mass, the pilgrims followed Claire from Loublande to her home at Rinfillières, the farm managed by the Ferchaud family. Rinfillières is west and north of the village of Loublande. From the Church of Saint-André it is reached by walking along a narrow road that leads west, past the spot where a life-size statue of the Sacred Heart now stands, to the junction. A road to the right leads to La Tessoualle and, eventually, to Cholet and Nantes. To the left, a road winds to a place where the entrance to the farm is clearly marked. From there, pilgrims followed a path from the main road down toward a creek, then up the western side of a hill to the residence and dependent buildings that make up the Rinfillières farm. In the spring the hills between the road and the Ferchaud house are a damp green broken by purple wildflowers and the yellow-gold of Scotch broom. In the summer the fields are dry and noisy when the wind blows. In the dead of winter, when the pilgrims first began to widen the narrow pathway with their steps, the trees dripped fog and rain and the hills were a mix of black and yellow-gray.

Along the way, there were silent prayers and prayers in unison. At the top of the rise, the pilgrims paused at the tiny chapel that Claire's grandparents had built in 1862 to Notre-Dame de la Garde—Our Lady of Protection.[6] The inspiration for the chapel was typical of nineteenth-century piety in that it involved the promise of a chapel in exchange for God's protection during times of disease, war, or famine. In the 1850s, when a typhus epidemic threatened the nearby village of Vihiers, Sister Saint-Luke convinced the pastor to protect the village's children by promising to build a chapel to Notre-Dame de la Salette. When the epidemic passed, regional dignitaries, including the archbishop of Poitiers, attended the ceremonial laying of the chapel's first stone in 1858. Four years later, the impressive domed monument was completed.[7] It still stands today, a vigilant sentry on the hilltop high above Vihiers. The Ferchaud's chapel was more modest: a tile-and-stucco structure barely larger than a tool shed. Claire's grandparents had built it in fulfillment of a vow they had made in 1856 during an outbreak of typhus, probably the same outbreak that had threatened Vihiers. Claire's grandparents had promised that if they survived the fever, they too would build a chapel in gratitude to Our Lady.

During the years following its construction, the chapel had been a local place of pilgrimage in difficult times. Times of war were surely difficult, and by late 1916 the statue of the Virgin standing in the Ferchaud family chapel had hundreds of written intentions placed at her feet. This was where the particular appeal of Claire to the families of soldiers became evident, because among the many prayerful intentions placed at the feet of the Virgin were photographs of soldiers—husbands, fathers, sons, and brothers—away at war.[8] Claire's vision provided additional meaning to their sacrifices. Not only were they fighting to defend France; they were fighting to *change* France.

Part of the appeal of Rinfillières and Loublande was that Claire's visions marked these sites as privileged places for prayers. After all, if Jesus appeared to Claire there, wasn't there a better chance that the prayers of others might be noticed too? Hence the accumulation of intentions, prayers, photographs, and ex-votos. But these gestures also pointed toward the political risk embodied in the tale of the visionary of Loublande. Did these pilgrims prefer to invest their hopes for an end to war in the visions and promises of the shepherdess of Loublande? What did that mean for political leadership in Paris? If Claire could end the war with victory for France, why wasn't Paris listening? A public consecration and a tricolor flag with the Sacred Heart—was that so much to ask?

Over time the subversive political potential of these demands—a modified flag and a national consecration in a secular, pluralist republic—would dominate the story of Claire, but for pilgrims to Loublande and Rinfillières her story was never simply, or even mostly, about that. Loublande would have been nothing without Claire, the charismatic presence. Getting close to Claire was the supreme wish of those who followed Claire prayerfully from mass at Loublande back to Rinfillières. The crowd scene at Rinfillières announced Claire's "arrival" as a minor celebrity.

Clergy and family members struggled to reconcile Claire's needs with the wishes of the crowd. It wasn't easy. Partly it was the pressure of knowing how far the pilgrims had traveled to see her. Partly it was the nature of the crowd itself—after all, it took a certain wealth and leisure to make the journey to Loublande. The crowd that gathered in the gravel courtyard outside the Ferchaud farmhouse included many regional notables—educated, leisured, well dressed. Some of them employed sharecropper families like the Ferchauds on their own properties. What they thought of Claire and her family, one can only guess, but a scene from early 1917 suggests that at Rinfillières, spirituality and celebrity trumped status and class.

Mademoiselle de la Pintière and her friends, a group of young women of noble background, installed themselves outside Claire's house on a late morning in mid-February of 1917. They became the kernel of a crowd that would not leave until its members had seen the visionary. They stood attentively in the Rinfillières courtyard, facing the modest, rectangular, white-stucco cottage. Mademoiselle de la Pintière described the scene and her feelings: "We experienced a new emotion because someone told us that we most certainly would not see Claire Ferchaud, that she was in bed. In spite of everything, we resolved to wait. . . . We waited a good hour. Little by little other groups arrived, and soon we were a veritable crowd."[9]

Inside the white farmhouse, Claire and her family watched the crowd grow. They could see that this crowd was stubborn and would linger despite the February cold and damp. Similar events on the preceding days, along with the unrelenting pressure of celebrity and her habit of nighttime prayer, had begun to exhaust Claire. Managing her admirers was becoming a problem. Public appearances failed to satisfy crowds fascinated by the details of Claire's existence—where she lived, what she wore, how she looked, the sound of her voice. Indeed, public appearances seemed only to make things worse. Even Claire's home offered no respite. By its very nature, it was now no different from any other pilgrimage site blessed by divine presence and open to the curiosity of the public. Celebrities in Paris were treated with greater dignity and respect.

Being denied contact with Claire frustrated a crowd that hoped to witness saintliness for their times; allowing contact, however, only encouraged others. In an attempt to balance access and security, the family experimented with a variety of forms of controlled contact. Mademoiselle de la Pintière described what was probably a common scene at Rinfillières. "We had been waiting about an hour when we saw a window open. Everyone rushed forward." The crowd, eager to touch a person touched by God, forgot its place and "behaved abominably." Arms and hands lunged through the opening, grasping for Claire's hand. Inside, frightened by the vigor of the assault, the family pushed limbs back outside. After three attempts they managed to close the window.[10]

Inside, the family pondered another approach. The house contained a *grenier,* a grain loft above the living area—a common feature in small farmhouses of the era. The grain loft included a loading bay that opened to the courtyard from just above the front door. Rather than risk opening a ground-floor window or door, the family would first address the crowd from the safety of the grain loft. As Mademoiselle de la Pintière and her friends watched, the grain loft door swung open. There, above the crowd, a member of the family leaned out, waited for the crowd to calm, then announced the ground rules for Claire's appearance: Claire was very tired. Nevertheless, she would come out and present herself to the crowd. No one would be allowed to approach her. No one would be allowed to shake her hand. "She has gotten up just for you," they were told.

A moment later, Claire emerged from the house. She stepped tentatively toward the well-dressed crowd. She offered a gracious bow, first to the left, then to the right. Then a look of deep sorrow came over her, as if a burdensome thought had entered her mind. She uttered just six words: "Priez pour moi, s'il vous plaît."

Claire's anguished, needy performance only stimulated the crowd. The desire to see her gave way to the desire to be close to her in her sorrow, to touch her. As Claire turned to retreat into the house, the crowd followed her. It pressed about the entrance as Claire slipped in, then it heaved inside, turning the household to chaos. An exasperated Madame Ferchaud—frustrated by the interminable drama, weary of her daughter's celebrity, and patently unsympathetic to the crowd—sought to drive them out by putting things in perspective. It was one o'clock, she pleaded, and she still hadn't done her dishes!

Just then, a priest arrived and restored order. The crowd reluctantly retreated from the home to the courtyard while the priest and Claire's family conferred. Moments later, the priest and Claire emerged from the house together. The presence of the priest restored dignity to the situation and order to the crowd, which listened politely and quietly as he made an announcement. "Listen," he said. "You can line up in single file in front of her but she is very tired and if there is the slightest scuffle I'll take her back inside!" In a manner reminiscent of schoolchildren in a playground, the priest arranged the crowd into two rows, with the idea that Claire would walk between them. Then he thought better of this arrangement, perhaps because it resembled a gauntlet—more fitting for a traitor or a vagabond criminal than a saint—perhaps because it left no line of retreat should the lines break and converge. Finally, out of consideration for her security as well as her state of fatigue, he stationed Claire in the doorway, where she could support herself by leaning on the doorframe as the crowd filed past.

"I really wanted to touch her," Mademoiselle de la Pintière later recalled. She no doubt expressed the desire of many in the crowd as they shuffled toward the doorway, standing on tip-toe to look over shoulders and glimpse the *voyante*. Members of the crowd planned their moment with Claire as they drew near. Mademoiselle de la Pintière took off her gloves as she approached. She wanted more than a simple handshake. She hadn't come for a gesture. She wanted to touch the *voyante*. Even more, she wanted relics. "I took all my medals and bound them together with a ring." Cupping the medals in the palm of her hand, she stepped forward and extended her hand. "Then, when I shook Claire's hand, the medals scattered, so I know that Claire touched all of them."[11]

If Claire's visions and message had made her a celebrity, she played one reluctantly. For Claire, accustomed to solitude, these moments with her public were wrenching. It was said that she suffered visibly during such ordeals; the receiving lines were an emotional gauntlet. Mademoiselle de la Pintière noted, and she was not alone, that Claire sighed as the crowds moved before her. Claire's eyes filled with tears. She turned her head aside, looking down with what onlookers understood as an air of profound suffering. Some wondered whether the Sacred Heart commanded such spectacles to fulfill some unknown purpose, for it seemed that Claire did not relish these episodes and that she was "shown" against her will.[12] Others speculated that the Sacred Heart sent her pain during these "exhibitions" in order to distract her and to spare her the sin of pride. But one might also ask whether Claire's expression didn't hint at a kind of Gethsemane, the pain of doubt before a final sacrifice? Or even the pain of despair at having escaped the torments of one life only to be confronted with the torments of another?

A NEW IMAGE OF THE SACRÉ-COEUR

Although Claire always insisted on the importance of the message she bore, one of the highlights of a pilgrim's visit to Loublande was a painting made from Claire's description of her visions. Perhaps Claire never sensed the need for a new image of the Sacred Heart but, as she would later recount it, Jesus did.

Claire did not invent the devotion to the Sacré-Coeur, any more than Marguerite-Marie Alacoque had invented it in the seventeenth century. Fascination with the heart of Jesus as the seat of divine love was almost as old as the Gospel stories themselves. It had been an object of intense scrutiny by the Catholic faithful, and subsequently by historians and art historians. Its primary message—the Christian theology of divine love for humanity—was conveyed in simple gesture: by representing Jesus either pointing toward his heart or, more rarely, holding out his heart as a gift of charity. Everything about the image was calculated to accentuate the immediacy and intimacy of Jesus's love for the beholder of the image. This image accorded with Catholic efforts to move away from an older frightening, sometimes angry and vengeful God—the Jehovah who sits in judgment of humanity.[13]

With varying degrees of success, artists created images of the Sacred Heart that expressed divine love and satisfied human curiosity about the human attributes of divinity. Artists represented the heart of Jesus in states of suffering, with an open wound from which blood oozed. The heart might appear ringed by the crown of thorns, for example, or, as in the case of the related devotion to the Immaculate Heart of Mary, transpierced by a sword. The bleeding heart of Jesus suggested a wounded love; it set one's relationship with God in an emotional register. The source of the wounds was humanity, for if Jesus held out his heart as a sign of his love, the wounds the heart manifested revealed that Jesus's love was unrequited. Given its rich and stable iconography, Claire would have understood the heart of Jesus as an index of Jesus's suffering. And given Claire's heavy investment in suffering as a pathway to Jesus, it was a devotion with obvious personal appeal. But it also projected outward. Jesus offered himself to men and women in a gesture of love, but the ring of thorns around his heart represented humanity's deafness to the appeal or, even worse, the hostility and culpability of humanity.

In this sense, the iconography of the Sacred Heart never quite overcame the spirit of divine reproach embodied by Jehovah; it simply recast it. The difference was that the results of human rejection of the divine were turned inward, not outward. In a strategy of representation that was passively aggressive, divine hurt replaced divine wrath. The image of Jesus that Claire revealed was significantly made over from images common for the time. Jesus appeared to her not so much as a loving God, but as a God visibly suffering from human rejection, a pose adopted, as she put it, "in order to strike the senses." Claire imputed to Jesus an aim, which was "to make me understand France's culpability."[14]

How could France's culpability strike the senses in a new and dramatic way? With Claire, Jesus took a form similar to that of the standard representation of the Sacred Heart but with certain striking innovations. In Claire's vision, the Sacred Heart of Jesus is pierced not by the standard transverse cut, but by a gaping vulviform wound (see figure 17, p. 136). Claire described the wound as caused by *coups de canif*—"multiple knife blows." As she told it, "a large wound seemed to cleave the heart, whence blood flows forth." It is unclear whether, or to what extent, Claire intended to suggest an eroticized suffering or even whether she was aware that not only the wound she described but even the knife that caused it evoke the image of the vagina (the Latin word means "sheath" or "scabbard"). In any event, from Catherine of Siena to Marguerite-Marie Alacoque by way of Jeanne de Chantal and François de Sales, an aesthetic of chaste eroticism characterized and, in a sense, drove the Sacred Heart devotion.[15] Eroticism aside, anyone aware of medieval and early modern precedent could not fail to notice at least the maternal nature of this representation of Jesus, because the blood that flows from his wounded heart possesses nurturing and life-giving qualities, and carries the promise of renewal. Claire's heart of Jesus resembled the place from which human life issues forth, an object of wonder from the earliest times.[16]

Moreover, Claire's vision of the Sacred Heart invites us to ask whether the feminization of religion in nineteenth-century France did not elicit more explicitly feminine representations of the Sacred.[17] Catholic religious practice in nineteenth-century France feminized—or, more precisely, demasculinized—as men abandoned the church. Should we be surprised to see shifts in the image of the Sacred? As men fell away from the church and as women came to dominate the body of the faithful, wouldn't these women, in time, come to see themselves as made in the image of God? Jesus as Mother had a long and distinguished pedigree, not only in form but also in temperament.[18] A Jesus whose response to human pride was one of pained rejection rather than a prideful rage of patriarchal fury should be seen, if not as an explicit feminization of representations of God, then at least as an improvement on inarticulate male rage.[19]

Indeed, in images of the Sacred Heart produced from Claire's visions, the first person of the Trinity is absent. Earlier versions of the Sacred Heart frequently featured a triangular relationship in which the individual gazes at Jesus of the Sacred Heart whose gaze, in turn, is fixed upward toward heaven; this Sacred Heart reminds us that Jesus is the Son of God and that Jesus intercedes with his father on behalf of humanity. Claire's Jesus confronted the viewer directly. Her version of Jesus of the Sacred Heart stood in a dialogic relationship with the individual rather than in an intermediate position. Claire's Jesus no longer insists on calling the viewer's attention to a paternal heavenly God.

Finally, Claire's vision of Jesus had grown. This was no longer the boy Jesus whom Claire had sought to embrace after her childish tantrum. Jesus had grown with Claire, and his preoccupations had grown too. The child Jesus had reproached Claire for her selfishness and her disobedience. The Jesus of Claire's adulthood had set his sights beyond Claire, now his ally and messenger, to consider the status of France itself. Their public career together had begun.

France troubled Jesus in 1916. That's what her vision told her. The sense of injury that Jesus once expressed to Claire regarding her selfish misconduct he now expressed with regard to the French nation. Jesus spoke to Claire of his heart. Gesturing toward his heart's gaping wound he explained its meaning. "The wound," he told Claire, "signifies the official atheism of France."[20] Like Claire, Jesus had been politicized.

Jesus's newly political persona spoke candidly of grave public matters. With so much at stake—not only theologically, but politically as well, in the context of heavily censored wartime speech—it was only a matter of time before ecclesiastical authorities felt compelled to investigate. Late in 1916, Claire was called to account for herself. She was to go to Poitiers to answer questions before an episcopal commission.

In the Footsteps of Joan

※

Public enthusiasm for Claire rose as despair about the war deepened. Early in January 1916, Erich von Falkenhayn, chief of the German general staff, resolved to raise the stakes in the war by concentrating his forces on the fortresses at a place called Verdun. The aim was to trap France in a war of attrition, to bleed the nation dry. The significance of the fortresses of Verdun was both symbolic and strategic. If concentrated attacks on Verdun, an exposed salient on the long Western front, forced France to abandon Verdun, the psychological effect could be devastating. But if France defended Verdun, it could do so only at the cost of great human loss. France defended Verdun, with catastrophic results for both armies. By the end of 1916, more than seven hundred thousand had died or been wounded. The majority of casualties were French, but the effects were nearly as shattering for Germany. The slaughter at Verdun was catastrophic, but it had not been decisive.

As the year of Verdun drew to a close, in the winter of 1916–17 Claire found herself engaged in a complex set of high-level negotiations, both divine and human. Claire had been called to Poitiers. She would have an audience with the archbishop. For the first time in her life, she would be asked to account for herself and her visions in a rigorous and systematic way. At the same time, her mission to save France was taking shape. Following her retreat to Saint-Laurent, Claire understood that she had great gifts and had been called to fulfill great deeds. The question was, how? Would her role be soldierly, in the manner of Joan? Or would it be diplomatic, as intercessor with those who held power in Paris? Claire and her visionary interlocutors were still working out her role in the weeks before the journey to Poitiers.

For a time, it had seemed that Claire might follow Joan into battle. Late in 1916, Joan of Arc spoke to Claire in bold and energetic terms. "Take the flag of the Sacred Heart," she told Claire. "Place yourself at the head of the army."[1] Admittedly, the suggestion had a picture-book appeal. A twenty-year-old shepherd maiden from the Vendée stands before legions of French soldiers, the legendary *poilus*. She hoists the flag of the Sacred Heart. She turns to lead the soldiers in a heroic charge across no-man's-land. The Germans, the *boches,* panic and flee in disarray. Like the original story of Joan, it had the right blend of simplicity, valor, and improbability. Add to that the prospect of the triumph of virtuous Right (France) over wicked Might (Germany) and the image of men taking courage from the example of an indomitable woman—it was a scenario with just the right mix of magic and crazy. Who knows? It just might work.

Alas, it was not to be. A short time later, the picture changed. Claire would not become a soldier after all. Instead, following a high-level dialogue, a diplomatic role began to take shape. As Claire described it, the scene opened with Mary on her knees before Jesus. She implored her son "not to send me to the battlefield." After a long, thoughtful silence, Jesus spoke to Claire, "My Mother wants me to keep you away from the front. I had decided that you would place yourself at the head of the army." There followed a reflective pause, followed by an alternative plan. "What I want above all is that you go to Paris. Go straight to the president. Tell him that I sent you to show him where to find salvation. Show him the image of my Heart covered with wounds; this large wound, it's France that caused it."[2] Claire would be a messenger, not a warrior maiden.

THE PROBLEM OF FEIGNED SANCTITY

Loublande falls within the administrative boundaries of Poitiers, a large diocese in the west of France. When news of Claire reached Monsignor Louis Humbrecht, the bishop of Poitiers, he did what any responsible administrator would have done. He appointed a committee.

Humbrecht had more on his mind than the challenge of wartime censorship or the potentially incendiary political claims coming out of Loublande. More than once the Catholic faithful—and Catholic clergy too—had been victims of what scholars and clergy call "feigned sanctity"—what anyone working within the vernacular would call a scam or a hoax. When Humbrecht heard of Claire, he wanted above all to avoid an unseemly incident, an affront to the dignity of the church or an attempt to prey upon the credulity of the faithful.

Humbrecht was alert to the risk that Claire Ferchaud represented; religiously inspired hoaxes were part of local history. In 1873, in the neighboring diocese of Nantes, a twenty-one-year-old woman named Marie Gagueny attracted national attention to herself by means of visions and reenactments of various tableaux from the Passion of Jesus. In March of 1873 she recounted to her parents a vision of the Holy Virgin, in which she was told that she would be marked by the five wounds that Jesus received at the Crucifixion—the stigmata—and that blood would flow from them. The stigmata were promised for a fixed date and time. They would appear on 21 April, a Friday, at ten in the morning.[3]

As news of the promised stigmata spread, the curious and the devout began to arrive at Blain, Marie's village. Marie's visions continued through the twenty-first and after. According to police reports, Marie suffered from catalepsy—a condition variously associated with schizophrenia or epilepsy. If so, her symptoms seemed to have blended—by intent or a kind of cultural induction—with conventional manifestations of spiritual ecstasy. Periodic seizures would certainly have lent her episodes an air of verisimilitude, conveying the impression that her entire being was given over to her spiritual unions. They could also induce pity, as when eight priests and some twenty lay witnesses looked on while Marie, lying on her bed, abruptly raised her arms toward heaven and asked the Virgin to cure her. On other occasions, trembling from her seizures became so intense that the result was not so much verisimilitude as panic. Those who witnessed one episode began to wonder whether she was possessed by the devil. They sprinkled holy water on Marie and her bed to drive out the demon and called a priest to hear her confession.[4]

Marie's stigmata fell short of expectations, but the crowds persisted. On peak days over two hundred pilgrims would descend on her village in hopes of getting a glimpse of the young visionary. A great and unspecified miracle was predicted for 2 May.[5] Meanwhile, every Friday Marie achieved an exalted state and reenacted the Passion of Jesus. During these episodes, Marie would place her hands and wrists side-by-side on her chest to represent Jesus, hands bound, standing before Pilate. Next, she placed both hands on her left shoulder as she acted out Jesus shouldering the cross. Then she would lie on her bed with her arms outstretched in a gesture suggesting crucifixion. She held that pose, hesitated, then let her head drop limply to her right shoulder. Finally, she would give out a sigh, marking the death of Jesus.[6] A sympathetic source gushed as if reviewing a theater spectacle, applauding her reenactment of Jesus's falls under the weight of the Cross ("les trois chutes sont épouvantables") and remarking of the performance as a whole that it was "ravissant!" A police reporter gave a more sober assessment, saying of Marie's Passion Play that it was "bien joué"—a role well played.[7]

Marie's comments, like Claire's, drifted from timeless spiritual topics to contemporary political ones. As one account had it, during one of her "ecstasies" Marie recounted a dialogue between Mary and Jesus in which Mary appealed to her son on behalf of France. "The Holy Virgin asked for grace for us," Marie explained. She "asked her son to bring peace and happiness to our country." Jesus resisted the appeals of his mother and shifted blame back onto a France of unbelievers. According to Marie, "Our Lord responded, 'I would like very much [to bring peace and happiness] but they will not convert; they don't want my grace, so they will be punished'."[8] Marie's Jesus, like Claire's, emphasized the theme of unrequited divine love.

What did the Catholic Church make of the young ecstatic? It temporized, apparently unsure what to make of her. It was difficult not to be impressed by the crowds the celebrated visionary drew, and for a while, the Catholic press reviewed her favorably. A laudatory piece on the "Stigmatisée de Blain" appeared in *Le Pèlerin,* the premier national Catholic publication of the day.[9] And then she dropped from sight—or, at least, from media commentary.[10]

By 1916, the Catholic Church had become vigilant with respect to such eruptions of popular religion. It would not let a case of holy celebrity go too far without subjecting it to scrutiny. Mere weeks before Claire captured national attention, a young visionary named Mademoiselle Clément generated public interest with claims of visions of Joan of Arc. In August of 1916, some two thousand pilgrims descended upon the town of Usson, south of Poitiers, to glimpse Mademoiselle Clément. Her supporters said that she glided more than she walked and that when she moved in fields of oats, the stalks she trampled sprung back upright after she passed. Mademoiselle Clément was the beneficiary of a phenomenon sometimes called "popular canonization" whereby the faithful, by their very numbers, confer celebrity, if not sanctity, upon religiously inspired individuals. Church officials considered it prudent to get involved early in these cases, lest they find themselves trapped between the evident public appeal of such figures and their own private doubts.

Indeed, Mademoiselle Clément was eventually deemed a hoax, her oracular utterances a product of a self-hypnosis induced by gazing at the setting sun. Moreover, in a development that showed how the stakes in the sanctity game had risen, church authorities performed a background check. The judgment was unfavorable. First, there were the parents. Discreet inquiries revealed that Mademoiselle Clément's father was not particularly devout and had little to recommend him; he was an unlikely father of a saint. Then, a review of Mademoiselle Clément's private life revealed few signs of piety. Rumors had it that Mademoiselle Clément had once dated a soldier posted to a local garrison. When that man moved on, she took up with another. Even the moments before her visions lacked dignity and reserve. Instead of preparing herself through prayer, she laughed and joked with those around her.[11]

Visions could generate notoriety, but without an impeccable record they would not generate sanctity. Sanctity in the modern era was getting no easier.

To Claire's credit, her personal life was above reproach. To the extent that Claire had faults, they ran, it was said, in the direction of an excessive piety. It was a family trait. By the time she was thirteen, Claire had developed the habit of a daily visit to Loublande for mass and communion, while one of Claire's older sisters had chosen a religious vocation, taken vows, and entered a convent in Nantes. When her parents organized a family trip to Nantes to visit her sister, Claire objected. "Et ma communion que je ne pourrais pas faire!" she exclaimed. "And what then of my communion!"[12] Was there such a thing as excessive piety? Was it a blessing or a curse that siblings should compete—one by religious vocation, the other through daily communion—to win the favor of the Heavenly Father?

The bishop of Poitiers called upon Claire to appear before his commission toward the end of 1916. In the meantime a vast public, eager to be close to a person who might prove to be a living saint, began to gather in greater numbers, revealing the convergence between sanctity and celebrity in modern times.[13] While Humbrecht counseled caution, the growing crowds at Loublande showed plainly that popular canonization—which requires no institutional validation—was getting underway.

SAYING GOOD-BYE TO LOUBLANDE:
CLAIRE GOES TO POITIERS

When Claire went to Poitiers, the seat of the diocese that included Loublande, in the final days of 1916, the men who had seen to her personal and spiritual development accompanied her. One of the three was the Reverend Audebert, young, even handsome, with his wire-rimmed glasses and fair hair parted on the side. The Reverend Bourget, who had helped to sharpen Claire's message and to turn this contemplative young woman into a messenger of God, also made the voyage. Monsieur Ferchaud, Claire's father, rounded out the group.

That Claire could command the time and attention of three men in such a way was a measure of her growing importance. And then there was the venue. Poitiers—episcopal seat, regional capital, ancient city steeped in history. To be summoned to Poitiers by Archbishop Humbrecht only confirmed her status as a figure of regional renown and growing national importance. Poitiers was itself a city of minor and major portents, starting with Notre-Dame-la-Grande, a captivating example of the Romano-Byzantine architecture cultivated in the French southwest. Within the church, a stained glass window recalled a moment in 1202 when the city was besieged by the armies of a foreign king. The mayor of Poitiers had invoked the protection of the city's three patrons—Radegonde, a saintly woman; Hilaire, its founding bishop; and Our Lady, *Notre Dame*. This heavenly trio responded to the mayor's appeal for rescue. They appeared in the night sky, disorienting the soldiers of the besieging armies. Their intervention saved Poitiers. In the context of 1916 and the present war and invasion, the similarities were obvious. Would a new constellation of forces—Claire, Humbrecht, the Sacré-Coeur—save France?

Claire's entourage surely felt the pull, as tourists today still do, of Poitiers' Palais de Justice, where Joan of Arc had faced her own episcopal inquiry in 1429. Anyone involved in the interrogation of Claire would have been hard pressed to ignore Joan's memorable precedent. Claire's appearance before Humbrecht's commission only added to

Figure 4.   Joan of Arc at Poitiers.
A stained-glass window at Notre-Dame-
la-Grande, Poitiers

the portents associated with this virgin visionary who promised
to drive out the invader and save France. The power of place and
precedent only heightened the sense of anticipation surrounding the
interrogation of Claire—that, along with the delicious prospect of
witnessing a national heroine in the making. As the epic elements

came into parallel alignment—wars, visions, maidens, Poitiers—Claire's story seemed less a matter of chance. Here, surely, was the hand of providence.

Just the same, some things didn't align, leaving room for the thought that mere circumstance, rather than some hidden hand, guided these affairs. Claire's interrogation did not take place in the Palais de Justice, by then a public building exclusively at the disposal of secular judicial authorities. Claire's audience was held in the more modest surroundings of the bishop's properties. Claire's episcopal commission also somehow lacked the luster and *gravitas* of Joan's. Joan's commission consisted of a formidable assemblage of eighteen distinguished ecclesiastics, including three Dominicans, a Carmelite, a Franciscan, and a Benedictine. It's hard to imagine that such a large group of theological scholars—confident in their learning, but diverse in training and affiliation—could easily be duped or cowed into consensus. Finally, an archbishop presided over this group of scholars, but it was an outsider—Regnault de Chartres, archbishop of Reims and chancellor of France—not the archbishop of Poitiers. Such a commission was designed to arrive at the truth regarding Joan, even if the truth disappointed or wasn't politically expedient.

Claire's commission, by comparison, was rather modest. It consisted of a committee of men—priests and theologians, six altogether—of strictly regional renown within the diocese of Poitiers. Among those Humbrecht appointed, four were close colleagues, including two of his lieutenants within the diocesan administration, the vicars-general Vareilles-Sommières and Lépine. He also appointed the hard-nosed manager and general secretary of his episcopal offices, the vicar-general Péret. To these three Humbrecht added Chaperon, the superior of the Grand Seminary of Poitiers.[14] Finally, Humbrecht decided to preside over the commission himself.[15] Thus, the commission was not an independent group of specialists charged to investigate and report to Humbrecht, but Humbrecht's own creation, a commission of close associates.[16]

The charge of Humbrecht's commission was to look into what was beginning to be called *les faits de Loublande*—the "facts" or "events" of Loublande—and to render a judgment. Claire's story was big, and Humbrecht was taking no chances—hence, his reliance on a hand-picked commission of close associates. For this same reason, however, Humbrecht's commission carried considerable risk for him: first because the lack of independence among its members reduced Humbrecht's chances of getting disinterested opinions; second because the lack of distance between Humbrecht and his commission meant that Catholic authorities would ultimately hold Humbrecht directly responsible for its actions. Although never discussed in these terms, Humbrecht's transfer out of Poitiers to another diocese two years later can be read as a negative judgment on his handling of the Claire inquiry.

As for the commission members themselves, it is not difficult to guess their attitude toward the task before them. The commission had drafted its questions with great care and in advance; they knew what they wanted to know.[17] The nuns of the Visitationist convent of Poitiers gathered Claire's writings for the commission. Thanks to them, as well as to Audebert, Bourget, the press, the word-of-mouth rank and file, and the rumor networks, the commission already understood the gist of Claire's visions and her mission. They surely wished that what they had heard about Claire would prove true. They had no reason to doubt the sober and well-intentioned men who had brought Claire to their attention. But they did not want to be the victims of a hoax, and they did not want to expose themselves or their bishop to ridicule. In short, they would be open to the possibility of sanctity but alert to the potential for fraud. And they would move quickly—does one keep God waiting?

For two days, on 28 and 29 December 1916, Claire and her entourage, minus her father, took their places before the commission.[18] For Claire, this would be the first time she would have to explain herself and her visions before someone other than a sympathetic spiritual counselor.

The transcript of the inquiry presents two portraits of Claire. The first is of a timid girl still finding her voice; the second is of an assured young woman able to hold her own in dialogue with her powerful and learned inquisitors.[19] Humbrecht himself opened the inquiry, pursuing a line of questioning that established the outlines of Claire's life and religious upbringing. His questions were gentle and nonconfrontational. By disposition or design, Humbrecht's questions cast him in the role of the "good cop."

Lépine, one of Humbrecht's "lieutenants," took up a more aggressive line of questioning. He took aim at inconsistencies in Claire's story. "On 25 September you announced the visit of the Holy Virgin for that night, but you don't talk about it afterward," he noted. "She came so often that I don't know what to say; I didn't write it down," she responded. Lépine homed in on an incipient anticlericalism in her remarks. "You speak of priests opposed to your mission; you say that Jesus is irritated with them. This is an error on your part, because everyone wants [your mission to succeed]. Why would Jesus-Christ be irritated because we demand proofs?" "Jesus isn't irritated," she countered. "He's distressed by those who oppose themselves to his plans."[20]

Lépine pressed the demand for proof, for irrefutable signs of the hand of God. "How can one know the wishes of God in a matter as grave as this if our Lord gives no proof? Did our Lord promise signs?" Lépine's phrasing suggests sympathy. He speaks of "our Lord" rather than "your vision," tacitly conceding the point that Claire truly had spoken to Jesus. Claire, noting that Lépine had confused his own desire for proof with the will of God, answered Lépine's request for signs shrewdly: "[God wishes] France to return to him." What mattered was the will of God—not Lépine's need of proof. Conceding her point, Lépine clarified his question, "I mean signs of your mission." "The Good Lord did not tell me to put myself at the head of the army," she replied, a reference to Joan of Arc, whose signs consisted of victory in battle. Claire's mission would not be fulfilled by military means.

Exasperated by the lack of progress, Humbrecht interrupted with a question that went to the heart of the matter, "These gentlemen want a sign before going any further." Claire responded with a remark that reminded them that she, not they, was God's true intercessor. "Monsignor," she said. "I'll ask him."[21] It was a comment that laid bare the subversive potential every visionary possessed: Who needs clergy when one converses directly with God?

Some of Claire's answers emphasized the wonder of her visions and the incommensurability of language.

QUESTION: How do your apparitions take place?
ANSWER: The voice strikes my ears, but my heart even more. As for the visions, it's inexplicable. I see as if with my own eyes, only better.
QUESTION: You say that our Lord took you on his knees. How did that happen?
ANSWER: His presence is palpable. I feel his presence in a way that I can't describe.

Finally, there was a great interest in Claire's stated purpose—to persuade the president of the French Republic to consecrate France to the Sacred Heart. Here, the skepticism of the commission is overt, especially in the face of such long odds. "Why this hope to impose an act of faith on an ungodly president?" Here, Claire's visions fortified her again. "I saw him on the path of conversion. His soul is very troubled. I've seen him pray many times." The transcript shows that at this point Claire began to sob.[22]

The commission also questioned Claire's two male sponsors, Father Audebert, pastor of Loublande, and Father Bourget, the priest Claire had won over during her retreat at Saint-Laurent. What of Claire's character? What was her motivation? Audebert, who had known Claire as a girl, noted that following her first communion, which coincided with the termination of her schooling, Claire had been particularly scrupulous in her religious observance. She declined a trip to Nantes on the grounds that it would interfere with her routine of daily mass and communion. Audebert conceded that he found this behavior "tedious." But Audebert also noted that he began to see Claire differently when, following a sermon about how Jesus wanted five victims and that one would come from the west of France, Claire volunteered, "It will be me."[23] Claire's quiet confidence had also swayed Bourget. He told the commission flat out that Claire was perceptive—she knew how to read souls.

Both men were asked about spiritual patterning. How much had Claire read about spiritual women—Joan of Arc, Marguerite-Marie Alacoque? They asked pointedly whether she had read of the life of Gemma Galgani, a young contemporary from Tuscany who had had visions, received the stigmata, and achieved international notoriety.[24] (Gemma Galgani was ultimately canonized.) Claire and her patrons generally conceded that Claire had read of such individuals, though by their responses they indicated how little they thought such influence mattered. In their eyes, Claire was not a copycat mystic. Claire was an original.

Claire's world was more visionary than discursive; in the end the commission was far more impressed by Claire's written testimony than by her responses under direct questioning. Claire was always more at ease when alone, whether at her desk crafting a language to describe her visions or on her knees at her bedside or in church in the reveries of her visions. She was not a woman made for dialogue—at least not of the human sort. Claire's autobiography and accounts written about her reveal a woman challenged by the presence, questions, and conversational demands of others. Claire felt inhibitions; articulating her thoughts was a challenge. She met questions with pained silence, sobs, or brief, one-sentence answers. Her most intense experiences were private ones.

Claire's contemplative tendencies made her marvelously receptive to spiritual influences. The solitude of writing activated her imagination and her sense of wonder, and her growing aptitude for writing made it possible for her to project her view of the world. Claire felt far more at ease trying to re-create her visions and their meaning in carefully crafted written statements in which her words sought to convey her sense of wonder. But her inability to express herself through the spoken word did not bode well for a woman whose public effectiveness would depend on a direct encounter with the president of the French Republic.

Bishop Humbrecht's commission did little to dampen enthusiasm for Claire or to halt the flow of pilgrims to Rinfillières. It heightened expectations. Virtually everyone knew that Claire was not the first visionary to emerge in troubled times to lead her nation and drive out an invader. Moreover, Joan of Arc had also undergone interrogation at Poitiers.[25] The symmetry—Joan the virgin savior of France in the fifteenth century, Claire the nation's virgin savior in the twentieth, each called to account by human authorities in Poitiers—was as evident to skeptics as it was to anyone open to the possibility of redemption.

But if Humbrecht respected the power of the human imagination, he seemed little concerned to offer the definitive public pronouncement that would channel and contain it. Humbrecht had convened the committee in late 1916; by March of 1917 its findings, as described by official diocesan publications, could only be characterized as equivocal. If Humbrecht had perceived Claire as an embarrassment, he would have pushed the commission to a speedy judgment against her, to cast a thunderbolt of condemnation that would have put the authority of the Catholic Church between Claire and her followers. Instead, Humbrecht let Claire's story and her notoriety grow. Humbrecht published an official statement in the weekly publication of the diocese of Poitiers, *La Semaine Liturgique,* in late March 1917. However, his statement said virtually nothing of consequence about Claire Ferchaud, her visions, or their authenticity. Humbrecht merely acknowledged that a commission had been named, that its members had met with Claire, that they were studying the matter, but that they had not reached a conclusion and cautioned members of the diocese against reaching premature conclusions, which, of course, is exactly what many proceeded to do.[26] Was the commission's deliberate pace part of a strategy? One can also imagine that Humbrecht's hesitation stemmed from his inability to reconcile his sympathy for Claire with his fear of the politically explosive potential of her revelations. Humbrecht was leaving his options open.

In this respect, too, Claire's experience at Poitiers was also like Joan's because the decision about Joan had also been open-ended. Joan of Arc had been pressed for signs. Seguin Seguin, a seventy-year-old professor of theology and dean of the faculty of Poitiers, had put this issue to her squarely: "God cannot wish us to believe in you unless he sends us a sign, to show that we should believe in you." To which Joan had replied, "In God's name, I have not come to Poitiers to make signs. But lead me to Orléans, and I will show you the signs I was sent to make."[27] Victory at Orléans was to be Joan's sign, her vindication. Claire would seek *her* vindication in Paris.

A Kind of Apotheosis

Claire Goes to Paris

❧

No modern army can prevail without the support of the home front—
at least not in the long run. That is why it is called a "front." Like any
other front, once it gives way, it soon brings an end to the war.

In modern times, states are as vulnerable to mercurial public opinion
as they are to armies. Impatience and war-weariness led to a spectacular collapse of the home front in Russia in early 1917, followed by a revolution that brought down Nicholas II, the czar of Russia. A new fear
haunted Paris and London—the fear that the new Russian government
would bow to public opinion and withdraw from the war. With Russia
out of the war, Germany could concentrate its forces—divided since
August of 1914 between the Western and the Russian fronts—on
French and British forces in the West. Even though Russia remained in
the war until the Bolshevik seizure of power in November of 1917,
German pressure on the Western front intensified and led to mutinies
among French troops in April and May of 1917.[1] In short, during the
opening months of 1917, the outlook for France and its allies had
sharply deteriorated.

Interest in Claire grew as 1917 began, and word spread of her interrogation at Poitiers. The increasingly desperate military situation in
France surely also had something to do with the public's willingness to

listen to someone—*anyone*—promising an end to the interminable slaughter. By the spring, most of the eventual 1.4 million French deaths in the Great War had already occurred.[2] Those who were still living and breathing and worrying in 1917 couldn't know this—and it would have been cold comfort if they did. From where they stood, the end of the carnage was nowhere in sight; the bodies and the bad news just kept piling up. Confidence in the men who led the country in war—politicians and generals—slouched toward its nadir. Public prayer and pilgrimage in places like Loublande channeled home-front anxieties, and they owed much to the public's deepening sense of powerlessness. The apparent inability of military and political leaders to bring the war to a conclusion contrasted markedly with the confident message of a woman who said she knew just how the war could be ended. The world of men had made a grotesque failure of the war; was it so odd to invest hope in a woman? In a peculiar but obvious way, curiosity about Claire served as an index of ebbing confidence in French public leadership.

Raymond Poincaré, president of the French Republic, was regularly briefed on such topics as the conduct of the war, troop morale, and the status of France's allies. When did he first learn of Claire? Public opinion and the morale of the "home front" were matters of regular concern, so it is likely that he heard of the *voyante* of Loublande, her plans for France, and the crowds that she was drawing long before he met her. He surely heard of Claire by 16 January 1917, when he received a letter from her, using the name that was now her public name, Claire de Jésus Crucifié: Claire of Jesus Crucified.[3]

Claire drafted and sent the letter with the knowledge and tacit approval of Humbrecht. (It was dated 1 January, so the letter must have been drafted around the time of the Poitiers interrogation, which concluded on 28 December, and sent immediately after.)[4] That conclusion is borne out as well by subsequent events. Like Joan of Arc's, Claire's interrogation at Poitiers was followed by actions. Validation would come from prodigious signs. Following *her* interrogation at Poitiers, Joan had set out with an army to raise the siege of Orléans. Military victory and her triumphant entry into an Orléans liberated from English control were the first of her grand public gestures. Claire's challenge was no less daunting. She set out to win over the president of the Republic, first through the written word, her most effective medium, then through her charismatic presence. Like Joan's, her fate would depend on the success of her endeavor.

Claire's letter to Raymond Poincaré amounts to the first systematic statement of her mission and her scenario for victory. France will triumph in this war, she declares, following a merger of powerful symbols. When the image of the Sacred Heart is placed upon the tricolor flag—symbol of France since 1789—it will mark the return of France to its Christian origins. France's allies will do likewise and place the Sacred Heart on their flags, too. Then, armed with their colors and their sacred emblems, the Allied forces will launch an assault at the same hour on the same day. "The enemy," Claire predicts, "will take flight and be pushed back across the border, with great losses. In a few days, the Sacred Heart will make us victorious."[5] Following victory, France and its allies were to be consecrated to the Sacred Heart in a solemn ceremony at the Basilica of the Sacré-Coeur on Montmartre.

In its basic features, Claire's program fit within a long pedigree of visionary designs for France. In the 1680s, Marguerite-Marie Alacoque, one of the founding figures in the modern Sacred Heart tradition, sought to send a similar message to Louis XIV, the Sun King. Like Claire, she experienced visions of the Sacred Heart. Those visions told her that Louis must consecrate the French realm to the Sacred Heart, that there must be a chapel built for this purpose, and that the banners and ensigns of the Crown must bear the image of the Sacred Heart.[6] The Basilica of the Sacré-Coeur, completed just as war broke out in 1914, was regarded as having fulfilled this long-standing demand for a "chapel." By emphasizing the tricolor flag and Poincaré's role in the consecration, Claire was, in effect, updating an already ancient Catholic patriotic vision and bringing it into the context of the crisis of the First World War.[7]

Figure 5. "France, the soldier of Christ": A postcard representation of how victory might be assured

There is no documentary evidence of Poincaré's reaction to Claire's letter, but he seems to have been unimpressed by Claire's vision for France. He did not respond or even acknowledge her letter, which amounts to a mute shrug of the shoulders. Claire, undaunted, resolved to take her message directly to the president. Early in February of 1917, she prepared for a journey to Paris.

SO *THAT'S* CLAIRE FERCHAUD

Claire left Rinfillières in the company of her father and the Reverend Audebert on 20 February 1917. She and her entourage traveled first to Cholet, where she spent the night at the elegant home of a patrician family. As their guest, the young visionary saw things she'd never seen before. A servant in livery met her car; she was offered a private room with a soft, silky bed. For a peasant from the Vendée, this was already a lot.

The next morning, she and her small entourage boarded a first-class carriage on a train that took them from Cholet to Tours and then Paris. It was midday on the twenty-first, a Wednesday, when the train began to slow as it entered the outer neighborhoods of the capital. That February Wednesday was the first day of Lent, traditionally a time of atonement. The most vivid impression Claire retained of her arrival was an ominously somber midday sky. The watercolor gray deepened as the train approached the station and the city. The gas jets that illuminated train cars and shops remained lit throughout the morning and afternoon. She interpreted this sign—"black night at midday" in her words—as ominous for France.[8]

When Claire first saw it in 1917, the Gare d'Orsay was still a relatively new structure, having been inaugurated on Bastille Day, 14 July 1900, just in time for the Universal Exposition of that year. Unlike the Gare Saint-Lazare, which made no pretense of being anything more than it was—an iron structure outfitted with glass, a barn for trains— the Gare d'Orsay was a cathedral of the age of industry, a pious gesture to the elegance of modern rail travel. It was a marriage of new materials with conventional aesthetics—an iron frame sheathed in stone—to create the wondrous effect of stone suspended in air. The sturdy iron frame meant that no columns were needed to support the massive barrel vault that hovered over the platforms and tracks, lifted by light-streaked puffs of steam. This was vast empty, sacred space, an elegantly enclosed volume of air into which trains and passengers rushed—a temple to the primacy of movement in the modern age.

In its vastness, the Gare d'Orsay was also a temple to anonymity. When Claire left Loublande for the Cholet train station and Paris, she left as a crowd's hero, the brave visionary who would save France. In Paris, she was just another anonymous traveler, probably one of dozens of provincials seeing Paris for the first time that day.[9] The spectacle was the city, not the visionary.

Stepping from the train onto the crowded platform, Claire experienced crowds in a way that she probably never had before. Unlike the crowds at Loublande and Rinfillières, this crowd was not fixated on Claire. Unlike the crowd she joined on pilgrimage to Lourdes, this crowd lacked a fraternal common purpose. This crowd moved about the platform in apparent randomness—in front of Claire, at her heels, jostling her bags. This crowd didn't know Claire and it didn't care.

If Claire felt fear and doubt at the Orsay station, she felt no better as she made her way across the city.[10] Claire's lodging in Paris had already been settled before she arrived. While in Paris, Claire would live at the Maison des Soeurs de la Sagesse, a convent in the fashionable sixteenth arrondissement, far removed from the city center.

In traveling from the train station to the convent, Claire would traverse the city of Paris, a city at war whose monuments were defended by sandbag walls. When Claire, her father, and Audebert exited the station, the Tuileries Garden and the Musée du Louvre were in full view just across the river. As they rode along the Seine, they had a choice of bridges. They could cross at the Concorde Bridge—passing the neoclassical National Assembly on their way to the vast Place de la Concorde. A bit farther down they could cross the elegant Alexander III Bridge—built for the 1900 Universal Exhibition and leading to the exhibition halls of the Grand and Petit Palais. Had they wanted a better view of the Eiffel Tower, they might have waited to cross at the Alma Bridge before making their way up the avenue George V. Wherever they crossed the Seine, their route would have taken them to the broad Champs-Elysées, which rose toward the Arc de Triomphe. At the Arc, they circled the monument 270 degrees counter-clockwise before exiting the roundabout at the avenue Victor Hugo and turning up an elegant tree-lined street in one of the more exclusive parts of the city.[11] They stopped in front of the convent, number 117. Claire wasn't in Loublande any more.

Alongside the fantastic appearance of the monumental capital, Claire would have seen the unmistakable signs of a city at war.[12] Paris in 1917 was a militarized city. Buses, like men, had been requisitioned; for the first two years of the war, Parisians had to do without them.

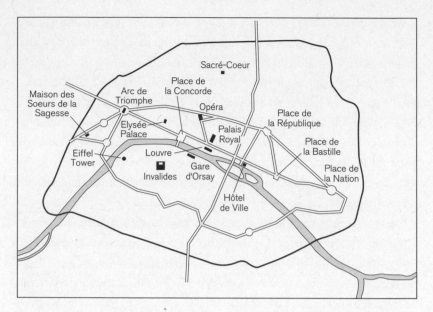

Map 3.   Paris: Landmarks and key locations. (Adapted from original by
Anthony Jonas)

Taxis were scarce. Livestock, a commonplace in the streets of medieval
Paris, could once again be found within the city, grazing in some of the
larger parks. With horses scarce and racing suspended for the duration,
Auteuil and Longchamps became pasture for cattle and sheep. If the image
of a dissolute and pleasure-loving "gay Paris" remained intact, the real-
ity was greatly diminished. Theaters and museums had closed in 1914;
three years later, many were still closed. Cabarets had adapted by offering war-related patriotic fare—*bleu blanc rouge* costume gave wartime
frivolity a veneer of patriotic respectability. Museums had reopened
with vastly impoverished collections: the masterpieces had been
relocated to provincial museums for safekeeping.[13] Rationing had created a black market in certain foods, forcing restaurants to struggle to
keep profiteering from driving them out of business. The Métro shut
down at 10:30 in the evening. Streetlights were dimmed by daubs of

blue paint and extinguished at 10:00, lest the city become too easy a target for bombardment from airplanes and zeppelins. By ten at night, the main exits from the city were barred to all but essential services.[14]

From the moment of her arrival in Paris, Claire's sentiments resonated with the bleak aspect of a city at war. Claire's heart was "aching and sorrowful." By the time she arrived at the Maison des Soeurs de la Sagesse she was reeling from the avalanche of events and the succession of novelties and wonders she had witnessed during the preceding hours and days. Claire, her father, and Audebert were ushered into the convent parlor, where they awaited the mother superior. Claire noticed the tall green plants—it was perhaps the first time that she and her father had seen large decorative plants growing indoors—and the somber mood of the large convent parlor.

The convent superior, Mother Pauline de Saint-Jean, entered the parlor. She greeted her visitors and began to speak to Father Audebert. Claire sat a bit to one side, not daring to move. Claire was disappointed by the appearance of the mother superior, which revealed little of the warmth and goodness she'd been told she could expect. The face, framed by the black fabric and white wimple, did not seem kind; her lips were thin and pinched, which Claire interpreted as a sign of emotional reserve.[15]

Mother Pauline spoke to Audebert rather than to Claire directly.

"So *that's* Claire Ferchaud," she said, turning slightly sideways and looking down toward Claire. "That's her, Claire Ferchaud," affirmed Audebert.

Claire noted a tone of irony in the mother superior's words. She heard it echoed in Audebert's reply. She didn't like it. It carried a palpable sense of disappointment. So *this* is the woman who would save France? Could anything good come out of Rinfillières?

"All of France talks of her," the mother superior continued. Claire's father, who had said nothing, spoke in her defense. "It's not for her enjoyment, you can be sure of that!" Mother Pauline ignored the remark. She turned to Claire. "I'll show you your room," she said. The conversation ended.

THE DARK SIDE OF THE FAIRY TALE

Perhaps the brooding sky that greeted her arrival was a portent. Perhaps it mirrored her inner state. If Paris was to be the scene of her triumph, her sojourn had gotten off to a nightmarish start. At the same time that she prepared for the encounter that would make or break her mission of national redemption, Claire was harassed by minor figures who seemed bent on humiliating her.

The Maison des Soeurs de la Sagesse was a convent. Attached to it was a boarding school for Catholic girls. It was not uncommon for girls to arrive and never leave, beginning their residency as boarding students and ending, following a religious vocation, as nuns. As head administrator for both establishments, Mother Pauline could be excused for seeing Claire as just another awkward adolescent girl who needed a bit of polish and a firm hand—in short, as another boarder at the school. Mother Pauline seemed to take every opportunity to chide and admonish Claire, as if she had written herself into Claire's scenario as the evil stepmother of fairy tales.

Claire described the convent atmosphere as glacial. It got chillier when Mother Pauline humiliated Claire before the entire convent community on her first day. As Claire was leaving the chapel by a side door, she let it close behind her. It slammed shut with a crash, startling everyone, including Claire. Mother Pauline was upon her in a moment. She ordered Claire to practice opening and closing the door to demonstrate "before all the sisters" that she knew how to leave the chapel quietly.[16]

While Mother Pauline infantilized her, others took a proprietary interest in Claire. The priest Jean-Baptiste Lemius arrived at the convent to announce that he would be Claire's confessor—a prized relationship with any spiritually gifted person. Lemius already knew a great deal about Claire. Bourget or other colleagues had kept him informed regarding Claire and her mission. Lemius would take over as Claire's spiritual adviser during the most critical phase of her career.

Lemius was not a stranger to Paris. He had once served as superior of chaplains at the Basilica of the Sacré-Coeur on Montmartre. Recently, however, he had been transferred from Paris to Bordeaux in what must have felt like a demotion. But he had been recalled to Paris with the encouragement of the bishop of Poitiers in order to facilitate Claire's mission. Lemius had recently written a book on France and the Sacred Heart, so her mission was no mystery to him. In a sense, he had drafted the blueprint for her mission. But on a temperamental level, a worse match for Claire could scarcely be imagined.

Lemius was a forceful speaker and a man of action. He wore his white hair swept back from his forehead. It billowed out above and behind his ears, like a white mane framing his face. His eyes were dark, deep-set, and narrow, giving them a focused and piercing quality. His strong chin jutted out, projecting personality. A crucifix as large as a pocketknife hung from his neck. He wore it tucked into his waistband, like a sword to be drawn at the first sign of the enemy.

Lemius understood Claire's message but he didn't understand Claire. As a man of action, he was impatient for results. He had little sympathy for the hesitant and sensitive young woman before him. Lemius understood visionaries, and he knew what they could do. For years he was the chief promoter and organizer of pilgrimages to Pontmain, where in 1870 a group of children claimed to have seen the Virgin Mary floating in the winter night sky, promising that prayer and penitence would soon bring an end to the Franco-Prussian war.[17] Lemius hadn't witnessed the visions, but he knew that visions represented a beginning, not an end. Almost single-handedly he turned Pontmain, a Breton backwater, into a major pilgrimage site. In the decades following the 1870s, railroad expansion and group travel made pilgrimage a precursor of modern tourism. Lemius made a name for himself by using the act of pilgrimage to put thousands of people on the move.

In 1893, Lemius was moved from Pontmain to Montmartre—a clear promotion. At Montmartre, he had put his prodigious skills to work promoting pilgrimage during the site's crucial early years. He believed

Figure 6.   The Immaculate Conception appears to a group
of children at Pontmain during the Franco-Prussian War. In
the winter sky are the words "Pray my children; God will
answer your prayers soon." Reproduced from *Notre-Dame de
Pontmain* (Abbeville, 1896)

in stimulating faith through action. Faith should be vigorous, hence he
supported pilgrimage and an array of networks and male fraternal
organizations for the Catholic laity, such as Les Hommes de France au
Sacré-Coeur.[18] From Montmartre, he promoted the idea that the Sacred
Heart should be attached to the French tricolor flag, a program he pursued through a publication, *Le Drapeau du Sacré-Coeur.*

Figure 7.   Masthead of *Le Drapeau du Sacré-Coeur*, fortnightly of Les Hommes de France au Sacré-Coeur. Archives nationales, Paris

For Claire, Lemius was a powerful ally. She was the gifted visionary; he was well connected in Paris and he knew how to get things done. At times he was also her manager and agent. For years he was one of Claire's most ardent defenders. He was also the bane of her existence— tendentious and overbearing.[19] From their first meeting he laid down the lines of authority. "You don't know how to make a confession!" he told Claire at the first of their regular encounters. She would later remember her weekly confession with Lemius as "torture," not at all like confession with the gentle Father Audebert, who indulged and comforted her. For Claire, confession was a time to think out loud, to follow her thoughts, her impulses, and her fears where they would take her, always in the safety of the company of a sympathetic soul. Confession could be like therapy to her. It clarified, through articulation, the sources of her inspirations and torments. But if the therapeutic analogy holds, then Lemius was an advocate of brief psychotherapy.

"The best confession is the one that takes only two and half minutes," Lemius told her. For Claire, this was like no confession at all.

Without talking things out, how was she to distinguish sin from mere defect? How could she know temptation from consent? Anguish was the dominant feature of her inner life. Her soul was "dominated by fear." So where was the consolation of confession? Lemius wanted only a catalog of sins, a laundry list. For Claire, this meant that she had to aggregate, to turn her anguish into a dry memorandum.[20] How could Claire unburden herself when she was enjoined from talking through her fears? Confession was a quick ablution for Lemius, not a talking cure. Lemius wanted brevity: unburden yourself and get on with life. But Claire's thoughts were never settled and tidy. And now, just as she faced the greatest challenge of her life and spiritual career in a strange and unsympathetic city, Lemius was leaving Claire alone to face the torment of her soul.

And Claire's torment was deepening. On 24 February, after three days in Paris, Claire was losing her protective entourage. Her natural father and her "spiritual father," Audebert, had stayed long enough to ease her transition; now they were going home. Claire fell into an emotional crisis. She wept. When Lemius arrived that evening to visit her, she was still overcome by grief. "My face was swollen from tears and sobs choked my throat," she recalled. Lemius, meanwhile, was no more disposed than earlier to play the role of nurturer. When Lemius spoke to her, her emotions overwhelmed her. She was unable to speak. Then Mother Pauline entered the room.

"Mother Superior," Lemius asked, "would you please bring an umbrella?"

"And what would you do with an umbrella?" she replied, playing along. "The weather is clear."

"No, the weather is not clear," Lemius replied. "On the contrary, it's raining, look at that," and he gestured toward Claire, her face bathed in tears.

As Claire later recalled the episode, both Lemius and Mother Pauline broke into mocking laughter.[21] What was to have been her triumph was turning into a humiliating defeat—*this* is the woman who would save France?—at the hands of individuals she thought would be her guardians.

For Lemius, the stakes were personal. In 1915, he had published a book in which he had boldly predicted the triumphant return of Christian France, a return to be manifested by the placement of the Sacred Heart on the tricolor flag of France. He had placed inspired women— Joan of Arc, Marguerite-Marie Alacoque—among a succession of patriotic saints. He had predicted that the "return" of France would take place during a national crisis, perhaps the present crisis of war. "Moments of great distress are always the most favorable moments for the reign of the Sacred Heart," he wrote. And then he asked, "Today, tomorrow, who will be the instrument of the Sacred Heart?"[22]

Lemius's book had provided the road map for Claire's career. The convergent paths traced by his book and Claire's story and visionary gifts had now brought them together—he from Bordeaux, she from Loublande by way of Poitiers. But to his dismay, the woman before him, the so-called Visionary of Loublande, was no Joan of Arc. This was a homesick peasant from the Vendée; her personality was crumbling before his eyes. How could she save France when she couldn't even speak? Sobs clutched at her throat. Comfort was something Lemius was unable to offer. He could only chide her and encourage her to get over the departure of gentle Father Audebert and accept him, Lemius, as her spiritual counselor.

"You'll have to get used to getting by without him," he admonished, "because I don't intend to bother myself with a two-bit little girl." Lemius could see Claire's mission coming apart. He was losing patience. "If you have only tears for me, I'll take the train back to Bordeaux this evening, and I'll write to Poitiers and tell them that it's over."[23] Claire's extraordinary adventure seemed to be coming to an end. Her throat felt choked. She couldn't answer. Lemius left.

Faced with these limitations and disappointments, Claire began to reshape her mission for France, to make it conform to things of which she was capable. Instead of her triumph, as she had once envisioned, she now began to imagine a kind of immolation. Perhaps her mission would not be victory after all, but the sacrifice of herself as a victim.

"I grasped little by little the true character of my Mission. It is sketched in strokes of fire and blood," she later recalled. Following the sharp rebuke from Lemius, she decided to offer her life for France.[24]

A WILDFLOWER AMONG ROSES

In fact no one was giving up on Claire just yet. It was apparent that the celebrity status Claire brought with her clashed with the culture of discipline and self-effacement that prevailed in the convent. Despite their severe attitude, Lemius and Mother Pauline of Saint-Jean sought to give Claire time to adapt to her new surroundings and still pursue her elevated role. They began to offer solace and diversion. One of the nuns from the convent, an assistant to Mother Pauline, was assigned to serve as Claire's companion at meals and to guard against loneliness and isolation. Also, it was arranged for Claire to accompany a group of young women from the convent boarding school on a field trip to Montmartre and the Basilica of the Sacré-Coeur on 25 February.

A boarding school on the avenue Victor Hugo would have served a clientele drawn from the wealthiest families of Catholic France. Claire sensed the difference immediately, the contrast between the "awkwardness of the modest peasant beside the distinguished demeanor" of the girls of the convent school. She reassured herself using the language of the fields and flowers. She thought of the "delicate violet that grows quietly at the bottom of a ravine and flowers sweetly, without ambition, but every bit as much the tiny creature of God as the splendid flowers of the rose garden beneath the palace windows."[25] In the company of these young women, Claire articulated for the first time a sense of a social difference.

The company of peasants, of people just like her, also accentuated her sense of difference. Pilgrimages to the Sacré-Coeur on Montmartre were often organized by theme, and the theme for 25 February was "the fields of France." Crowds of peasants took their place in the basilica. Claire no longer felt dwarfed and submerged by the daughters of privilege around her, her convent school companions. She no longer felt like a violet, a wildflower among cultivated roses. Claire looked into the "weathered faces" of the peasants and she noticed the "calloused hands." She felt a shiver of pride and thought to herself, "Jesus, *we* are the ones who love you."[26]

Claire was smart and she was learning quickly. She was learning that celebrity played differently in Paris than in the provinces. As she moved around the Sacré-Coeur, heads turned to follow her and she heard voices murmur *la voyante* ("the visionary") as she passed.[27] But even here, where one would have expected fascination with her to peak, the scene was nothing like what she had known at home. There were no fawning crowds, eager to touch her or to brush something against her. Parisian indifference was compounded by the preoccupations of a city at war. Claire was learning that Paris was detached, even jaded, and that charisma was allied with context.

In Paris, interest in Claire was decidedly more aloof, more clinical, even among those likely to be well disposed toward her and her message, like Jean-Baptiste Lemius and Mother Pauline of Saint-Jean. There were others. Édouard Loutil was one of the more powerful Catholic spokesmen of his day. In his day job, Loutil was pastor of Saint-Jean-de-Montmartre, the lovely Romanesque church that serves as the parish church of Montmartre. Loutil moonlighted as a regular contributor to the Catholic daily newspaper *La Croix,* where his militant message was encapsulated in his pen name, Pierre l'Ermite (Peter the Hermit), the name of a clergyman who had preached the Crusades.[28] In 1901 Loutil, in the guise of Pierre l'Ermite, had advocated his own kind of crusade by urging French Catholics to celebrate the national holiday of 14 July by displaying tricolor flags emblazoned with the Sacred Heart.[29]

Claire had embraced this cause as her own, so Loutil ought to have been sympathetic to Claire and her message; however, in a private audience with him, she found him cold and steely, like Lemius. Claire was "timid and trembling" as Loutil questioned her closely. She felt confused. She was used to thinking of priests as incarnating Jesus, but these men were not at all like the compassionate, androgynous Jesus of her visions, the man whose gaping heart bled. Loutil's questioning made her feel like a suspect. She lost her spontaneity. She lost her composure.[30] Claire was closing in on herself. She sought solace from a parish priest at Saint-Honoré d'Eylau, a church near her convent on the avenue Victor Hugo. He didn't help. Instead, he told her candidly that her project would fail. That night, she prayed that she be allowed to go home.[31]

WITH THE PRESIDENT OF THE REPUBLIC

Claire's break came through Lemius, who, for all of his hostility, retained an abiding interest in Claire, if not a grudging respect. Lemius had a history of establishing privileged spiritual relationships with spiritually gifted women, and his role as founder of a Catholic women's organization, Les Femmes de France, in 1898 can be seen, in part, as a way of institutionalizing this penchant.[32] But Lemius also tended to establish proprietary relationships with the women he guided. And although Claire's reputation owed much to Lemius's tireless campaigning on her behalf, he was reluctant to let anyone else assume his function as her privileged interlocutor.[33] After his departure from Paris, Lemius argued against assigning Claire another spiritual counselor—a great hardship for someone like Claire who felt a great need to talk about the things she experienced. As Claire reflected on their relationship later in life, she remarked that Lemius wanted no one else "to lay claim to what he considered his property."[34]

Other things besides advocacy and a sense of ownership bound them. Lemius had a lively imagination and sensed the action of spirits around him. His sensibility was not as acute as Claire's, but they shared an openness toward a realm of unseen things. Lemius was also keen not to be duped. This combination of credulity, skepticism, and self-doubt preyed upon him, generating an inner turmoil that took the form of demons and haunting figures. When Lemius decided to see the archbishop of Paris about an earlier visionary protégé, Marie-Adèle Garnier, he experienced a frightful carriage ride, pursued by demons on his way to the episcopal offices.

"I will never forget that short ride," he wrote,

> as soon as the carriage began to move, I began to feel agitated, fright-ened as I rarely had been. It seemed to me that all Hell swirled about me, to the point that I held the carriage door part way open, as if I were in danger. Relieved to set foot on the sidewalk, I heard within myself a mocking voice say that I was the plaything of a visionary and that the Archbishop was going to get a good laugh at my foolishness.[35]

Demons from hell or projections of his own doubts, Lemius under-stood these creatures as obstacles in his mission of advocacy on behalf of a saintly woman.

True to form, Lemius was well disposed toward Claire, despite his gruff demeanor and his impatience with her anxieties and her need for talk. He served as Claire's advocate, promoting her and her story among sympathetic notables in Paris. Among them was Baudry d'Asson, a deputy in the French legislature representing the Vendée, a département near Claire's home. The Revolution of 1789 had abolished titles of nobility, but this deputy was known among his friends and admirers as the "marquis" de Baudry d'Asson. Baudry d'Asson was a distinguished name, associated with royalism and counterrevolution-ary politics in the west of France. He had heard of Claire from contacts in his district. When Lemius was recalled from Paris to Bordeaux by his superiors, he put Claire in touch with Baudry d'Asson. It turned out to be Claire's most important introduction.[36]

Baudry d'Asson took Claire to his large home in Paris, where she was treated as a novelty and a living saint, as she had been in Loublande. It gave her back some of what the mocking, skeptical treatment of Mother Pauline of Saint-Jean had taken from her. Baudry d'Asson assumed the role of personal emissary, a reversal of status—national politician serves the cause of peasant visionary—that flattered Claire and her cause. Finally, Baudry d'Asson got Claire's stalled initiative moving again. He did it in the same way that Bourget had when he sought to draw out Claire during her retreat at Saint-Laurent. He asked her not to speak, but to write.

The result was a second letter to President Poincaré. The letter is brief, its main point to reaffirm the cornerstone of Claire's campaign: the Sacred Heart was to be placed on the French tricolor flag. Only then would France triumph over the invading enemy.

The letter also contained an explicit threat for Poincaré. "If you refuse to believe," Claire wrote, "great chastisements will rain down upon your person."[37] But Claire's closing was upbeat, "Joy to all French hearts because, in spite of religious persecution, God wants to reign as Master and King over France." She signed her name in a way that contrasted her own smallness—"a little girl sent by God"—with Poincaré's high office, a contrast that highlighted the improbability and mystery of her campaign. The letter was dated 27 February and Claire gave as her address "117, avenue Victor Hugo," the address of the convent where she resided. Baudry d'Asson relayed Claire's letter to Poincaré and, in so doing, laid the foundation for Claire's audience with Poincaré a few weeks later.[38]

Claire's appointment with Poincaré was set for 21 March at the Élysée Palace, the official residence of the president of the French Republic. The drama of the encounter was not lost on Claire when she later recounted the story as a portrait in incommensurates: the powerful man, the powerless woman; immense political power, immense spiritual power; the president, the peasant.

Claire covered herself with a veil, a not unusual accessory for the time that nonetheless heightened the drama and mystery surrounding her visit to Poincaré. The marquis de Baudry d'Asson escorted her. When Claire and Baudry d'Asson arrived at the Elysée Palace, they crossed the esplanade that led to the entry. They were invited in and then led into a room draped, improbably, with red damask.[39] Her appointment was for 4:45 in the afternoon, but their wait, and the tension, dragged on. Claire felt a tightening in her heart, but she held off an emotional crisis of the kind she experienced with Mother Pauline and Father Lemius. That tears and sobs did *not* render her speechless was a measure of the emotional maturity and composure she had acquired in the month since her arrival. Paris had been good for her after all. Baudry d'Asson suggested that they recite the rosary together. When they finished their prayer he remarked, "It's not very often that these walls hear prayer!"

After about twenty minutes, the door opened and a man in livery entered. He bowed, and then made a sign to Claire to follow. Claire, still veiled, traversed a series of galleries before arriving at the office of Raymond Poincaré, president of the French Republic.

When Claire revisited her encounter with Poincaré from the distance of many years, she described Poincaré as a simple man whose face revealed a troubled, even fearful, spirit. But her original transcript of their dialogue suggests a man comfortable in his position, a man who listened politely to Claire as he would listen to any concerned citizen who had come a long way to help her country in a time of war.[40]

After apologizing for disrupting his day, Claire began by asking Poincaré if he had received her letter. He acknowledged that he had. Claire then introduced the reason for her visit, "God had sent me to inform you of his will. The Sacred Heart speaks to you. He wants official France to recognize God for its master. He wants his heart painted on our national colors and he awaits this homage from the head of state."

Poincaré responded by emphasizing the limitations of his office. "Yes, but I can't do that. The laws have been voted. I can't change them unless the Chamber [the legislature] changes, and I don't believe it will."

"Well then!" she replied impatiently. "Why don't you do it yourself? You are the head of everything and God awaits this act in order to bless you."

"But one cannot undo the laws that have been made, and no one can change the national flag."

"Monsieur le Président," she responded, emphasizing the authority of his office. "There is no harm in putting a religious emblem on the French flag, because it's God's wish; and I say to you that France will only be saved by the reign of His Heart, and this reign—He wants it solidly established by official France."

Claire's comment was an apparent *non sequitur* —putting the Sacred Heart on the flag did not violate French law because it was God's will. But the remark revealed Claire's perspective—human laws cannot stand in the way of divine will.

Poincaré moved on. "Why this sign and not another?" he asked.

Claire offered a brief history of Christian emblems and military victories, including the Roman emperor Constantine for whom, the story went, a Christian emblem had been decisive. In the present war, she asserted, victory will only come with the Sacred Heart on the flag.

"But France has won wars in the past without the Sacred Heart on its flag," noted Poincaré.

Their discussion then turned to the subject of personal Sacred Heart flags among soldiers. From the beginning of the war, individual soldiers had stitched or pinned Sacred Heart tricolor emblems to their uniform caps and lapels. The government had banned such gestures as a violation of discipline and unauthorized modification of the uniform. Poincaré defended the government's policy. Claire characterized it as a form of religious persecution.

The remainder of their conversation turned on three questions. In the face of Poincaré's claims that only the legislature could change the national flag, Claire asked that he introduce such legislation himself.

The second item concerned an image that Claire had brought with her. It was a new image of the Sacred Heart, based upon her visions. A nun at the Saint-Laurent convent, where Claire's journey had begun, had painted the image. It had since been reproduced and distributed widely as a holy card as part of the campaign undertaken by Claire's supporters to get her message out. The image had worked wonders before. Claire unrolled the painting and showed it to Poincaré, who, according to Claire, looked at it without comment. "Pas un mot," she recalled. Not a word.

Finally, Claire raised the third issue, which involved a public petition on behalf of the Sacred Heart flag. "If the majority of the French people ask for the Sacred Heart flag, would you refuse it?" she asked.

As Claire recounts it, Poincaré insisted that he would not. But this highlights the historical problem of this encounter, namely, that we have only Claire's word for how it played out. Claire's account of it reads like a transcript, as if she somehow had committed the entire conversation to memory, then wrote it down at her first opportunity. And her account strongly suggests that she believed that she had succeeded, that she had extracted from Poincaré two solemn engagements: that he would propose a law to the French legislature calling for the Sacred Heart flag, and that he would not oppose a public petition calling for the same.[41] If Poincaré undertook either of these engagements—which is unlikely to say the least—he kept neither. In short, with respect to outcomes, Claire's account provides better evidence of her credulity than of her credibility.

The Sacred Heart
and the *Union Sacrée*

Claire's Story Goes Public

❦

Raymond Poincaré, it was said, had a stone where his heart should be.[1] If so, he had concealed the fact from Claire, who left his office feeling that somehow she had touched him, that they had an understanding. In fact, he had merely humored Claire before sending her on her way.

It was probably a familiar role to him; as president he must have received dozens of concerned citizens who approached him with all manner of schemes, from blueprints for whizbang secret weapons to surefire plans for victory. In Claire's case, the stakes were somewhat higher. Poincaré was trying to hold together a delicate domestic coalition and he needed Catholics who supported Claire as much as he needed Catholics of a more sober variety, as well as centrist republicans and leftists. By humoring Claire (and her political sponsor Baudry d'Asson) Poincaré labored to hold together a fragile alliance he called "the Sacred Union."

Poincaré's fate was to preside over France during seven of the most difficult years of its history, arguably the apex of French influence in the world. The European war initiated in 1914 by the German and Austro-Hungarian empires led to four years of destruction from which France, and Europe, would emerge greatly diminished. In some ways, the war had been foreordained, given the resentments that had lingered in France since the last war between France and Germany in 1870. Poincaré was born in Bar-le-Duc, Lorraine, in 1860. This made him old enough to remember the summer of 1870, when the German army swept through northeastern France. He would also remember how the Germans had occupied large parts of France, including his hometown, until a defeated nation paid war indemnities. Like most French of his generation, he remembered the feelings of resentment when he learned that the Germans had annexed Alsace and much of Lorraine; the people of Bar-le-Duc remained acutely aware of the annexation because it brought the German border within miles of their town.[2] Poincaré did not need reminding about what the defeat of 1870–71 had cost France and what the present war meant. He didn't need instruction on the subject of patriotic sacrifice. Nationalism, for Poincaré, was not an idea. It was reflex.[3]

But getting a deeply divided French public to set aside its differences was not an easy task for Poincaré, or indeed for anyone with public responsibilities in France between 1914 and 1918. Poincaré himself coined the term Sacred Union *(union sacrée)* as an expression of the idea that to rally to the "sacred" cause of victory against Germany was a sacred duty. Poincaré introduced the Sacred Union as the cornerstone concept of his first speech of the war, delivered before the legislature on 4 August 1914.[4] Sacred Union was meant as a gesture of patriotic reconciliation across the political spectrum. It invited those Catholics who still felt alienated from a Republic they viewed as anti-Catholic to set aside their doubts.

The Sacred Union was also a gesture to the French Left, which also felt alienated from the Republic and the body of the nation. Well before the outbreak of war, working-class and socialist leadership had seen in war the possibility of revolutionary transcendence. Class mattered, they argued; nations did not. Workers should greet any declaration of war with a massive strike that would paralyze the country and make war impossible. The government took this revolutionary threat seriously and drew up a list of socialists and trade unionists (the famous "*Carnet B*") who were to be arrested as a preventive measure in the event of war.

Uncompromising revolutionary socialists, anticlerical republicans, ardent Catholics—Sacred Union meant that they all somehow had to reconcile their irreconcilable differences for the sake of France's survival.[5] They did, mostly. Patriotic enthusiasm was so widespread and so deeply felt that the Left abandoned the general strike as unrealistic and impractical.[6] Not until 1917, when despair and defeatism began to take hold of soldiers, did the idea of transcending war through revolution again get serious attention. The famously anticlerical Jules Guesde, one of prewar socialism's most ardent and intransigent opponents of socialist membership in "bourgeois" governments, accepted an invitation to join the wartime government.[7] In a bizarre twist, the chauffeur of Guesde's state-supplied automobile turned out to be a priest mobilized for the war.[8]

There were limits to Sacred Union, however. Although Poincaré's first wartime cabinet included such socialists as Guesde and an array of moderate and radical republicans, it did not include any prominent Catholic politicians. The obvious choices, Albert de Mun and Denys Cochin (who would join a later cabinet), were left out. And there was some dissension from the Catholic grassroots. Before the war was even a month old, Poincaré had received letters on the nature of the war and how it would be won—or lost. On 29 August 1914, mere weeks into the war, Poincaré sat down to summarize an increasingly urgent concern— he was beset by mail from Catholics critical of his leadership in the war. "My mail," he confided to his diary, "becomes heavier. It consists of criticisms, complaints, recriminations, as well as petitions from priests or women, demanding insistently that I consecrate France to the Sacred Heart."[9] Poincaré's private complaint shows that Claire's visit—indeed, her entire campaign—was merely one manifestation of a popular movement that had pursued victory through the Sacred Heart from the opening weeks of the war. These letters, in fact, show that nothing that Claire said to Poincaré at their famous meeting at the Elysée Palace on

21 March 1917 was news to him. What set Claire apart was not her message—that had been heard before. What set her apart were her visions, which sought to elevate this message from the partisan realm of political opinion to the unassailable realm of divine command.

A CAMPAIGN ON THE HOME FRONT

Early in 1915, recently mobilized soldiers streamed through the Perrache train station in the city of Lyon. Under the glass-enclosed ironwork, they struggled with duffle bags and backpacks, bumping into each other and the civilians who cluttered the platforms. Among the few women in this teeming crowd was a woman who gripped a handful of emblems. She moved against the flow of men, making eye contact, approaching individual soldiers as they made their way to the train. Some walked past her. One, a Breton, stopped. At first glance, the emblems looked like small reproductions of the French tricolor flag, with its vertical bands of blue, white, and red. On closer inspection, the flags turned out to be embellished with images of the Sacred Heart of Jesus in the middle of the white band. It was an ensign that blended faith and nationalism, the emblem of the Sacred Heart superimposed on the national flag.

The soldier paused to examine the image, then gently refused. "Look," he said. "I have one that's better than that." He pulled out a hand-made tricolor similarly adorned with the Sacred Heart. He showed it to the woman.

"When I went away to join the army, my mother gave me this little flag. She said, 'Keep this, my son. It will protect you.' It has been with me ever since."

This incident was widely reported in the months and years to follow.[10] In sermons and editorial essays it worked well as a way of introducing two key ideas: the solicitude of the home front, represented by the woman; the simple faith and filial piety of the French soldier, represented by the Breton. The theme of the story—how war transforms men and nations and puts God back at the center of their lives, both symbolically and in fact—became the dominant theme of a drive to mobilize the Catholic laity on behalf of a war to save France.

The incident was surely not the first of its kind. Scenes like it had been played out at train stations throughout France since the beginning of the war.[11] It also resonated with one of the most powerful episodes of the *last* war, the Franco-Prussian War. In December of 1870 a general complained that his regimental colors, a simple white heraldic cross on a blue field, were not more emphatically religious. "I have what you need," a fellow officer commented as he unfurled a banner on which the Sacred Heart emblem and the motto "Sacred Heart of Jesus, Save France" had been embroidered. The general and his men later followed this Sacred Heart banner into battle, with results that were deadly and inconclusive but also regarded as heroic and prophetic, especially with the outbreak of war in 1914. When, in 1914, the soldier produced the Sacred Heart emblem before heading to the front, his gesture knitted past and present, defeat and revenge, 1870 and 1914.[12]

The distribution of Sacred Heart flags to departing soldiers was a common feature of many tearful *adieux* in 1914 and later. Many of these flags were standard tricolor flags, modified at home. Early in the war, nuns from the Visitationist convent at Paray-le-Monial made certain that soldiers were offered such flags, along with Sacred Heart medals and scapulars, as their trains passed through town on their way to the front. The items were so popular that they exhausted their supply.[13] The Apostleship of Prayer, originally a Sacred Heart prayer network headquartered in Toulouse, took it upon itself to produce and distribute small Sacred Heart flags. During the course of the war, their distribution center would send out hundreds of thousands of such flags.

In Lyon, the train station incident of 1915 was cited as the catalyst for a national movement to consecrate France to the Sacred Heart and put the Sacred Heart emblem on the tricolor flag as a symbol of a divine compact. The woman in question, never identified, was so moved by the incident that she rallied her friends. They formed a sewing circle

Figure 8.   A Sacred Heart safeguard

and began to embroider small Sacred Heart banners to distribute to soldiers departing for the front. Soon the women were struggling to keep
up with demand, especially as they began to send the small banners to
the chaplains among soldiers. Embroidering Sacred Heart insignia
even on small tricolor flags and banners soon became impractical. Fate,
providence, or dumb luck had situated their effort in Lyon, which, by
1914, had centuries of experience of specialized textile manufacture.
Industrial know-how and capacity took over from the embroidery
circle. At first, the design was machine-woven; then, when demand
ballooned, it was printed on prefabricated tricolor flags.[14]

Ultimately, the enterprise was constituted as a charitable society, an
oeuvre, with headquarters facing the Saône River on the quai Tilsitt.
The Oeuvre de l'Insigne du Sacré-Coeur assumed responsibilities that
included management, production subcontracting and oversight,

publicity, sales, and wholesale distribution of Sacred Heart emblems. Unlike the charitable embroidery circle it replaced, the Oeuvre did not engage in direct distribution of emblems. Its business was not that of the women of the embroidery circle, passing out hand-made emblems *gratis* on train station platforms. The Oeuvre operated as a wholesaler, selling emblems in quantity to individuals, who in turn distributed the emblems in train stations, churches, and, via mail, to soldiers and chaplains at the front.

Such a complex operation required full-time management. According to a police source, three Jesuits assumed leadership of the Oeuvre, while the League of French Women (*La Ligue des Femmes Françaises*) provided financial support.[15] The Jesuits no longer existed legally in France, having been forced to cease operations years earlier in the aftermath of the Dreyfus Affair.[16] So it is not entirely clear how the three men named—Gressien, Dechabannes, and Perroy—could have been Jesuits. Some Jesuits had preferred to leave France rather than leave their order. Others had left the order in order to remain in France as parish priests. For them, their Jesuit training no doubt remained an important part of their pastoral mission and their identity. And many Jesuits who had left France returned with the declaration of war in 1914.

Whether returnees or "crypto-Jesuits," these three men led an operation that became one of the most effective propaganda machines of the war. They had the good business sense not to attempt to do everything in-house. They focused on design, publicity, and distribution, and contracted out manufacturing to Varichon, a Lyonnais firm.[17] By the winter of 1915, the Oeuvre had a large repertoire of items for sale on the theme of the tricolor and the Sacred Heart. It sold tricolor flags with the Sacred Heart on the white middle band. It sold various tricolor insignia with the Sacred Heart emblem above the inscription "Hope and Salvation of France" (*Éspoir et Salut de la France*). In addition to items made from fabric, the Oeuvre also sold emblems printed on cellophane—easier to pack, lighter and less expensive to mail, and a concession to wartime materials shortages.[18]

The Oeuvre's publicity campaign focused on the national and regional Catholic press, although local and national speaking campaigns also played a role in mobilizing buyers, donors, and distributors. The national Catholic daily newspaper, *La Croix,* carried notices, as did *Le Messager du Sacré-Coeur de Jésus,* the monthly bulletin of the Apostleship of Prayer based in Toulouse, and *Le Pèlerin* and the *Bulletin de l'Oeuvre du Voeu National au Sacré-Coeur de Jésus,* both monthly publications.[19] Diocesan bulletins also promoted the drive to multiply the number of Sacred Heart emblems at the front. By July of 1917, the Oeuvre had produced over half a million Sacred Heart insignia.

Getting sufficient quantities of religious emblems and Sacred Heart flags to the front remained a persistent problem throughout the war. Demand remained high, but civilian and military authorities became increasingly vigilant in the face of what they regarded with alarm as a seditious movement, injurious to national unity at a time of national peril. Flags, emblems, and scapulars were shipped surreptitiously, stuffed in packages alongside jellies, jams, and preserves; slipped into letters; stashed among folds of linen. At one point, a collection of Sacred Heart emblems, printed on cheap paper, was slipped into the chaplains' semimonthly bulletin, *Le Prêtre aux Armées.* There, on a centerfold insert tucked between pages 728 and 729, the readers of *Le Prêtre aux Armées* would find forty-eight Sacred Heart emblems, ready to cut and distribute to soldiers. A private benefactor had underwritten the printing costs.[20]

By the end of the war, the quantity of Sacred Heart paraphernalia shipped to the front was staggering—12 million Sacred Heart insignia, 1.5 million Sacred Heart banners, 375,000 Sacred Heart scapulars, and some 32,425 tricolor flags outfitted with the Sacred Heart. Charles Marcault, a vigorous supporter of the Sacred Heart campaign, estimated that this resulted in a full-size Sacred Heart flag every thirty meters along the thousand-kilometer front and a Sacred Heart banner or insignia every sixty centimeters.[21] In short, the front was saturated with Sacred Heart emblems; it would have been hard to die without falling on one.

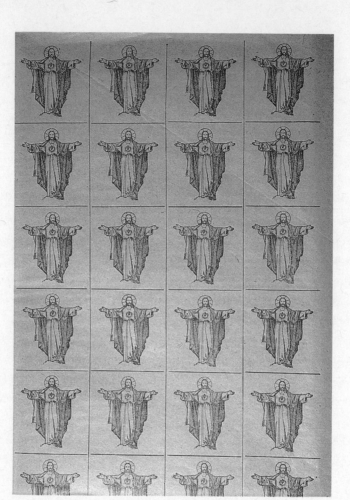

Figure 9.   Clip-and-pin safeguards distributed to French troops in a centerfold to *Le Prêtre aux Armées,* 1 January 1917

Not dying, of course, was on the minds of most soldiers and here, too, once in the field and in the hands of soldiers, Sacred Heart objects fulfilled a number of functions. For the front-line soldier, a Sacred Heart scapular, medallion, flag, or banner served as a talisman. As stories of incidents involving the Sacred Heart and miraculous brushes with death made their way back to the home front, they were snatched up by the Catholic press in whose hands they were used to suggest a vast spiritual renewal in the trenches and the hand of God visibly at work on behalf of France and its soldiers. "My protective banner, which I always wear under my coat, recently saved my life," reported one artillery man who, in a moment of mortal peril repeated, "Coeur de Jésus, Éspoir et Salut de la France!" until the danger passed.[22] An officer and his soldiers endured a forty-eight-hour bombardment at Verdun. Afterward, everything was in tatters—rifles, gear, blankets, clothing—but not a man was touched, a fact he attributed to "my little Sacred Heart banner."[23]

Surely one of the tragedies of war is that death is indiscriminate; when lead and shrapnel fly, death harvests the good along with the wicked. And yet some soldiers claimed that the Sacred Heart improved their odds. Indeed, a lieutenant writing in 1916 claimed that displaying the Sacred Heart made the difference between life and death. "The bombardment became intense and I unfurled our [Sacred Heart] banner. Our post remained untouched. Shortly after, we were relieved by another unit, which lacked a banner. They took a direct hit."[24]

The Catholic newsweekly *Le Pèlerin* ran a story from a sergeant who wrote that, thanks to the Sacred Heart, his unit had no casualties during a five-hour barrage. They had placed a Sacred Heart banner in the middle of the munitions depot they were serving. Throughout the barrage, the banner—and the munitions—remained intact. "As a result," he wrote, "now everyone wants a Sacred Heart banner."[25]

"Your results may vary," it might be added, if anachronistically. While the thrust of these anecdotes and personal testimonies was that the image of the Sacred Heart was as good as armor against bullets, shrapnel, and artillery shells, occasional events made it clear that past performance is no guarantee of future results. Early in 1917, one young lieutenant, Sacred Heart banner in his hands, led his men some fifteen hundred meters across no-man's-land. He and his men took the first line of trenches from the Germans, miraculously without casualties.

Figure 10.   "Le fanion protecteur des poilus français."
Illustration of a Sacred-Heart lance-pennon, for an
article on Sacred Heart talismans at the front, *Le Pèlerin,*
16 June 1918

However, as he moved on to the second line of trenches, he was hit in
the chest and died instantly. The best that could be said for him was
that he had died heroically. The Sacred Heart accorded him a good
death.[26]

One could easily multiply such examples. *La Croix, Le Pèlerin, Le
Messager du Sacré-Coeur,* along with dozens of local and diocesan publications, are full of such tragic and miraculous accounts of men in
battle. For soldiers, these gestures gave meaning to a war that seemed

meaningless. As the short war of 1914 faded into the interminable war of mud, blood, and attrition, devout soldiers and the merely recently devout found that the Sacred Heart gave their lives and deaths eternal meaning. War meant that these men had lost control of their lives. Thank God that they could at least assert control over the manner of their death. And if their death included a desperate or courageous display of faith, if it gave them a grip on the promise of eternal life, well, why not?

The Sacred Heart emblem was a piece in thousands of quiet acts of desperation or heroic acts of faith. On the home front, the mounding up of such stories flowed into efforts to make the war a soldier-by-soldier referendum on the future of France. For as soldiers crafted for themselves a transcendent story that gave meaning to their lives and those of their comrades in their final moments, back home these stories were put to work to prepare a kind of political and national redemption that seemed to threaten Poincaré's Sacred Union. The Sacred Heart pointed toward national redemption. On the home front, the Sacred Heart went to war for the soul of France.

Consecration by Proxy

❧

Spirituality has a history, just like anything else. One of the most endur-
ing features of the spirituality of wartime is the sense, even conviction,
that war serves a divine plan—war gets theologized. Theologizing war
is an ancient reflex, as old as Athena watching over the Greeks at Troy,
as old as stories of waters parting to save a people and closing again to
crush an army. Theologizing war was also a powerful reflex in 1914.
Spirituality, not to mention spiritualism, enjoyed a remarkable recovery among European men and women after 1914.[1] How else to com-
prehend the enormity of such a disaster except as in the service of some
grand design?

When Claire Ferchaud began to talk about the wonderful things
that she saw and heard, she added her story to a mix of projections,
prayers, and predictions regarding the transcendent power of war.
Claire's supporters saw her story as convergent with a way of understanding the war that had already found its voice and its audience.[2]
Claire's detractors, those who ultimately prevailed against her, were far
less sympathetic to what they regarded as a ploy to yoke her story to an
existing campaign for national renewal and a divine promise of victory.

The Catholic spirituality of the Great War, like that of the Franco-
Prussian War of 1870–71, drew heavily upon the images and themes of

the cult of the Sacred Heart. Commentators made much of the fact that the consecration of the Basilica of the Sacré-Coeur, announced for October of 1914 by the archbishop of Paris, had to be cancelled because of the outbreak of the war—a symbol of the unfinished business of national consecration and a portent of the lengthy conflict ahead. The Sacred Heart remained an important image for France's understanding of the war over the coming months, long before Claire's rise to prominence as a national figure. In September of 1914, the Jesuit priest Joseph Calot had spoken of the divine nature of war and of its moral significance for France. His remarks were published in the monthly bulletin of the Apostleship of Prayer, *Le Messager du Sacré-Coeur de Jésus.*[3] The war, according to Calot, was the justice of God and a sign of the "strange mercifulness of His Heart," for war awakens a people into what Calot called "patriotic faith," defining the *union sacrée* as the literal sacred union of a Christian people.[4]

Calot also explicitly linked the war effort to long-standing beliefs about the special relationship between France and the Sacred Heart. He revived the idea, implicit in the vision of Marguerite-Marie Alacoque and made explicit during the crisis of the Franco-Prussian War, that fulfilling the demands of the Sacred Heart of Jesus would lead to French military victory. Addressing the Sacred Heart directly, Calot remarked, "You have asked for a national temple and a national consecration as the price of victory. The temple is complete; already each of its stones climb toward You like a cry of repentance and of faith, hope, and love; [it stands as a] splendid memorial . . . of the eternal alliance concluded between You and France."[5] Thus, from the opening weeks of the war, partisans of the Sacred Heart revived their calls to fulfill the divine request—as a condition of French victory—of a national consecration of France to the Sacred Heart of Jesus. France's consecration was central to a Catholic war-scenario that ended with the nation's resounding triumph on the battlefield. Consecration meant victory.

During the opening years of the war, the French episcopate frequently spoke and wrote in similar terms about the war, France, and the Sacred Heart of Jesus. The bishop of Meaux traced the special relationship between France and the Sacred Heart, starting with the fact that Jesus "had deigned to appear to the Blessed Marguerite-Marie on our soil." Moreover, the Sacred Heart had demanded not only a special devotion "from Christian souls" but also "a social and national cult. One might say that He wanted to make France the fatherland of his heart."

The bishop of Meaux called upon the people of France "to profit from the plague we are undergoing to examine our past faults." The miracle of the Marne was a manifestation of the vigilance of the Sacred Heart, according to the bishop, and he expressed confidence that the consecration of the basilica was the result of divine will, a desire to see "an entire people" offer its thanks.[6] He closed with a political appeal, calling on France's secular leadership to reconcile with God and to take steps to renew "the centuries-old alliance between Christ and the fatherland," to fulfill its evangelical mission in the world. He compared the conversion that he envisioned for France's political leadership to that of Saul on the road to Damascus, knocked down from his horse by a gesture of God. Saul halted his persecutions of the Christians, converted to the faith, and embarked upon a life of Christian evangelism under the name Paul of Tarsus.[7] The patriotic devotion of the Sacred Heart, according to the bishop of Meaux, entailed the re-Christianization of public life in France. The *true* Sacred Union was not the present wartime political truce but the triumph of public faith over secularization and nonbelief.

Such were the public and printed pronouncements regarding France and the Sacred Heart. Even if the interested parties couldn't agree on whether the Sacred Union *was* Christian patriotism or merely a colorful metaphor for a political truce, it nonetheless obliged all parties to abstain from partisan and divisive remarks that might weaken national resolve. Statements about culpability and redemption through the patriotic deaths of the righteous, however, suggested that indirect and implicit critique did not fall within the terms of the Sacred Union.

In private, or at least off the printed page, openly critical commentary still applied. The gloves had clearly come off when, at Paray-le-Monial late in 1915, the Jesuit priest Henry Perroy placed the Sacred Heart squarely in opposition to the French Revolution. In a classic trope, he reminded his audience that Revolution had substituted the tune "La Carmagnole" for religious hymns.[8]

The Revolution was the point when France turned from God, but, for Perroy, there had to be a turning back. In fact, he argued, the turn toward redemption had already taken place—in 1870, when "France showed its faith once again by building the people's temple of the Sacré-Coeur on Montmartre. . . ." This act would be the first in a new national saga, not of postrevolutionary decadence but of national regeneration through an alliance with the Sacred Heart of Jesus. Perroy asserted that the "miracle" in the miracle of the Marne—when the German advance was stopped a hundred kilometers from Paris—was not hyperbole; it was literally a miracle earned through urgent prayer at Montmartre.[9]

The main lesson of autumn 1914, however, was that the Basilica of the Sacré-Coeur had been entrusted with "the mission to protect the city," a mission accomplished by France's victory in the Battle of the Marne.[10] This made the treachery of "official France," by which Perroy meant the republican authorities who had sought "vainly to halt the construction [of the Basilica of the Sacré-Coeur]," all the more conspicuous. The miracle of the Marne, then, had a three-fold significance: as a miracle, as a victory of the Sacred Heart of Jesus, and as a revelation of the treasonous efforts of those republicans who had sought to halt the construction of the very basilica that had saved Paris. Perroy's assertion that the war was divine chastisement, but that victory revealed the designs of the Sacred Heart for France, was often repeated during and after the Great War; to this, he added a corollary: that its republican leadership was blocking France's path to victory. The enemies of the Sacred Heart were not just enemies of Christianity and Christian France; they were also the enemies of victory. Here was rhetoric with potentially explosive consequences, a rhetoric that threatened to shatter the Sacred Union because it cast doubt on the patriotism of political leadership. If the leaders of the Republic ignored appeals to secure victory by consecrating France to the Sacred Heart, weren't they guilty of criminal acts? These were not dispassionate debates about the place of belief in public life. This was about treason.

How could Catholic France demonstrate its gratitude for the divine promise of the Sacred Heart if secular leaders thwarted it at every turn? While some Catholic rhetoric moved from despair about secular leadership to suspicion of treason, the French Catholic hierarchy eagerly sought a proxy for a recalcitrant government.

CONSECRATION: THE SEARCH FOR SURROGATES

French victory would come through the Sacred Heart: that much was clear. Moreover, the consecration must be national. As conventionally understood, this had ritualistic and symbolic consequences. This meant that Jesus not only required construction of the "temple" of the basilica, but also the placing of the Sacred Heart symbol on the nation's flag—sign of the compact between France and the Sacred Heart—followed by a consecration of France to the Sacred Heart in a solemn ceremony involving France's leaders.

It was evident to many, however, that given the stubbornness of the current national leadership, no national consecration would soon be forthcoming. How, then, to demonstrate the fidelity and zeal of Catholic France? In the face of official indifference, a national consecration would be no easy task. Short of an improbable religious conversion among the members of France's government, that is, a modern "road to Damascus," it was simply unrealistic to look to Paris for a national consecration, although some Catholics, including Claire, apparently did.

In the meantime, however, the Sacré-Coeur's adherents needed an interim solution; municipal consecrations to the Sacred Heart were one

element of it. The idea of using local or municipal consecrations as substitutes or proxies for a national consecration goes back to the late seventeenth century, to the time of Marguerite-Marie Alacoque herself.
When it became evident that Louis XIV would not consecrate France
to the Sacred Heart, Marguerite-Marie's brother, the mayor of a local
village, organized a ceremony with the help of his brother, the pastor of
the village church. Together, they consecrated their village to the Sacred
Heart, a scaled-down version of the royal consecration demanded in
their sister's visions.[11] The city of Marseille had been consecrated by its
municipal leaders in 1722 as part of a campaign to combat the scourge
of plague.[12] Amiens had been consecrated in 1766, Poitiers in 1814, and
in the 1890s there had been a spate of municipal consecrations, mostly
in smaller towns and villages. The movement toward municipal consecrations climaxed in 1901; it was discouraged and suppressed by the
government between 1901 and 1905.[13] The late nineteenth-century
municipal consecration movement was part of the "deep background"
to the government's suppression of unauthorized religious orders in
1901 and the explicit separation of church and state in France in 1905.

The particular interest of these turn-of-the-century consecrations is
that they conspicuously employed the use of the Sacred Heart emblem
on the white band of the French tricolor flag. Parisian newspapers
reported in May and June of 1901 that mayors and municipal councils
in towns and villages throughout the French southwest (Gers,
Aveyron) and west (Loire Atlantique, Finistère, Manche) were holding
consecration ceremonies. In the same year, the Catholic daily newspaper called on households to display the Sacred Heart tricolor on 14
June, making the annual liturgical feast day of the Sacred Heart a kind
of Catholic national holiday, in opposition to France's secular national
day: 14 July. Pierre l'Ermite used his column in *La Croix* to promote the
event. Sacred Heart tricolors were reported displayed in Tourcoing,
Tours, Mende, Châlons-sur-Saône, Limoges, Lorient, Roubaix, and Le
Havre, as well as Paris. Republican authorities ordered these flags taken
down, citing an 1894 law. Below the radar of vigilant republican

Figure 11.   The masthead of *Le Petit Berrichon—Croix du Berry* featuring a
Sacred Heart flag, published 4 August 1901, at the peak of the campaign of
municipal consecrations

officials, however, small towns and villages such as Graye-et-Charnay,
Miery, Cuvier, Plenise and Plenisette (Jura), Saint-Paul-de-Salers
(Cantal), Chavoy, Saint-Brice, Saint-Senier (Manche) used Sacred
Heart flags in municipal consecration ceremonies.[14]

Municipal consecrations served as substitutes for a national consecration. They also became a ritualistic way of registering dissent.
Republican authorities understood this subtext, but they also construed
the consecrations as an infringement on religious pluralism. What
room could there be for other beliefs—or for nonbelief—in villages
consecrated to the Sacred Heart? Accordingly, they were forbidden.
But the possibility of such consecrations surfaced again in modified
form with the outbreak of the war, when the Catholic hierarchy
searched for a different kind of proxy to carry out a national consecration to the Sacred Heart.

June is traditionally celebrated as the month of the Sacred Heart; when the war broke out in August 1914, the French episcopate planned a national consecration for the following year, in June 1915. Léon-Adolphe Amette, archbishop of Paris and therefore guardian of the Basilica of the Sacré-Coeur, took the lead in organizing the event and coordinating the efforts of the French episcopate. This meant, first of all, securing the cooperation of the cardinalate—typically, but not exclusively, the bishops of France's leading dioceses: Lyon, Paris, Bordeaux, etc. It also meant forging a consensus about what this consecration would mean. Practically, this meant drafting a statement that would be endorsed by the cardinals.

Cardinal Amette's drive had remarkable results. Under his leadership, the cardinals agreed to a strong statement on the meaning of the consecration. And since words should be accompanied by action, their statement called for a national consecration that would be celebrated in every parish in every diocese on the same day—11 June—of 1915. Given its scale and simultaneity, the consecration of France to the Sacred Heart of Jesus was to be like no other event in the history of the French church. In every diocese, in every church, Catholic France would gather at the same hour to consecrate the nation to the Sacred Heart.

By the spring of 1915, Cardinal Amette had a statement drafted and ready to distribute. It would be used throughout France, in diocese after diocese, to rally the Catholic faithful to the national consecration. In Luçon, the heart of the département of the Vendée, Amette's statement was incorporated into a call to participate. Since it *was* the Vendée, a region where the Sacred Heart had served as an emblem of counter-revolution, the statement's publication became an occasion to recall the historic importance of the Sacred Heart to local identity.[15] As the bishop of Luçon put it, "The program outlined in this letter will be greeted nowhere more eagerly and joyfully than in our Vendée, the holy land of the Sacred Heart."[16] Diocese by diocese, the announcement was repeated, in preparation for the national consecration of 11 June.

Little surprise that the project soon ran afoul of the public authorities. After all, such a ceremony would be premised on the failure of
France's national leadership to carry out the consecration on its own. As
such, it was a kind of public rebuke, inconsistent with the spirit of the
political truce of the Sacred Union. However, it wasn't only the fact of
the ceremony that riled the French government; more worrisome was
the list of regrets written into the ceremony, cast as a list of putative sins
of the French people. Each one identified a specific offense against God
committed by the people of France. Together, they took the form of an
amende honorable, a formal demand for forgiveness, a practice that in
earlier times had frequently included the appearance of the penitent, in
sackcloth and ashes, on the steps of the church.

There would be no sackcloth and ashes in 1915, but the tone of the
amende honorable was the textual equivalent. Indeed, the *amende* showed
how persistently the Sacred Heart could be used as the focal point for
counterrevolutions big and small, because the list of republican failures
expressed a desire to return to a status quo ante—a rejection of the secular and pluralistic ideal of the Republic. The *amende* had a penitential
tone, a doleful sense of sin and regret, organized around an inventory of
offenses, including specific acts of legislation. The "Amende Honorable
et Consécration de la France au Sacré-Coeur de Jésus" demanded
pardon for "private and public" offenses and included an oblique reference to the recent (1905) separation of church and state in France. The
statement sought pardon on behalf of those who, through "blindness
and ingratitude," had misunderstood France's "divine mission."[17]

According to the text of the *amende,* the reading of each offense was
to be followed by a statement of assent from the people: PARDON,
Ô SEIGNEUR JÉSUS! Surely the most problematic portion of the *amende*
was the list of offenses that unambiguously alluded to specific pieces of
legislation approved under the Third Republic. The list included not
only the fairly standard references to "the violation of your command-
ments" and "blasphemy of word and pen" as well as "the depravation
of morals," and "the unbridled love of luxury and pleasure," but also

explicit references to civil marriage and legislation on divorce and lay education. The *amende* was set off by a statement from the archbishop of Paris to the effect that the *amende* and consecration, given that they would take place "on the same day and in the same form in all our churches" would "assume a national character" and "might obtain for us more promptly from God, victory and peace."

These statements drove the government to act. The immediate concern of the government was the soldier in the trenches. The idea that victory might be hastened by asking pardon for the secularizing legislation of the Republic was simply too much to accept, for it threatened to undermine the morale of soldiers and their confidence in their political leaders. Moreover, it looked like a coordinated assault on the Sacred Union. Alexandre Millerand, minister of war, acting on the orders of Prime Minister René Viviani, telegraphed a message alerting censors to the offensive nature of the *amende.* "The text of the litanies aims at the work of laicization of the Republic, for which pardon is asked. The insertion of these passages in diocesan bulletins or other publications is forbidden."[18] The ceremony would not take place.

There was no collective response from the French episcopate, at least none that wartime censorship would have allowed, but a kind of guerrilla warfare, carried out diocese by diocese, arose. In the diocese of Luçon, the text of the consecration and *amende,* dated 26 May, was printed and apparently distributed.[19] The Catholic daily newspaper *La Croix,* published in Paris and widely regarded as the organ of official Catholic opinion in France, succeeded only in publishing the accompanying letter of Cardinal Amette. The letter explicitly referred to the *amende,* describing it as "attached," that is, published alongside, but it was not.[20] In Montauban, in the French southwest, the diocesan bulletin was censored and the text of the *amende honorable* did not appear, but local authorities reported to Paris that diocesan clergy were resorting to subterfuge: the bishop of Montauban had the text passed "from hand to hand" so that parish priests could read it aloud at mass the following Sunday.[21]

No attempt was made in Lyon to circulate the *amende* surreptitiously. Instead diocesan leaders opted to promote another form of consecration by proxy—the consecration of families, not as an alternative to the diocesan consecration but in addition to it. The diocesan bulletin of 11 June called for the "enthronement of the image of the Sacred Heart in the home and the consecration of the family."[22] Family consecrations had been popular during the Franco-Prussian War of 1870–71,[23] and they were promoted in various dioceses thereafter, notably in the Paris region with the encouragement of Cardinal Amette.[24] Family consecrations, the Lyonnais bulletin claimed, were intended to produce three results: the apostleship of the family by the family, the preparation of the national consecration of France to the Sacred Heart, and the defense of family against the Masonic Order (*la franc-maçonnerie*). The effect of this was to revive the accusation that the Third Republic, like the Revolution of 1789, was the result of a conspiracy, led by the Masonic Order, to undermine Catholic France.

By the late nineteenth century, Freemasonry in France was a social network for aspiring and established republican politicians. Many republican political leaders in France were members of the Masonic Order, with the result that the Masons operated as a kind of informal caucus for politicians on the republican Left, a republican boys' club, and a gateway to formal politics. Given the antagonistic relationship between republican politicians and the Catholic Church in France, the Catholic hierarchy tended to see the Masonic Order as an organized network of the church's opponents.[25]

SACRED UNION OR SACRED HEART?

The bishops' initiative sought to consecrate France parish by parish, diocese by diocese in June of 1915. The republican establishment felt that the bishops' initiative threatened both the government and the Sacred Union war effort. Government censorship and suppression of the *amende* limited the campaign of 1915. Instead of the impressive image of a home front mobilized by prayer and penitence—and the government revealed as out of touch with the wishes of the citizenry— the campaign of 1915 had to settle for partial or isolated gestures.

At the same time that the bishops' home-front initiative was coming apart under pressure from politicians and wartime censors, a citizens' initiative to reach soldiers at the *real* front was building momentum. During the war, public life centered on the soldiers and their effort to bring victory and drive out the invader. What if the soldiers themselves were to demand a consecration? What would the government have to say *then*?

On 8 June 1915, the Institut Catholique—France's Catholic university—hosted the annual meeting in Paris of La Fédération Jeanne d'Arc (the Joan of Arc Federation) , a Catholic women's group. On the agenda for their annual meeting was a plan to push front-line soldiers to demand a national consecration. Enlisted men had been at the center of public life since the onset of the war in August 1914. A demand for a consecration from soldiers would be irresistible. The challenge the women faced was two-fold: first, how to get news to soldiers about the campaign for a national consecration? Second, how to get Sacré-Coeur emblems past an increasingly vigilant military censorship?

Father Berthay, a member of the editorial board of *La Croix,* spoke to the women. He acknowledged that reaching the troops with the message of a consecration of France to the Sacred Heart would not be easy. Even his newspaper, the national Catholic daily, had been banned in certain units. He knew, however, that copies were getting through nonetheless, mostly because they were shipped along with other things. He suggested the use of lower-profile sources of information—tracts and leaflets—the sorts of things that could easily be slipped into letters and care-packages. When Berthay concluded his remarks, a member of the federation rose to her feet. She seconded Berthay's suggestions, proposing that small tricolor flags, marked with the Sacred Heart, also be surreptitiously sent to the front. In response, Berthay quickly noted that soldiers were no longer permitted to wear such insignia.[26]

At least not openly, he should have added, because at the front, such insignia were getting past vigilant censors and getting through; at the front, they were worn inconspicuously inside a lapel or on the underside of caps. The availability of Sacred Heart emblems, like news about a consecration, was very uneven at the front. In June of 1915, army officials halted the distribution of Sacred Heart flags, medals, and leaflets. They also seized a bundle in the possession of a soldier known to be a member of the antirepublican political group Action Française.[27] But the crackdown was obviously incomplete and spotty; Sacred Heart flags, tracts, and songsheets were readily available at a military hospital in Troyes in the same month of the same year. A song containing the lines "O Tricolor Flag, to bring victory, France decorates your colors, with the beloved Sacred Heart" circulated among troops.[28] Meanwhile, the Oeuvre de l'Insigne du Sacré-Coeur, headquartered in Lyon, continued to send hundreds of thousands of Sacred Heart insignia in packages marked "linens" or "preserves."[29]

Sacred Heart emblems arrived in unsolicited packages, sometimes sent to soldiers with whom the Oeuvre's members had only tenuous contact. Soldiers, eager for any distraction from the war, devoured mail from any source. In some ways, this was simply an extension of the phenomenon of the *marraine,* the godmother, a woman who "adopted" a soldier and sent gifts and letters as a sign of support from the home front.[30] Antoine Redier described a fellow soldier who was shocked to receive a large package from "a pious lady he hardly knew." Just the same, receiving a package was a grand occasion and, surrounded by his friends, he opened it. Out came several pairs of socks, soap, cigarette papers, tobacco, handkerchiefs, candy, and a large envelope labeled simply: "To a Soldier of France." Inside the envelope were a letter and several religious emblems. The soldier shared the contents of his package, including the emblems.[31] The next day, Redier sat down to have a smoke with a fellow soldier he described as "an anarchist." Out of the anarchist's pocket came a pack of tobacco, a pipe, a fresh bar of soap, and a Sacred Heart medallion. Redier was an officer, and he noted that

Figure 12.　A Sacred Heart holy card.
Bibliothèque nationale de France

all of the men under his command had such insignia, in their pockets, around their necks, pinned to their shirts, on their greatcoats, and inside or even on the front of their caps. When he thought about it, he was reminded of "those peasants of Normandy who put medals around the necks of sick cows, in order to heal them." But on further reflection,

Figure 13.   "The 28th Brigade Remembers Its Fallen Heroes," from *Le Monde Illustré,* April 1919. The Sacred Heart flag of the 28th Brigade drapes the altar at an outdoor memorial service

he concluded that these gestures went beyond superstition. Attaching a medal was "a positive act," an act of faith.[32]

Such efforts to reach out to front-line soldiers didn't rely solely on the near-random sending out of packages to the troops. From the opening weeks of the war, they also made use of a network of chaplains serving troops at the front. The number of recruits actually assigned to chaplain duties was rather small at the beginning of the war. A decree of 5 May 1913 mandated an allocation of four chaplains to the stretcher-bearer teams of each army corps. In the language of the decree, these four were to consist of "two ministers of the Catholic cult, one Protestant, one Israelite." This ratio was arbitrary; there was no attempt to calibrate the number of chaplains to actual demand.[33] Catholics, at least nominal Catholics, made up 99 percent of the population of wartime France. And while religious practice among men baptized Catholic tended to fade as they approached adulthood, it was still the case that Catholic chaplains were underrepresented in proportion to chaplains of other faiths. Additional Catholic chaplains were assigned to infantry and cavalry divisions, two and one respectively, but here too the figures were arbitrary.[34] After all, what difference would a chaplain or two make in a unit of well over ten thousand men?

The insufficiency of these allocations became clear only with the onset of war. Ironically, anticlerical legislation of the prewar period was part of the solution. Republican political leadership had stripped male religious orders and seminarians of their exemption from military service. The loss of exemptions put clergy and clergy-in-training in military service, but not always in chaplain roles. In the opening weeks of the war, during the first flush of enthusiasm for the Sacred Union, Albert de Mun, a prominent Catholic politician, negotiated with Prime Minister René Viviani for permission to increase the ratio of chaplains to soldiers. De Mun clinched the deal by offering to supply a cadre of *volunteer* chaplains, at virtually no cost to the treasury of the Republic.[35] Once approved, this would be sustained by charitable contributions, which in turn could be doled out to support the chaplains in the field. But next to the challenge of securing political approval for putting clergy next to soldiers in the battlefield, fundraising was a trivial matter.

Many who joined the ranks of volunteer chaplains were members of religious orders, notably Jesuits, condemned as an unauthorized religious order in the 1880s and later. Members of these suppressed orders had left France rather than renounce their vows. With the declaration of war in 1914, many such priests ended their exile. Some joined the army as simple soldiers, but most believed that a combat role was inconsistent with their vocation and sought to serve in the ranks of de Mun's volunteer chaplains. The minister of war had authorized nearly four hundred such volunteer chaplains.[36] These members of the clergy served out of a sense of patriotic obligation but also with the certainty that war presented a unique opportunity to reach a notoriously "unchurched" part of the French population: the adult male.

Coordinating the fundraising and distributing the funds were responsibilities that fell, especially after de Mun's death late in 1914, to General Geoffroy de Grandmaison, de Mun's collaborator in social Catholicism, and François Veuillot, son of the Catholic journalist Louis Veuillot. Grandmaison succeeded de Mun as president of the Comité pour les Aumôniers Militaires (Committee for Military Chaplains) headquartered on the rue de Bellechasse in Paris. Both Grandmaision and Veuillot worked at fundraising to support the chaplains, and both maintained a correspondence with chaplains in the field. Together they sought to use the chaplaincy to fulfill a version, adapted to wartime, of the social Catholic vision that de Mun had articulated. Their vision was one in which chaplains, as leaders, watched over the spiritual development of soldiers with as much concern and zeal as commanding officers supervised their charges' training and physical well-being.[37] But the vision was always about more than just the salvation of individuals. The war presented a unique opportunity to reach an entire generation.

War and the proximity of death sharpened the search for meaning in life. For some soldiers, of course, war changed nothing. War, like life, was a dark pageant of pain, struggle, and tenuous fellowship shattered by separation in death—in sum: a tragedy. War was life as usual—only less of it. For other soldiers, such as those disposed toward the vision of the socialist Left, war led to speculation on the emptiness of nationalism, the irreducibility of class, and proletarian revolution as the only possible way out—a transnational dream of war transcended through revolution. For many other soldiers, of course, the experience of war favored religious renewal, with an emphasis on the purpose of life and the meaning of death. For them, war changed everything. It tore them out of their routines and placed them in a world in which daily confrontations with the senselessness of war drove them toward nihilism, despair, and—finally—a desperate groping after faith.

Individual crises of faith were one thing; coordinating these episodes into a grand, national regenerative gesture—a consecration—was quite another. For some, the distinction was never sharply drawn. Certainly de Mun's aim in organizing the volunteer chaplains was to provide comfort and administer the sacraments to men about to face death in battle. But as the war dragged on and the drive to organize a national consecration took shape, the chaplaincy initiative took on the aspect, at least for its critics, of a privileged channel constructed to proselytize a captive clientele: the front-line soldier.

During the opening months of the war, and following the death of de Mun, Veuillot and Grandmaison assembled a network linking battlefront and home front, with Veuillot at the interface. The extent of their efforts over the years following was largely hidden from public view. Shortly after the war, however, Veuillot and Grandmaison collaborated in a remarkable account of their chaplaincy project. The book, *L'aumônerie militaire pendant la guerre, 1914–1918,* was published in 1923. It describes in considerable detail the extraordinary network linking military chaplains in the trenches with Catholic donors on the home front.[38] Grandmaison and Veuillot credited de Mun with the vision of organizing volunteer chaplains. De Mun, Grandmaison noted, knew that the patriotism of priests would drive them to volunteer for chaplaincy duty. He also knew that he could rely on the generosity of donors to fund them; indeed, de Mun raised over 100,000 francs in the opening months of the war.[39]

For the priests, full of zeal, who responded to the call for volunteers, wartime service was a kind of paradise. Service to the soldiers freed them from parish routine and the supervision of the church hierarchy. It gave them an unusual liberty to follow their troops and serve them as they saw fit, free of stifling episcopal constraint.[40] Moreover, the troops, for the most part, were more receptive to the chaplain's message than

was the typical parishioner back home. Grandmaison liked to emphasize what was unique and dynamic about the chaplain's role. He liked
to talk about chaplains as directors of "parishes on-the-move." Theirs
was the dynamic, opportunistic role of a missionary, not the static,
routine-laden obligations of the parish priest.[41]

LETTERS FROM THE FRONT

One of the consequences of Veuillot's central role in the chaplaincy
effort was that he, probably as well as anyone else, was able to gauge the
sentiments of the front-line soldier because he was the recipient of a
vast quantity of uncensored letters from chaplains in the field request-
ing funds. It is unclear how much money Veuillot ultimately had at his
disposal beyond the 100,000 francs that de Mun had raised, but he doled
it out liberally in sums of 150 and 200 francs per request.[42]

In writing to Veuillot for help, the chaplains recounted details in the
spiritual life of the soldiers in their care. Their aim, of course, was to
convince Veuillot of the good work already being done among the soldiers and the possibility of doing still more with the financial support of
Veuillot and his backers. This being the case, we should be aware that
there is a measure of interest guiding these letter-writers, but it is interest driven by a commitment to serve others as well as to appear worthy
in the eyes of the likes of Veuillot.

The letters reveal troops in a variety of mental states, their vulnerabilities exposed by the experience of battle: men terrified by the prospect
of death, men resigned to their fate, men eager for distraction from war,
men restored by faith, men driven to compulsive behavior by the fear
that the slightest departure from routine would alter their good luck.

The letters also reveal something about the prejudices and powers of
observation of their authors; indeed some fall fairly easily into cliché.
Father Guéguen served among the stretcher-bearers of the 61st Infantry,
which comprised a great many soldiers from Brittany. Although he often
wrote with sensitivity and insight, he occasionally indulged in fairly

Figure 14. A soldier from the Vendée, celebrated in stained glass, holds a tricolor flag and wears a Sacred Heart tricolor pinned to his chest. Window by L. Fournier, 1944, in the Church of Saint-Pierre, Les Lucs-sur-Boulogne (Vendée)

broad and somewhat patronizing remarks. Guéguen observed the abiding faith for which the Bretons were famous. "I told you our Breton soldiers were religious. Hé oui!" he told Veuillot. But he also observed some soldiers' almost obsessive use of religious symbols and rituals. He noted that Breton soldiers would recite the rosary endlessly in the trenches, "in order to keep from falling asleep." And he reported that an officer had told him "that they lay out their cartridges in the form of a cross."

Moreover, these soldiers' respect for religion (and their distrust of medicine) was such that "when they are wounded or seriously ill, their first wish is to go to confession."[43] Bretons cared first for the soul, then for the body. Although the French Republic (and French high culture with it) had regarded the Breton language with suspicion and as a marker of "backwardness," Guéguen found the use of Breton to be crucial to his pastoral mission. He occasionally gave his sermons in Breton, a gesture that Breton soldiers found reassuring, leading some to complain that his sermons "weren't long enough." In the end, Guéguen wondered at the symbolic and ritualistic obsessions of the Bretons. "This is natural for them," he wrote, in a remark that mixed awe and condescension.

While Breton soldiers set the standard for faith and practice, revealing a daily culture framed by Christian emblem rituals, some chaplains reported encountering other soldiers woefully lacking in religious training or sentiment. Indeed, some chaplains seem to have been unprepared for the spectacle of atheism, agnosticism, and irreligion that they encountered. One chaplain described "an unbelievable ignorance." And not just ignorance; he also encountered real hostility to belief among soldiers, along with a "stupefying prejudice."

But if some chaplains were unprepared for bouts of anticlericalism and irreligion, others were unprepared for displays of fervor and fellowship, and they were stunned at the sight of men who, at "frequent evening prayers and open-air masses," sought to triumph over death, conquer fear, or find consolation. Many priests found the experience of ministering to entirely male congregations at the front both novel and emotionally overwhelming, particularly since the number of practicing male Catholics in France had dropped precipitously during the course of the nineteenth century. Armed with folding, portable altars (donated through Veuillot's network), priests followed the movements of the troops in their care, offering sacraments when and where they could. Nature itself crafted sacred architecture for these mobile communities of faith. Some priests wrote of masses among a stand of trees; trunks defined the nave, while high above tall branches joined to form Gothic arches.[44]

Such natural shrines added to a variety of improvised sacred spaces, including barns and abandoned houses transformed into chapels. In the network of trenches, devout soldiers constructed elaborate underground chapels from the earth and reinforcing beams. Sometimes priests assembled altars from the debris and bric-a-brac of materials found at the front. A zinc countertop salvaged from a shell-shattered *bistro* served as an altar at one mass.[45] It was an ironic emblem of reconciliation. Priests remembered well the prewar Sunday mornings when they had stood on the steps of their churches to watch women and children file in for mass while their husbands, fathers, sons, and brothers drifted into nearby cafés, where they leaned on zinc counters for drink and conversation: the profane rituals of male companionship. Sunday-morning male sociability amounted to a weekly ceremony marking the estrangement of men from the Catholic faith. To conduct a sacred ritual for soldiers on a café countertop—*there* was an image generating a powerful sense of return.

War put priests at the center of the lives of the men they served. Some chaplains groped for superlatives adequate to their experience; they were overwhelmed by their importance to the men around them. "Military chaplain?" wrote one. "What a rare grace for a priest, to have lived such a life, to have lived such a dream."[46]

Such was the optimism of the early war. As the war dragged on, renewals of faith sometimes faded, and religious skepticism returned in tandem with cynicism about the war. The conviction that the war would end quickly was widespread during the autumn of 1914. The letters of chaplains reveal a corresponding conviction about the significance of the war for an awakening male spirituality. The chaplains' stories of individual reconciliations with faith in the closing months of 1914 corresponded with a spike in religious practice on the home front. For some Catholics the return to religion in the trenches and on the home front, taken together, seemed to point toward a reconciliation of France with the Catholic Church, as if the war was a providential act designed to bring France back to the bosom of the church.

The Unraveling

~❖~

On 25 June 1917, as morning mass in a makeshift church came to an end, a military chaplain asked his congregation to stay for a brief ceremony. The chaplain, a man named Devezy, handed out half-page sheets in small stacks to be distributed among the men. "The completed forms," he called out, "will be sent to Montmartre and placed on the altar of the Basilica of the Sacré-Coeur." As the forms were passed from hand to hand, Devezy gave instructions. "Those who wish to consecrate themselves to the Sacré-Coeur," he said, "need only complete the form, sign it, and return it to me."

Devezy told the soldiers that the consecration was "purely individual, or familial"—in other words, it was not to be one of the regimental consecrations that had already attracted the attention and condemnation of authorities. Just the same, Devezy sensed trouble when he noticed among the soldiers that day a commanding officer, a colonel, who "practically never attends mass." The colonel witnessed mass and the distribution of the consecration leaflets. But as the men filed out, he called out to them. "I forbid you to sign these forms," he told the soldiers. "They [the Catholic clergy] are trying to organize a collective petition, [and] haven't the right."[1] The colonel collected as many of the leaflets as he could, then dispatched a bicycle messenger to all the

118

surrounding encampments with orders to seize any consecration sheets and send them to headquarters.

Devezy was about to confront the colonel but then thought better of it. The following day he sought out the colonel and asked for an explanation. The colonel explained that what the chaplains had intended was far from benign. "You planned a collective petition [through the consecrations]. You wanted to gather signatures in order to show to the highest ranks of the clergy how many men could be counted upon for a religious movement." Chaplain Devezy protested that he intended nothing of the kind. The colonel responded by describing an elaborate conspiracy theory: the Sacred Heart was a Jesuit cult; the Jesuits were leading a covert consecration effort; the Jesuits were a powerful international political party. He also claimed that the Jesuits were ardent supporters of France's enemy, Kaiser Wilhelm II. To this theory of a treasonous Jesuit conspiracy against France, the colonel added the threat of an imminent Jesuit coup d'état at the Vatican. The Jesuits were plotting to capture the pope and take him to Spain to make him serve as their agent! Devezy, stunned by the colonel's increasingly improbable imaginings, protested that the colonel was obviously mistaken. The colonel would hear none of it. "You," the colonel told Devezy in a sympathetic tone, "you are a decent man; you walk in the simplicity of your conscience. You don't know what your leaders are doing!" Devezy concluded that further discussion was pointless.

The chaplain summarized the incident for François Veuillot by remarking wistfully, "I would like to be able to tell you that our Sacred Heart feast day was lovely; in fact it was, but it ended strangely. . . ." The colonel's bizarre international Jesuit conspiracy theory—involving papal abduction and German imperial complicity—was not the first woven around the Jesuits.[2] Nor do we have any reason to doubt the authenticity of Devezy's bewilderment. He and many like him genuinely believed that the soldierly consecrations should be taken at face value, as profoundly private spiritual acts. From his perspective—and his candor is as evident as his disappointment—his men were doing nothing more than seeking spiritual consolation during a most difficult and dangerous time in their lives.[3] It probably never occurred to him that the consecration initiative he promoted was taking place within a national debate over the war and the future of France.

Just such a debate—which threatened to tear apart the Sacred Union—was underway on the home front. Claire was a major figure within it.

THE 1917 PETITION CAMPAIGN

The struggle between chaplain Devezy and his commanding officer has many of the features, allowing for scale, of the epic struggle between Catholics and the government over the Sacred Heart consecration in 1917: alarm, disingenuous claims, specters of vast conspiracies, bewilderment, exasperation. With Claire's help, the national debate added the prospect of a shift from personal redemption to national redemption.

Lay Catholics, with the support or acquiescence of the hierarchy, carried out a national petition-drive to persuade the government to lay the grounds for victory by consecrating France to the Sacred Heart. Leadership of the Catholic episcopate in France does not rest with the archbishop of Paris—that distinction belongs to the archbishop of Lyon, known as the "Primate." However, attention focused on Paris and its archbishop because Paris was the nation's capital in virtually all other domains and because leadership for the drive came from Paris and radiated outward from there. Petition headquarters, Le Secrétariat du Sacré-Coeur, was on boulevard Raspail in Paris.[4] The secrétariat announced the drive in May of 1917 in the Catholic daily *La Croix*. The message was picked up by many weekly diocesan bulletins, the semiofficial *semaines religieuses*.[5]

Cardinal Amette, archbishop of Paris, kept his distance from the petition-drive, at least publicly. Presumably he did this to avoid confrontation with the government, not because of any basic philosophical difference. Although some Catholic clergy had ambivalent feelings

Figure 15. Léon-Adolphe Amette, archbishop of Paris

about the Sacred Heart devotion—particularly concerning the more overtly political goal of a national consecration—Amette was not among them. He was the eager patron of the project to complete the Basilica of the Sacré-Coeur on Montmartre; he had placed the Sacred Heart emblem on his own episcopal coat of arms; he had enthusiastically endorsed the ill-fated 1915 attempt to carry out a consecration of France diocese-by-diocese and parish-by-parish.[6]

What set Amette apart was that Claire's magic didn't work on him. Unlike Audebert, Bourget, and Humbrecht—who had fallen under her spell at first contact—Amette remained suspicious of Claire. When Claire appealed to the archbishop for permission to spend a night in adoration at the basilica on Montmartre, Amette hesitated. Night prayer at Montmartre was reserved to men, he noted. Claire persisted. But how could a peasant woman stand up to a powerful archbishop? Shortly thereafter, in an episode that must have felt as though she was pulling rank on him, Claire wrote to Amette of a vision in which Jesus reproached her. "I brought you here so that you would spend a night in this church," her vision told her. "Go again and tell the Cardinal that you cannot go home until you have his authorization," scolded Claire's visionary Jesus.[7]

Amette relented and authorized the nighttime vigil, but he appears to have been angry that Claire sought to manipulate him with a vision in which Jesus scolds the cardinal archbishop of Paris. And he wondered about the other visions too, visions that seemed to pave the way for Claire and her ambition. Were visions driving Claire? Or was Claire driving the visions? In a letter to Montmartre authorizing the vigil, he made it clear that although he was granting Claire's request, he had doubts about her visionary claims. "I disapprove of the insistent demands of Claire Ferchaud [that she make a nighttime vigil at Montmartre]. I have trouble believing that this insistence truly comes from Our Lord. I am inclined to believe that this young lady is sincere, but she could be a crank and under the power of suggestion."[8] Amette was smart. He insisted on a quid pro quo. In exchange for his permission to carry out the vigil at the Sacré-Coeur, he ordered Claire to return home to Loublande the day following.[9] Rather than confront her directly with his doubts, he sought to placate her, then remove her.

Amette was a keen judge of character, but his desire to avoid confrontation gave free rein to some of Claire's advocates and close allies. In fact, the distinction that Amette sought to maintain—advocacy of a national consecration but skepticism of Claire—proved difficult to maintain in practice. The two were becoming hopelessly entangled. Whatever the origins of the idea of a national petition, it is certain that Claire had it firmly in mind when she went to visit Poincaré, because she put the question directly to him. "If the majority of the French people demand the Sacred Heart on the flag," she asked, "would you refuse it?" "Maybe not," responded Poincaré, a political roué who had surely seen his share of earnest schemes. "We get petitions all the time."[10]

The petition idea had been seconded shortly after Claire's visit with Poincaré by a certain Mademoiselle Blanche de Béarn, who spear-headed the campaign, with Claire serving as its figurehead. Blanche de Béarn never had an audience with Poincaré, as Claire had had. But she was able to gain an audience with Amette on 18 April in order to seek his approval for the petition. According to Blanche de Béarn, Amette stated that he personally did not favor the idea but added, in a charac-teristic gesture of indirection, that he would not forbid it.[11] The risk for Amette, of course, was that the ongoing campaign to change the flag and bring about a national consecration, causes that he ardently sup-ported, would be hopelessly confused with the story of Claire, of whose bona fides Amette was growing increasingly skeptical.

Amette did manage to establish a certain critical distance from the national campaign. Although the Catholic daily newspaper *La Croix* was headquartered in Paris, it was by no means the official organ of the archdiocese of Paris. The archdiocese had had its own weekly publica-tion, *La Semaine Religieuse de l'Archdiocèse de Paris,* since the middle of the last century. *La Croix*'s readership was national, not Parisian, and it appealed to that readership when it ran an announcement of the petition-drive in its edition of 6–7 May 1917. *La Croix* gave a Paris address, 133 boulevard Raspail, for the Secrétariat du Sacré-Coeur—the organization leading the petition-drive. As headquarters for the initiative, *La Croix* noted, the secrétariat would serve as clearinghouse for the petition cam-paign in favor of a national consecration to the Sacred Heart. It was the place to go to obtain blank petitions and to submit completed ones.

Amette moved quickly to distance himself from this initiative. Two days later, in the edition of 9 May, *La Croix* ran a clarification: although the headquarters for the drive was in Paris, Amette's diocese, the archbishop had authorized neither the secrétariat, nor the petition-drive. The newspaper counseled its readers to consult their respective bishops as to the status of the petition-drive locally; there was no consensus among the bishops of France, hence no blanket authorization.

The published clarification was intended to reassure the government of Amette's neutrality on the issue, not to discourage the campaign. Amette had not *opposed* the initiative; he simply had refused to authorize it—a gesture of benign neglect. In the absence of any text or speech attributable to him, Amette's views can best be understood symbolically. Three weeks earlier, on 22 April, Amette had been the central figure in a ceremony that had taken place at the Cathedral of Saint-Denis, just north of Paris. Saint Denis, a third-century martyr, was commonly regarded as the first bishop of Paris. By going to the cathedral built in his name, Amette emphasized his role as the spiritual leader of the nation's capital. The ceremony had its liturgical dimension, but the key symbolic moment came when Amette took the "banner of Saint Denis"—a stand-in for the national flag—and pinned a Sacred Heart emblem on it. Amette's gesture, which took place in the middle of the national petition campaign—and four weeks after Claire's meeting with Poincaré—was a kind of dress rehearsal for the addition of the Sacred Heart to the tricolor. As if to drive the point home, just as the national petition-drive was getting underway in early May, the Catholic newsweekly *Le Pèlerin* ran a color photo on its front page. The photo showed the altar of the Cathedral of Saint-Denis decked out with flags. In the foreground, plainly in view, was a tricolor bearing the emblem of the Sacred Heart.[12]

Elsewhere in France, the supporters of the drive had their ardent advocates.[13] In Poitiers, notably, archbishop Humbrecht called upon all diocesan clergy to work to bring about the success of a petition that would, he noted, "realize the demand [for a national consecration]

Figure 16. Masthead of *Le Pèlerin,* 13 May 1917, with a color photograph of the altar at the Cathedral of Saint-Denis decked out with flags, including a Sacred Heart tricolor

made by Our Lord to Marguerite-Marie two centuries ago."[14] A petition circulating in one town of his diocese had already accumulated some fifty signatures when it was presented for signature to the mayor, who promptly seized it and reported it to the provincial administrator. The petition specifically noted the vision of Marguerite-Marie Alacoque and the demands for a chapel, a consecration, and a Sacred Heart emblem on the flag.[15] Thousands of petitions were duly sent to the Secrétariat du Sacré-Coeur in Paris.

CHARGES OF TREASON: THE GOVERNMENT ACTS

The campaign for a national consecration—petitions, emblems, ceremonies, photos, newspaper reports—continued to build during the opening months of 1917. The campaign was to peak on the first Friday of June, the month of the Sacred Heart.

Claire continued her public campaign. She also maintained pressure on Poincaré, writing to him again on 1 May 1917. She chided him for reneging on his promise to her to introduce legislation to modify the French flag. At the same time, Claire's visionary world was becoming more elaborate. The boundary between this world and the world of her visions became more porous; one might even say that the boundary had begun to collapse. She claimed, in her letter, to have received knowledge of a Masonic plot to destroy France. The plot would soon be uncovered; many high government officials would be put to death. Claire's visions were becoming richer and more detailed, and her rhetoric was becoming more alarming. Her message had always implied that only the stubbornness of government officials stood between France and victory. Now her message was unambiguous. It amounted to a charge of treason on the part of France's highest officials.

In the face of resistance among key secular and religious authorities, Claire sought to go over their heads by writing directly to French military leaders. On 7 May 1917, she wrote to fifteen high-ranking generals and commanders, repeating the claims that she had made in her March letter to Poincaré. She revealed, moreover, the fact of her audience with the president himself, which surely came as a surprise to many of the letter's recipients. She repeated the claims of a Masonic plot to undermine France and recounted a charmingly improbable vision in which the betrayal of France had been averted only because Jesus had cut "an electric wire that would have delivered the secret of France to the enemy."[16] Claire's message forced a choice between competing allegiances—either Claire was wrong or the government was in the hands of traitors.[17]

But the government had already resolved to act to halt a movement it regarded as divisive and potentially destructive of the Sacred Union and the war effort. Indeed, from the point of view of secular leaders, it must have been difficult to distinguish the official campaign on behalf of the Sacred Heart led by leading members of the French episcopate and the rogue initiative associated with Claire and her lay supporters.

In late May, leading members of the government sought to bring an end to these campaigns, both on the home front and in the army. Jean-Louis Malvy, minister of the interior, instructed provincial administrators, known as prefects, to forbid the addition of any emblem to the tricolor flag. Then, on 25 May, in order to alert and mobilize supporters of the government's position, he sent a dispatch to the press. The dispatch denounced the petition-drive and noted that the prefects had been advised to defend the secular nature of the national flag. Prefects asked mayors to post the interdiction in public places.[18] There were incidents and challenges to the decree. In Châtellerault, schoolchildren drew Sacred Heart tricolor flags on paper and posted them on doors and windows around town. At Civray, an individual circulating a petition was asked whether the sentiment behind the petition wasn't seditious (*frondeur*). The person circulating the petition, a certain Madame Jouillat, situated her conduct in the republican tradition of popular sovereignty, noting that when the government sees the entire country demanding something (in this instance, the Sacred Heart flag), it will give in to the general will.[19]

As if to emphasize the gravity of the situation and the determination of the government, an example was made of the archbishop of Tours, who displayed in his cathedral a tricolor flag on which the Sacred Heart was clearly evident. When the archbishop refused to remove the Sacred Heart emblem, the government pressed charges.[20] For the most part, government officials and church leaders avoided confrontation that might erupt into civil disturbances. Public officials also pressed charges against the director of a seminary at Montmorillon when they learned

that Sacred Heart tricolors were on display there. The seminary director removed the flags and was assessed a symbolic fine of one franc.[21]

So much for the home front. The minister of war, Paul Painlevé,
sent a confidential memorandum to commanding officers in which he
catalogued the various elements of the Sacred Heart campaign, including the mailing of hundreds of thousands of unsolicited Sacred Heart
banners, flags, and medals to front-line troops. The memorandum
described a network of army chaplains, mobilized priests, and sympathetic officers who served as recipients, distributors, and agitators.
Painlevé also described numerous attempts to carry out consecrations
of entire units to the Sacred Heart, cited as a violation of freedom of
conscience and the separation of church and state. Marshall Philippe
Pétain attached a cover memorandum in which he seconded Painlevé's
remarks and prohibited the wearing of all but approved military
insignia.[22] The government's position was emphatic. Neither among
the troops, nor on the home front, would a grassroots campaign in favor
of Claire Ferchaud or a consecration of the nation to the Sacred Heart
be permitted.

TRUE BELIEVERS SWAMP LOUBLANDE

As the struggle between the government and the sponsors of the petition deepened, Claire's mission entered a new phase. Claire's voyage to
Paris, her sojourn in the capital, and her audience with Poincaré only
added to her notoriety and her mystique. Back home, her celebrity and
spiritual authority continued to grow. Her activism was unrelenting as
the summer of 1917 gave way to autumn and winter.

She had not returned to the farm at Rinfillières following her departure from Paris; she had gone first to Saint-Laurent and then to a kind
of convent-house made available to her in Loublande. Five colleagues
joined her. The women dressed in black outfits that resembled religious habits, and they lived as members of an unofficial religious community. By February 1918, there were eight "sisters" in Claire's

community. They were known collectively as "Les Réparatrices Nationales"—the National Atoners.[23]

Rumors about Claire began to circulate. One rumor had it that Claire knew that she would die an early death, at the age of twenty-four. (She was then twenty-two.) Another had it that Claire had predicted a new devastating setback for the Allies, a defeat so great that even the faithless would recognize in it the hand of God. The Enemy would approach the city of Paris, sending France and its allies reeling. Then, on the verge of annihilation, the Allied armies would rally and triumph when they placed the Sacred Heart on their flags.[24] For skeptics like Amette, the archbishop of Paris, such increasingly eccentric pronouncements only substantiated initial doubts. For Claire's supporters, tormented by an unending war, these same bold pronouncements only added to her allure and heightened the sense of alarm and urgent anticipation.

A renewed German offensive in the spring of 1918, the second Battle of the Marne, seemed to validate Claire's prediction of near-calamity for France. So did the approach of another June (and another month of the Sacred Heart). Hundreds gathered at Loublande for the first Friday of April 1918. Loublande had no hotel, but local residents managed to set up makeshift rooming facilities. Even these were quickly overwhelmed by the demand; pilgrims had to find lodging in neighboring villages. Some simply spent the night in the church. Such expedients added not only to the fatigue but also to the festive atmosphere of Loublande. Bourget, for whom all the hubbub was a confirmation of his early faith in Claire's mission, rose to the occasion and preached on the theme of national redemption through the Sacred Heart, highlighting the observation of the bishop of Poitiers that the "goal" to attain was the "social reign" of the Sacred Heart through the flag of the Sacred Heart.[25]

Loublande became the privileged backdrop for a series of speakers who had promoted the story of the visionary of Loublande. Among them was a priest named Mathéo Crawley-Boevey, reportedly of

Peruvian origins, who had spent the war years on a speaking tour in France.[26] Crawley-Boevey was by all accounts a dynamic and indefatigable promoter of the Sacred Heart devotion. By 1918 his speaking engagements had taken him to nearly all of the dioceses of France, where he had run "missions" to break the liturgical routine and restore flagging faith.[27] The tradition of domestic missions is a long one in France, dating back to the Old Regime and, ultimately, to the missionary activity of the founding bishops of Gallo-Roman France. By the early nineteenth century, these missions had taken on a dramatic quality, notably after the Revolution of 1789, when the missions' programs often included the spectacular burning of revolutionary emblems in bonfires of repentance for revolutionary acts.[28] In short, internal missions and missionaries operated within a tradition that blended theatrical and liturgical elements.

Crawley-Boevey, a man of unusual charisma, descended upon Loublande in May of 1918.[29] From his experience on the road as itinerant preacher, he had learned how to read an audience and how to appeal to its sensibilities. By all accounts he was handsome, young, and energetic, and he had a gift for drama and spectacle. Admirers noted how Crawley-Boevey's French, spoken with a Peruvian accent, added to his exotic allure. Defending Crawley-Boevey against his critics, who disliked his "fanaticism," an anonymous writer in *La Croix* conceded that Crawley-Boevey's strength was not "eloquence." "That's not what he aims for," noted the sympathetic commentator, who compared him instead to a kind of traveling salesman, hawking rare goods and cure-all remedies, a snake-oil peddler, a barker for a carnival sideshow. "His thick exotic accent makes him resemble an Indian doctor from the depths of the virgin forests who is promoting a fruit, discovered in a tree, capable of healing all illnesses."[30]

Hence, the carnivalesque quality of Crawley-Boevey's sojourn at Loublande. During his ten days there, Crawley-Boevey reassured his listeners of the unprecedented nature of their times. He described Claire, in exalted terms, as proof made manifest of exceptional divine solicitude. "Praise God, residents of Loublande," he preached. "You are blessed and privileged. The Lord has given forth from your land His Liberator of France! The Angel who will save the fatherland! Victory will come not from Montmartre, nor from Paray-le-Monial—it's from Loublande that Peace will come." Later Crawley-Boevey would reproach himself in his characteristically exalted style for having had the temerity to preach to Claire and her "sisters" at Loublande when it was they, "these Saints, who taught *me* what faith is. The Angels and the Saints, if they came down to earth, would bow down before them!" During his stay he operated a veritable tent revival meeting, a ten-day mission-spectacle, including sermons and nighttime candlelight vigils in which he praised Claire as "the Liberator of France" and acclaimed Loublande, improbably, as "the vestibule of heaven."[31]

Crawley-Boevey was a hard act to follow. Jean-Baptiste Lemius, Claire's demanding spiritual counselor in Paris, somehow found the courage. Lemius had personality to spare and bowed to no one but God. He followed Crawley-Boevey's exotic revivalism with grand theater of his own in early June 1918, at the peak of enthusiasm for Claire. The program, announced in advance, shows a fevered activity over nine days (a novena)—one whose relentless pace would certainly have generated fatigue but also a collective sense of mystery and exhilaration. Activities for the seventh, the first Friday in June, were to begin at nine o'clock on Thursday evening with a torchlight procession, followed by a nightlong outdoor vigil (weather permitting) with masses at 1:30 AM, 3:30 AM, and 5:30 AM. Masses continued into Friday morning, culminating in an outdoor mass at 10:30 AM. In the afternoon, there would be another procession to the new Loublande cemetery, where vespers would be chanted, followed by a solemn return procession. Lemius appointed himself the featured speaker.[32]

René Guérin, chaplain of the Poor Claires of Alençon, captured something of the atmosphere of celebrity and theater surrounding Loublande in those days. Guérin noted that Claire was reportedly ill and had been absent from the program on one day during his visit.

It hardly mattered. Claire's celebrity had surpassed Claire the person. "The pilgrim at Loublande," he noted, "is more attentive to what Claire represents than to the person herself." Claire played well in the heartland, but events—faith, hope, notoriety—had overtaken her. In effect, she had become an emblem; Claire the person had been effaced by Claire the persona and the cause that she and her advocates had created.[33]

The public career of Claire Ferchaud, the visionary of Loublande, had entered its final phase. Her supporters—Humbrecht, Bourget, Lemius, Crawley-Boevey—had made Claire a vehicle for a project of national renewal. Her message was now fully developed—penance, prayer, Sacred Heart flag, national consecration, triumph of Catholic France over the secular Republic. As the stakes were thus raised for all concerned, skeptics and opponents of Claire among the Catholic clergy found that they had to move more aggressively. From the beginning, Claire's message had exercised polarities of attraction and danger. The chief attraction, shared by all visionaries, was the promise of sanctity for one's own time: vision comforts faith. But Claire's attack on public authorities as traitors—attacks that were once veiled but were now overt—amounted to the opening salvos of a renewed civil war.

The Unmaking of a Saint

When war broke out in August of 1914, Father Servant, pastor of Saint-Gervais parish, had an idea. He would write a private history of the war. He took out a pen and a bound booklet of lined paper. He opened the booklet to the first page. With his pen he scratched the letters *JMJ* at the top of the page. His gesture consecrated his journalistic efforts to three sacred personages: Jesus, Mary, and Joseph. Beside these initials he wrote the numeral *1*—the first day of the war. In the days, weeks, months, and years to come, he followed the logic of his first gestures unrelentingly, tracing the letters *JMJ* at the top of each page and adding to the count of the number of days in a war that seemed to stretch on into infinity.

The title Father Servant gave to his enterprise—roughly translated, *As the Ink Flows: My Impressions during the War of 1914* (*Mes impressions au courant de la plume pendant la guerre de 1914*)—was overtaken by events. The war did not reach its end until November of 1918, by which time the number of days Servant duly noted had exceeded fifteen hundred. Servant had filled *eight* thick tablets with thoughts, souvenirs, and press clippings. He had confided his hopes and doubts to unknown readers—to us. His reflections found their way to provincial archives in Poitiers, where they were discovered in the course of research for this book.

Servant's *Impressions* are a precious resource. They provide a glimpse of wartime France and the mentality of a rural priest. Servant understood from the outset that he, like France, was caught up in an event that would change his world forever. Much that he could see of this new world he didn't like. Soldiers from his parish and region (the Vendée) had occupied the Rhineland after the signing of the armistice. While serving in the occupation, these men had learned to dance—a social and moral horror to someone of Servant's day and background. German women—he called them "*bochesses,*" a delicate feminine version of the pejorative term *boche* applied to the German enemy—had boldly approached French soldiers and invited them to dance. Now the soldiers were home. Thanks to the *bochesses*, they had developed a taste for dancing and brought it back with them to France. "Now everyone in the Vendée dances," Servant fretted, "and piety is none the better for it."[1] The war had shaken up the stagnant, immobile communities of rural France. Things would never be the same.

Then there were the Americans. Servant looked upon them with a mix of anxiety and admiration. He was particularly apprehensive about African-American soldiers: "I admit that I don't have much sympathy for these descendants of Ham," he noted. (Ham was one of the sons of Noah and the ruler of Ethiopia, hence regarded as the biblical ancestor of all black people.) Servant comforted himself with the thought that "the Americans [he meant white Americans] don't either. . . . they hang them from time to time." "Yet another element that will not improve the French race," he concluded.[2] But Servant also admired "American qualities." In a private editorial commentary—perhaps the draft of a sermon—entitled "The Americans and the Future of France," Servant expressed the view that French intermarriage with Americans would be a good thing. "Today I saw some women approach some Americans, whom they judge favorably," he noted. "Someone who reads a great deal and knows the aptitudes of [the French and American] people told me that the infusion of new blood would fortify the French race; the Americans would give us the spirit of initiative in industry and commerce that we lack." Servant's comments blended concepts of race with received wisdom about national traits. The French "race" was weak, he believed, and lacked entrepreneurial zeal, which the Americans possessed.[3] Intermarriage would reinvigorate tired French blood.

Besides providing us with insights into the hopes, fears, and prejudices of an early twentieth-century Frenchman, Servant's running commentary during the war years also allows us to track the career of Claire. Because he is primarily interested in recording his impressions of the war, the diary becomes a useful index of when and how Claire's notoriety imposed itself on Servant, commanding his attention and finding its way into his commentary and his understanding of the war. Thanks to Servant's memoirs, we have a sense for when Claire first appears on the public's "radar," when she reaches her apogee, and when she falls from sight.

Of course, Servant is not an impartial observer. As a priest, Servant is receptive to Claire's message, and he manifests the varieties of attitudes toward her—ranging from fervent support, to skepticism, to hostility—and the complex emotions that her career was provoking throughout France. Reading Servant, we see that Claire embodied some of the clergy's most cherished traits—innocence and a capacity for vivid faith—but also aroused deep suspicions: of fraud, inadequate clerical guidance, and the risk of unorthodoxy. Servant shows us Claire as a potential saint-in-the-making, but also as a potential threat to an institution that guards an ancient spiritual heritage and protects the faithful from false prophets and their own credulity.

Servant first writes about Claire in March of 1917, on the "971st day of the war." His remarks reveal affection for Claire and an early optimism. "Our little visionary of Loublande," he writes, "works for the Sacred Heart and for France." By June, however, his tone has grown muted; he understands more clearly the complexity of the situation and

Figure 17.   A prayer card based on Claire's visions, taped
into the wartime journal of Abbé Servant

the risks involved. "We are entering the month of the Sacred Heart. A
petition is being signed to put the image of the Sacred Heart on the
French flag," he notes matter-of-factly. Servant is aware of the opposition of the government and the publicly ambivalent position taken by
Cardinal Amette, the archbishop of Paris. The clergy itself is divided
and fearful that unrealistic expectations generated by Claire and the

petition-drive will end in disappointment. "Some go forward; others hold back," he noted. "People are getting carried away with the visionary of Loublande. People pray to the Sacred Heart, but they say that they won't believe any more if the war isn't over by the 15th of June."[4] Claire had inspired millenarian hopes; so had the petition-drive. A population exasperated by unending war was drawn to promises of a spectacular conclusion to the war. Servant worried that when those hopes were betrayed, hope would collapse and faith with it, putting "religion at stake."

Servant even questioned whether the kind of "Joan of Arc" redemption that Claire was promising really made any sense in the early twentieth century. "Are we worthy of divine intervention as in the time of Joan of Arc?" he asked, linking personal doubts about Claire with a gloomy conviction about France's decline. "There are hardly any men at religious services in our region," he noted. "I presided over First Communion at a neighboring parish—there weren't any boys. . . ."

And then there was the army. "As for the morality of the French army, at least in the depots and in the services at the rear, where they employ women, it is deplorable. . . ."[5] Servant had trouble believing in Claire's promise of divine redemption, because he couldn't believe that France was worth the trouble!

And then there was the confusion of dates. By July of 1918, Servant confided to his journal his concerns about how the Catholic leadership had handled Claire's story. He faulted Archbishop Humbrecht of Poitiers for concentrating popular anxiety and millennial expectations on certain dates, only to see them come and go without result. "Popular rumor said that victory would come by a miracle of the Sacred Heart in February 1917, then [in June] on the feast of the Sacred Heart, then in February 1918 with Our Lady of Lourdes, then for the month of June [again]," wrote Servant in July of 1918, his exasperation clearly evident. "Monsignor [Humbrecht] has announced victory on set dates, but incorrectly, several times. . . ."[6] As steward of faith, Humbrecht had failed in Servant's eyes.

DOUBTERS EXPRESS THEIR MISGIVINGS;
THE VATICAN TAKES CHARGE

Servant was not alone in his doubts about Claire and her supporters. Among Catholic laity, there were those who rejected the petition drive and were skeptical of Claire's claims. Their attitude was important to public officials who rejected the impression that Catholic opinion on these issues—Claire, the Sacred Heart flag—was monolithic. "I know many clerical families that disapprove of the petition drive," wrote the subprefect of Châtellerault to his supervisor at Poitiers. "They don't want anyone to alter the flag."[7]

The position of Catholic clergy was somewhat more delicate given their unique mix of allegiances—to the laity, the hierarchy, the *patrie,* their consciences, their faith. Some clergy openly championed the cause of the Sacred Heart flag and annexed Claire's cause to it. Others, such as Cardinal Amette, had doubts about Claire but apparently saw little harm in the union of the patriotic symbol of the tricolor flag and the religious emblem of the Sacred Heart. Still others had grave reservations about both.

The bishop of Périgueux opposed the circulation of the flag petition in his diocese on the grounds that it was at odds with religious pluralism in France. "Given that Protestants, schismatics, Mohammedans, and unbelievers must march behind this same flag, this [petition] seems pointless and dangerous," he wrote. The bishop of Nice emphasized less lofty concerns in his weekly diocesan bulletin. "To attempt this [the Sacred Heart flag]," he wrote, "would only provoke refusal, opposition, perhaps acts of blasphemy and, even among Catholics, regrettable disagreements."[8]

A private letter brought national attention to these differences when it was published in a leading French national daily newspaper, *Le Figaro,* on 4 May 1918, apparently without the knowledge or permission of its author. Given that the letter was not intended for a public readership, it was candid and blunt. The fact that it was written by a Jesuit of French nationality (the order avidly promoted the Sacred

Heart devotion)—a cardinal, in fact, stationed in Rome—gave the letter particular weight.[9] It laid bare the misgivings of part of the Catholic clergy.

On the pages of *Le Figaro,* Cardinal Billot's critique became an "open letter" raising doubts about the Sacred Heart flag, as well as about Claire and her visionary enhancements of the Sacred Heart saga. What would it mean, Billot asked, to put the Sacred Heart, a symbol of love and peace, on the national flag during a time of war? What would it mean if the Germans, many of whom are Catholic, were to do likewise? "Then we would have this Heart," Billot noted, "leading French to slaughter Germans and Germans to slaughter French."[10] Billot constructed a horrifying scenario in which nationalism trumped religion, as French Catholics and German Catholics slaughtered each other in the name of the same Sacred Heart.

Supporters and opponents picked up the story. It became an object of commentary in such quasi-official Catholic publications as *La Croix,* the national Catholic daily newspaper, and *Le Messager du Sacré-Coeur de Jésus,* as well as partisan pro–Sacred Heart periodicals such as *La Foi Catholique,* and several ephemeral publications.[11] Billot's letter reassured those who were skeptical of Claire or who had doubts about putting a religious emblem on the tricolor flag. For Claire's supporters, while they never doubted Billot's good intentions, the letter became yet another occasion to trot out their theories of conspiracies to laicize France and thus bring about its ruin. One commentator remarked that the choice was between the reign of God and "the social reign of Satan in the tyranny and (lay, Masonic, germanic) anarchy of revolutionary socialism."[12]

Among some soldiers at the front, fascination with Claire and the controversy surrounding her message remained at fever pitch. Troops were understandably eager for any news that might bear on the outcome of the war. But news about Claire and her promises, much less the controversy surrounding Billot's critique, had a hard time getting past vigilant censors. A chaplain ended his letter to Canon Péret, a fellow clergyman of the diocese of Poitiers, with a question he hoped would not be out of place. "Would I be indiscreet if I asked you your views of Loublande? In my division, we talk about it a lot, especially among the officers."[13]

As public debate surrounding Claire and her mission threatened to rage out of control, the Vatican stepped in. Bishop Humbrecht's management of the affair came under particular scrutiny. Humbrecht had only accelerated the pace of Claire's career by inviting her in December 1917 to undergo examination by his episcopal commission in Poitiers. Eighteen months later, Humbrecht's commission still had not reported its findings, but everything that had happened subsequently suggested approval. Humbrecht's management strategy combined benign neglect—Claire was free to pursue her mission unimpeded—and tacit endorsement. This attitude was consistent with Humbrecht's counterrevolutionary politics. Humbrecht was an ardent supporter of the antirepublican group l'Action Française, whose scornful antiliberalism and paramilitary street politics anticipated the themes and motifs of the interwar radical Right in Europe.[14]

The unofficial portion of the weekly bulletin for Humbrecht's diocese frequently carried stories and favorable commentary regarding Loublande, Claire, and her mission. These only added to her notoriety, encouraged her supporters, and provided copy that could easily be picked up by regional and national newspapers.[15] Moreover, each subsequent step in Claire's public career—her voyage to Paris, her pursuit of an audience with Poincaré, her letter to the generals—carried the implied support of Humbrecht because his stance of public ambivalence gave Claire critical room for maneuver, to provide the validation by signs that he and his commission had demanded.

During Claire's sojourn in Paris, Humbrecht had authorized a gesture that stopped just short of full public endorsement. One of the nuns who had hosted Claire's retreat at Saint-Laurent-sur-Sèvre had made a painting of Jesus based upon Claire's description of her visions.[16] The painting became the signature image of Claire's campaign for a national consecration, and it caused a sensation when put on display for the pilgrims in the parish church at Loublande. While in Paris, Claire, her father, and her spiritual patron sought out a publisher who would reproduce the image in quantity as a prayer card (see figure 17, p. 136).[17] Such an act typically requires episcopal approval, an *imprimatur,* which Humbrecht granted. The publisher, Boumard Fils of Paris, duly noted Humbrecht's imprimatur on the back of the card. He also included a prayer to the Sacré-Coeur attributed to Pope Leo XIII. The combination of Claire's graphic vision with Humbrecht's imprimatur and the papal prayer implied a level of support that Claire, in fact, did not enjoy. To the laity, it looked as though Claire's vision, her mission, had the endorsement of the highest authorities of the Catholic Church.[18]

The climax came in late spring of 1918 when the approach of the feast of the Sacred Heart in June once again raised hopes and inspired imaginations. Indeed, copycat visionaries were beginning to emerge. On 7 June, a nun calling herself Louise of the Eucharist appealed to the archbishop of Paris to bless a Sacred Heart flag at Montmartre and take it to the president of the Republic for transmission to the front. She claimed that Jesus had conveyed this command to her in a vision.[19]

Claire and her advocates had collided with a broader initiative in favor of a Sacred Heart consecration as the key to ending the war. Those who, like Amette, doubted her, who felt that they'd seen through her, were obligated somehow to distinguish publicly between Claire's message, centered on her conversations, visions, and growing notoriety, and their own. In the growing confusion of rogue initiatives, exotic preachers, and do-it-yourself visionaries—and in the fog imposed by wartime censorship—subtle distinctions were easily overlooked.

The Vatican's position was clear. In May of 1918, with the end of the war in sight, it discouraged all Catholic activism regarding the Sacred Heart flag.[20] A year earlier, in May of 1917, Humbrecht had forwarded to the Vatican a complete account of Claire's career, including flattering testimonials and glowing accounts of her visions. There was also a handwritten letter from Claire and a cover letter from Humbrecht endorsing the entire dossier. A dryly formulaic reply to Humbrecht, sent more than a month later, summed up the Vatican's lack of enthusiasm for Claire. "Monsignor," it began. "The Holy Father recently received a *mémoire* regarding a young woman of your diocese, along with a self-written letter from the same intended for His Holiness. The Sovereign Pontiff deigns to recognize these documents and he asks me to thank you for sending them."[21]

Translation: "We'll get back to you."

The bland, bureaucratic tone of the letter almost suggested that the Vatican got letters every day from people who spoke to Jesus. Maybe it did. Humbrecht persisted. Privately, he remained a candid advocate of Claire's claims to divine inspiration. "Without going too much into details," Humbrecht wrote to the archbishop of Reims, "I will say that my personal conviction is that the revelations made to the child of Loublande are divine in origin. However, being a responsible bishop, in an especially grave matter, I am proceeding slowly, too slowly for some. . . ."[22]

Publicly, Humbrecht was more circumspect with his words, but his gestures spoke volumes. He continued his tacit sponsorship of Claire's mission by presiding personally over the grand opening and consecration of the private chapel at the Loublande residence of Claire and her acolytes.[23] Indeed, Humbrecht's gesture prepared the institutionalization of Claire and her message, perhaps even the establishment of a women's religious order organized around her message and her mission. The arrival of five new acolytes in July of 1918 suggested as much.

Shortly thereafter, Humbrecht's episcopal commission, which still had not reported officially, was abruptly shut down. The spectacular public events at Loublande—the novenas, the endless pilgrimages, the itinerant preachers, the outdoor prayer ceremonies, the eerie torchlight processions—were ordered halted. In September, the Catholic newspaper for the Poitiers region, *La Croix des Deux-Sèvres,* reprinted a notice from the diocesan bulletin of Poitiers on the matter of Loublande. The message was terse. The Loublande "affair" was in the hands of the Holy See. The Vatican's Holy Office, direct descendant of the

Figure 18. The unofficial convent at Loublande shared by Claire and her acolytes, photographed in 1998

Inquisition, would undertake a full review of the matter of Claire, her visions, and her prophecies. Meanwhile, the meetings in Loublande would end. The episcopal commission was closed. A week later the same newspaper announced that Humbrecht had been named archbishop of Besançon, a city and diocese on the other side of France.[24] It was a lateral move and it was abrupt. Humbrecht had been sacked.

The Vatican clampdown on Claire, her supporters, and the atmosphere of spectacle at Loublande left Claire in a kind of limbo in September of 1918. The armistice and Allied victory in November tended to dampen public interest in Claire too, by removing the issue—the war—that had given Claire's redemptive message such urgency. But Claire's supporters revived interest in her mission and her message with the news that Ferdinand Foch, commander in chief of the Allied armies on the Western front, had consecrated his armies to the Sacred

Heart in a private ceremony in July of 1918, mere weeks before the successful conclusion of the war.

The story of Foch's gesture seems credible. Sitting in his presbytery in Saint-Gervais on 8 December, Abbé Servant picked up his copy of *La Croix* and read that Foch had indeed consecrated his armies to the Sacred Heart while asking for victory and "a glorious peace for France." Private connections in Paris told him that Foch had confided his vow to Cardinal Amette himself. "His vow was well answered," concluded Servant.[25] With or without Claire, Catholic France was encouraged to understand Allied victory in transcendent terms.

Claire's supporters, however, went beyond attributing the victory to Foch's gesture. They sought to link it to Claire's mission. Some corroborated the claim by noting the appearance of an ex-voto in the crypt of the Basilica of Saint-Martin at Tours bearing the words "11 NOVEMBRE 1918—FOCH—MARÉCHAL DE FRANCE." An enamel Sacred Heart tricolor was affixed to the ex-voto. In 1918 and well after, Claire's supporters attributed Foch's consecration and Allied victory in the First World War to Claire and her mission to save France, although nothing about Foch's gesture, including the ex-voto in Tours, could be linked explicitly to Claire.[26]

Vatican opposition, meanwhile, was unflinching. In the spring of 1920 the results of the Vatican's inquiry into "the facts of Loublande" were made known—the quotation marks denoting the skeptical tone and conclusions of the inquiry. The cardinals, members of the Holy Office, had pored over the visions, revelations, prophecies, and writings associated with "the facts of Loublande." In a report dated 10 March 1920, the Holy Office concluded that the phenomena associated with Claire "could not and may not be approved." The following day the pope accepted the conclusions of the Holy Office and ordered them published in the *Acta Apostolicae Sedis,* the official publication of the Holy See.[27] The Vatican's rejection of Claire's message and career was forceful and definitive. Claire, who defined her adult self through her spiritual persona, experienced it as "a death sentence."[28]

THINKING ABOUT CLAIRE

"Suffering" was a mode that Claire understood and accepted, even embraced; melancholy regret was not. When she failed to rouse Raymond Poincaré to action, Claire reinterpreted her message as one of vicarious suffering rather than dwelling on her ineffectiveness as divine messenger.

And yet, during her long quarantine in Loublande, Claire had occasion to reflect on her career and her antagonists. "I learned the word [hysteria]," she remarked, "without knowing the symptoms of this sickness." Nor, she later admitted, did she fully take in the implication of this diagnosis. "It wasn't until much later that I understood what this meant," she protested. "I underwent all this without resisting the diagnosis."[29] Claire eventually learned from Vicar-General Péret, Archbishop Humbrecht's lieutenant, why a nun was always with her at mealtime during her sojourn in Paris: in order to monitor her food intake. Claire claimed that eating was a source of suffering to her and that she ate "out of fear of disobedience"—a remark which suggests that issues of authority were at least partly to blame for her discomfort, her ambivalence toward food, and her professed inability to eat. Sometimes Claire complained she couldn't swallow because of a lump in her throat that she described, tellingly, as a *boule d'hysterie*.[30] She had drawn upon a common expression, not fully aware of the array of clinical associations it invoked.

That Claire's message and ambition would be constrained by the language of pathology—and that this precise language would be employed against her by members of the Catholic Church—constituted a supreme irony, for the diagnosis of hysteria had achieved a special status—at once scientific and political—during Claire's lifetime. In fact, the secularizing cultural trend against which Claire struggled owed much to a man named Jean-Martin Charcot, whose work with psychologically disturbed patients in Paris aimed, in part, to medicalize the ecstatic experiences of saintly women by means of the clinical language of pathology.

Charcot's work at the Salpêtrière Hospital in Paris focused on the somatic manifestations of psychological disorders, an insight that had great influence on Sigmund Freud when he studied with Charcot in 1885. Although Charcot couched his research in the disinterested language of positivist science, it nevertheless quite easily fit into contemporary political debates. Charcot's patients included women who experienced religiously inspired states of exaltation, states that Charcot sought to explain away with the clinical language of hysteria.[31]

Charcot aimed to help his patients, to be sure. Successful therapeutic outcomes are what physicians are trained to seek. But Charcot made no secret of his skepticism of religion. By reducing the spiritual experiences of the saintly ecstatics of the Catholic Church to psychological disorder, Charcot's aim, at least in part, was to diminish their power and, by extension, weaken the church. Charcot doused saintly reveries with cold clinical language.[32] By shifting the context in which extravagant saintly behavior was observed from the church to the clinic, by shifting the vocabulary from spirituality to science, Charcot turned saints into hysterics. In short, for Charcot, mysticism was pathology.

"Hysteria" was a word anyone (even a peasant) of Claire's generation was likely to know. In fact, it had already entered the vocabulary of everyday life as a synonym, somewhat hyperbolic, for any agitated emotional state.[33] But over the course of her atypical career, Claire became sensitized to hysteria's more specific clinical meaning, to the current fashion for diagnoses of hysteria, and to the risk that she would become entrapped in it. She eventually understood that the keen interest some had taken in her was motivated not by admiration but by clinical curiosity. She was startled to learn that this curiosity extended beyond anticlerical physicians to members of the Catholic clergy alert to the possibilities of fraud and wary of the formidable power of visionaries, especially when combined with the modern phenomenon of celebrity.

Indeed, some of Jean-Martin Charcot's more celebrated hysteria cases were capable of inducing symptoms in public settings, that is, on demand and while under observation. Charcot was famous in clinical

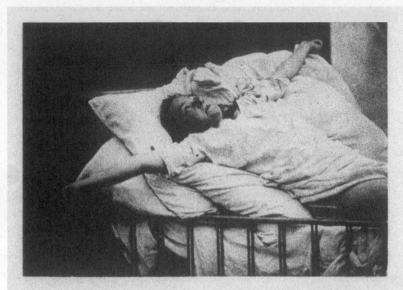

Planche XXV.

ATTITUDES PASSIONNELLES

CRUCIFIEMENT

Figure 19. "Impassioned affects: 'Crucifixion.'" Photograph of a hysteria patient at the Salpêtrière Hospital, Paris. Reproduced from Désiré Bourneville and Paul Regnard, *Iconographie photographique de la Salpêtrière* (Paris, 1896)

circles for his patients' "performances"; their capacity to perform on cue in Charcot's medical theater was part of what built his formidable reputation. These exhibitions attracted a large clinical audience as well as leisured and well-to-do members of the general public. Through photographs and illustrations in newspapers and periodicals, as well as in medical journals, they reached the wider general public. The histrionic displays of Charcot's patients had their place in a city whose appetite for spectacle was apparently limitless.[34]

Charcot's profile of clinical hysteria readily accommodated many female religious visionaries of early twentieth-century France. Their notoriety depended to a great extent on their ability to perform on cue for the vast audiences of pilgrims they drew. One of Claire's contemporaries, the Visionary of Blain, apparently was able to induce her episodes through intense concentration while in a state of repose; another brought about a kind of autohypnosis by staring at the setting sun. In both cases, the ecstatic episodes of the would-be saints were accompanied by involuntary movements, or "acting out."

In this, however, they were different from Claire, whose spirituality was not a spirituality of display, of histrionics. Her behavior matched neither the calculated gestures of a manipulator nor the tormented public eruptions of pathology. Claire's gift was for private spiritual communion, typically taking the form of dialogue. There was little in the way of exhibitionism in the way that she underwent her spiritual experiences or described them to others.

But hysteria was an elastic category by no means limited to pathological histrionics and an appetite for display. It referred to an array of symptoms related clinically to psychological distress. This elasticity is what made hysteria so useful as a concept, but also so dangerous, because it provided a clinical language by means of which rogue figures like Claire could be consoled, classified, and contained.[35] Hysteria, ironically, was thus a common ground upon which anxious clergymen and anticlerical scientists such as Charcot could meet. At the height of her public career, some of those around Claire watched for signs that her visionary gift correlated with telltale somatic symptoms. These symptoms included choking sensations, tightening of the throat, anorexia, sleep disorders, and other features fitting a dissociative/hysterical profile. At Poitiers, the archbishop's lieutenant, Vicar-General Péret, focused intently on Claire's eating habits. Unlike Humbrecht, his credulous boss, Péret had private doubts about Claire's spiritual gifts. Péret wondered whether Claire's gifts should not more appropriately be understood as pathology. Péret, whom Claire found "cold," questioned

Claire intensively on matters related to her eating and sleeping habits as well as on her "personal life." He apparently entertained the possibility that Claire's propensity for suffering—her avoidance of food, her extended bouts of nocturnal prayer—explained both the onset of her visions and their pathological origins.

Indeed, Claire manifested a preoccupation with food that extended even to revulsion at the prospect of eating. Ingestion disgusted her, suggesting a troubled relationship with herself and her own body. When she entered the dining car during her famous train voyage to Paris, she was filled with disgust for those seated at table and was revolted by the "animal action that seemed to absorb these human bodies." Yet she found herself unable to turn her eyes from "the carnal spectacle" of self-absorbed chewing. She finally overcame her revulsion through spiritual reflection and was reasssured of their humanity by seeing them as "souls redeemed because they were loved by God."[36]

Claire's vexed relationship with food was linked with her aesthetic of suffering. Self-deprivation was an important part of her spiritual path, as it had been for many others. Self-denial is a path to others and to God. In Claire's case, it also intensified the interest of those around her, and she sensed this preoccupation. At the Maison des Soeurs de la Sagesse, where she was housed while in Paris, she at first refused to eat at all, even when the mother superior led her to the dining table. "Suffering nourished me," she remarked. "I touched nothing."[37] In the disciplined environment of the convent, however, she was not allowed to deny herself food for long. She was served and supervised at mealtime by a companion, from whose "surveillance it would have been difficult to escape."[38] She later complained of the large portions she was expected to eat.

Claire's remarks and recollections suggest that she felt as though she had been backed into a diagnosis of hysteria. It was as if some of those around Claire, from whom she might have expected greater sympathy, had betrayed her. They had accepted Charcot's anticlerical gambit, his reduction of demonstrative feminine sanctity to the clinical language of

hysteria—and were now using it against one of their own. Stripped of
its anticlerical origins, hysteria had become another tool in the critical
assessment of spiritual behavior, an aid to the culling of the flock.

Claire's aesthetic of suffering was also, however, an aesthetic of
ecstasy and intimacy with a divine partner. Claire often juxtaposed the
denial of food with spiritual nourishment and intense, private moments
of exaltation. If, as she remarked, suffering nourished her, it was
because suffering brought Jesus to her, replacing torment with bliss.
She expressed the wish "to be alone with my Jesus. . . .We love each
other so." Spiritual succor, she claimed, sustained her. Jesus nourished
her. She sought the solitude that would potentiate an even greater intimacy with Jesus. She looked forward to a time "when I will do nothing
but drink long drafts at the sacred fountain."[39] Pathological or not, suffering was a pathway that took Claire to a world much sweeter than the
one she left behind.

The path that led to the private pleasures of the imagination also led
her to the great challenges of her public career. A decisive moment in
Claire's youth was her parents' decision to remove her from school.
This decision, she realized, imposed a very bleak outlook. It took away
control of her life, along with any prospects other than the ones pre-
scribed for her by the circumstances of her birth. Without education
and the social contact of school, Claire knew her life would henceforth
be circumscribed by farm work and only intermittent contact with
people outside her family.

Bright, curious, and blessed with a stubborn independence, Claire
found freedom in the cultivation of her spiritual life. In a devout community and a devout family, a woman's decision to pursue spiritual
enrichment was the *only* independent decision that could not be gain-
said. Who would dare turn a woman away from God? From there,
however, the challenges increased as Claire found herself and her
prodigious visionary gifts yoked to the political and religious ambitions
of others. She was a vector, a visionary force, to which others sought to
attach more specific meaning. Her message developed its sharp political

edge after her decisive encounter with Bourget on retreat at Saint-Laurent. Indeed, prior to Saint-Laurent, one could say that although Claire had great gifts, she had no message; she was talent in search of content. In sum, Claire bound up her fate with that of her sponsors—with Bourget, Lemius, and others who saw in Claire a providential figure, a form of political redemption, and even a vehicle for their personal ambitions.

After Saint-Laurent, Claire's message began to take shape. It started as a kind of *bricolage,* a makeshift, combining elements of the political culture of Catholic France—especially of western France, famous for its intransigent antirepublican politics—informed by a fervent devotion to the Sacred Heart. The devotion to the Sacred Heart had constituted a form of protest against the secularization of French law and politics after 1789. In fact, the devotion asserted that Jesus sought to rule in French public life. By binding her visionary gifts to local political culture and the saga of the Sacred Heart, Claire succeeded in extracting herself from the control of her parents and the bleak destiny held out to a poor peasant woman. It also meant that Claire, like the Sacred Heart devotion itself, wed the personal with the political.[40] Jesus's will to power—that is, the imputation of his desire to rule uncontested in France—was embodied in the devotion to the Sacred Heart. Claire embraced Jesus's will to power and made it her own.

In earlier times, Claire's message—that secular, postrevolutionary France was a dead end and that recovery of glory was contingent upon the nation's re-Christianization—would not have been nearly so controversial. But neither would it have been terribly unique. By Claire's day, this style of intransigent Catholic politics was passing out of favor, at least officially. When the conservative, antimodern Pope Pius IX died in 1878, his successor, Leo XIII, urged French Catholics to reconcile with their Republic. Reconciliation was slow in coming, but by 1914 it had made significant progress. The *union sacrée,* which called on all French citizens to put aside their differences in the name of national defense, was itself a manifestation of it. So, too, ironically, was the image of the Sacred Heart on the tricolor flag—a juxtaposition of symbols that an earlier generation might have viewed as profanation. In contrast, Claire's message, with its emphasis upon betrayal and the adversarial relationship between Catholics and the French Republic, aimed to undermine such reconciliation. In a sense, Claire was conscripted into a wartime battle over the future of France by people for whom reconciliation with the secular Republic was no more conscionable in a time of war than in a time of peace. For Claire's advocates there could be no sacred union, no *burgfrieden,* no civil truce. On the contrary, war was the moment to exploit exposed vulnerabilities.

Claire's message challenged France's secular political leadership, who had no trouble seeing in her the counterrevolution—the Vendée—embodied. But she challenged the Catholic leadership as well, whose own initiatives on behalf of a Sacred Heart flag and consecration were put at risk by her campaign. The French episcopate saw in the war an opportunity that might come along once in a generation. A yearning for transcendent personal meaning during a time of war drove many men—in a nation conventionally indifferent if not hostile to religion—back into the arms of the Catholic Church. The Catholic hierarchy sought to integrate this wartime religious revival with a long-standing goal of re-Christianizing public life in the name of the Sacred Heart—hence the coordinated diocesan consecrations and the efforts of chaplains to consecrate military units. How Claire's initiative differed from theirs would be lost on the French public, particularly given the information fog generated by wartime censorship. Indeed, the distinction was lost on Humbrecht, one of the hierarchy's own.

That Claire would ultimately be sequestered in her unofficial community of sisters in Loublande—and hemmed in by the taint of "hysteria"—was a measure of the unease with which some members of the Catholic hierarchy beheld her and her message. That message, although still active in the regional culture in which she was raised, was not so much wrong as "untimely" and embarrassing to a mainstream religious culture that was moving on in fits and starts.

Claire's sponsors backed her despite the hesitations of parts of the Catholic hierarchy. Claire's supporters labored hard to shape her message and her image, working with her on her presentation and, especially, her prose. Given her palpable discomfort in the presence of others, Claire was an unlikely messenger. Personal gifts and qualities she had, but physical courage was not among them. It was in this regard that she was least like Joan. Indeed, the written word was the only form of public communication with which Claire felt any ease. Even there, she had to overcome some significant early handicaps, as one would expect of someone whose schooling was interrupted at an early age. Late in life, Claire developed a great facility of language, and her writing took on a graceful, even lyrical quality. But as a young woman, her grammar and syntax were rife with error; anything intended for the consumption of Claire's public had to be heavily edited. Her successive handlers were willing to do this for her, most likely because they felt that public confidence in her statements would suffer if they were rendered in a form the average *lycée* student would find laughable. Father Bourget, it was later revealed, had gone over her famous letter to the generals and given it "orthographic correction."[41]

One wonders how extensive these corrections were and whether they were confined to matters of orthography. That was the suspicion of Abbé Servant, who sensed that Claire was a vehicle for others whose sophistication, if not ambition, were greater than hers. Servant confessed that he had trouble reconciling Claire's inadequate grasp of basic French grammar, syntax, and spelling with the claim of his colleague, the parish priest at Loublande, that Claire's writings had earned the admiration of a theologian and a professor of canon law. Servant noted the account of a reporter for *Le Petit Journal,* who visited Loublande at the height of the public fascination with Claire. Above the tiny chapel at Rinfillières, the journalist noted a sign made by the young visionary. "On est priés de fermez la porte," it read. Rendered in similarly twisted and ungrammatical English it might be translated as, "You are pleased to closed the door."[42]

With time, Claire claimed to see even many of her local supporters and handlers turn diffident as she and her story collapsed into obscurity again. A few remained loyal. Baudry d'Asson, the local politician who had secured Claire's audience with the president of the Republic, was among the faithful. After the war, he secured the consecration of his district, the département of the Vendée, to the Sacré-Coeur.[43] He also helped to organize the construction of a votive church—a scaled-down version of the Sacré-Coeur on Montmartre—in the departmental capital of La Roche-sur-Yon. The church still stands and is in use today, although it was never completed on the scale originally imagined. Its fate faithfully mirrors that of Claire. The front elevation is of an impressive scale for a provincial capital and attests to a certain ambition. Two domes in the Romano-Byzantine style that recall the Sacré-Coeur of Montmartre surmount the structure. Above the steps, the words "La Vendée au Sacré-Coeur" gleam in tall gold letters from the façade. From inside, however, the nave feels shallow and out of proportion with the rest of the structure. Support for the ambitious enterprise dried up, just as it had for Claire, and the project had to be scaled back. On closer inspection, one sees that the nave ends abruptly just beyond the transept. As donations dwindled, construction of the sanctuary and the remainder of the nave had to be abandoned and terminated hastily with a concrete wall. A curtain partly conceals, partly softens, the wall's sheer mass and abruptness. The church—a grand but truncated space that literally hits the wall—serves as an illustration of aspirations abruptly brought up short, as a scale model of Claire's career.

Over time, Claire reinterpreted her earlier acclaim, returning relentlessly to religious imagery to explain her confinement and predicament. The fascination and adulation of the pilgrims to Loublande she saw as a necessary preliminary to her ultimate betrayal, her "Calvary," as she liked to think of it. "My Calvary is complete," she noted toward the end of her life. She called her fate a "crucifixion" with "its cortege of traitors, cowards, false witnesses, and a mocking crowd, the same crowd that had kneeled beside the path of a humble little girl of the fields and now treats her as a madwoman . . . a trickster . . . a girl possessed."[44] Claire's mood blended ironic melancholy with a sense of bitter triumph. Her language suggests that she saw her experience as mirroring that of Jesus, whose triumphant entry into Jerusalem, like her triumphant departure for Paris, was mere prelude to trial and execution. But it also suggests that she was aware of others who had gone before—holy women who achieved notoriety only to be condemned as mad, conniving, or possessed. Joan of Arc, rather than Jesus, would have been the more appropriate analogy. At least that was the view of one of her admirers, a keeper-of-the-flame who summed up her story with the remark, "They burned Joan, but sequestered Claire."[45]

The remark flatters Claire, highlighting some similarities, while obscuring some telling differences.[46] Claire was like Joan in that one of her aims was for France to prevail in a war with an invader, but there the similarity ends. Joan's words were followed by actions. She was a visionary—she heard voices—but she was also a warrior. Claire was not a warrior, except in a metaphorical sense. Most tellingly, Joan loved leadership, action, and the challenge of engaging with others. Claire was at her worst in such situations, choking up, sobbing, unable to speak, as if the real struggle lay within. Even so, in defense of Claire we might note that it took a martyr's death and the safe distance of nearly five hundred years for the Catholic Church to embrace Joan and initiate steps leading to her canonization, the Cooperstown of sanctity. Joan was burned in the square in front of the Cathedral of Rouen in 1431. She wasn't canonized until May of 1920, mere weeks after the Vatican's repudiation of Claire.

Claire's message, intensely political and alleging treason and betrayal by high government officials, departed markedly from the more pacific and apolitical sanctity of her contemporaries and immediate predecessors. Thérèse Martin's nickname, "the Little Flower," sums up her spiritual persona—gentle, delicate, spiritually precocious. Although she was aware of the political spirituality of Joan—she once performed the role of Joan of Arc in a convent play—Thérèse focused on individual acts of charity rather than on the high-stakes struggles of national politics. This was a world away from the spiritual persona of Claire, who, in retrospect, seems to have been entrapped in the political and spiritual culture of Pius IX, the antimodern and counterrevolutionary pope of the nineteenth century. From La Salette (1846), to Lourdes (1858), to Pontmain (1870), and, finally, Loublande, young people had achieved notoriety following spectacular visions and divine messages forecasting imminent doom or imminent rescue from it.[47]

Unlike Claire, Thérèse never saw Jesus. She never saw the Virgin or heard her weep for France. But her rapid canonization (Thérèse was canonized in 1925, a mere twenty-eight years after her death, something of a record in modern sainthood) signaled a new standard for saintliness in the twentieth century. One can easily imagine these parallel inquiries—ending in canonization for Thérèse and seclusion for Claire—as a battle of proxies standing in for the broader direction of the Catholic Church itself.

Perhaps an early death would have made a difference. Joan, of course, had had the "advantage" of a martyr's death, while Thérèse courted death and finally embraced it at the age of twenty-four. Claire had no such dramatic end, although the prediction of her own youthful death—it was once said that she predicted that she would die at twenty-four "after much suffering"—suggests that she understood how important such an end could be.[48]

Claire's presentiment of an early death for herself also betrays an important insight: the challenge she posed resided perhaps not so much in her message but in the fact that she was *alive*. After all, to validate Claire's visions in any way while she was alive would leave the Catholic Church, and the revealed truth of which it was guardian, at her mercy. Yet, despite her own gloomy predictions of an early death, Claire in 1920 was a sturdy specimen. She languished in good physical health. Death eluded her, while her continued existence posed difficult questions. What place can there be for visions and visionaries in a religion of

Figure 20. Thérèse Martin ("the Little Flower") as Joan of
Arc in a convent play. © Office Central de Lisieux

revealed truth? Can some visions be valid and others not? Who can
gainsay someone who converses with Jesus? The prospect for mischief
from a living saint had no horizon.

Claire languished in Loublande. She and her acolytes lived with all
of the constraints of life in a religious order—confinement, dress

restrictions, clerical supervision—and none of the advantages: recognition, a spiritual legacy, a female autonomy of sorts. Claire called it her "long Calvary." Unlike Joan, there would be no fiery end for Claire, only a slow death by neglect, a process she experienced, tellingly, as an "immolation."[49]

Interest in Claire enjoyed a brief reprise in 1940 as France collapsed in the face of Nazi Germany's invasion. The enormity of the disaster induced at least some to think of Claire and the Sacred Heart flag. As the crisis of May–June 1940 deepened and as the German army advanced on Paris, an old admirer, Cardinal Alfred Baudrillart, head of France's Catholic university (the Institut Catholique), met with the archbishop of Paris, Cardinal Suhard, in a capital that was evacuated and nearly deserted. The conversation between the two men was so full that Baudrillart recorded it as a litany of items: "relations between bishops, between charitable works, between French and foreign soldiers, clergy of diverse dioceses, relations with the Pope, with the Italians. Charity even toward the enemy, etc., etc."

Baudrillart was overwhelmed. He was weary. He continued: "Wisdom of measures adopted, sincere words. Devotions, public prayers, the Sacred Heart on the flag. Mass at Lourdes. Loublande and Claire Ferchaud. The priests of Saint-Laurent-sur-Sèvres."[50] Baudrillart was taking notes on what to say, enumerating a "to-do" list, and giving himself stage directions ("sincere words"). His rushed staccato phrases fall short of limpid clarity, but they do suggest a coordinated response to the war, a program consisting of populist initiatives, religious spectacle, and mass rituals: Lourdes, the Sacred Heart, public prayer, and Claire.

Baudrillart, as one of Claire's advocates, thought her message relevant in the circumstances of France's invasion, defeat, and imminent occupation. That Baudrillart would go on to embrace the New Order and the Vichy regime is relevant in this context.[51] Those members of the Catholic hierarchy who, like Baudrillart, advocated a collaborationist position with the Nazi occupier were, like everyone else, stunned by the defeat. Unlike everyone else, they were inclined to see the bright side, the gilded fruits ("*fruits dorés*") of French defeat. Among the gilded fruits was the collapse of the Republic. Defeat had delivered France from the "corrupt regime" of secularization and the Masonic lodges—antirepublican themes familiar to Claire and her supporters.[52]

The revival of interest in Claire and her story was brief, perhaps because the Vatican's clampdown on Claire and Loublande was still in place and, in fact, had been reaffirmed in 1940.[53] Although it was said that Marshall Pétain, head of the collaborationist government of wartime France, acknowledged receiving a Sacred Heart tricolor in January of 1943, it seems not to have been associated with Claire, her story, or her supporters. The bishop of Carcassonne, Monsignor Pays, presented the flag to Pétain on behalf of a group calling itself "l'Oeuvre de Jésus Ouvrier" (Jesus the Worker). When the same group asked Pétain to consecrate France to the Sacré-Coeur, he declined, on the grounds that the moment was "not opportune."[54] Perhaps the bishop of Carcassonne had forgotten that Pétain was among those who had struggled to contain the Sacred Heart initiative in the last war.

In 1964, the Vatican lifted its 1920 prohibition, and the chapel at Loublande was opened to the public. The gesture did not signal a fundamental change in Rome's view of Claire, her visions, or her mission; more likely it simply reflected the fact that a tragically youthful death—the kind that builds legends and makes saints—had eluded Claire and that at sixty-eight, Claire threatened no one. Meanwhile, her youthful penchant for visions and public notoriety had been tempered. After some forty years, it was safe for her quarantine to end.

Claire was seventy-five years old when she died in 1972, on 29 January.[55] By then her fame, even as a regional celebrity, had declined. While researching her life story, a local newspaper reporter noted that her death prompted "strange memories" among those, then already quite elderly, who had experienced the Great War as children. They recalled that during the war Claire's message taught them to look to the heavens with new hope. Claire had predicted that one day a tricolor flag would appear in the sky. On it they would see a Sacred Heart.[56]

Prologue as Epilogue

The Story of Jonas

❦

I was awakened to the power of Claire's story by a chance encounter I had in the spring of 1998. I didn't know Claire's story very well then, but I knew enough of it to be curious about her, and to want to know more. I rented a Renault Twingo at the Angers train station, then headed southwest toward her home town of Loublande.

I'm not sure what I expected to see. I knew that Claire was a farm girl, a peasant, so I wanted to visit her home, to see the fields she had helped to cultivate and the pasture where her animals had grazed. I knew she was a visionary, so I wanted to visit the parish church where she had first disclosed her visionary gifts. I hoped to photograph the landscape and vegetation, especially the stands of Scotch broom where she had first seen Jesus face to face. I thought that I might talk to someone who had known her.

As I parked along the main street that runs through Loublande, I noticed an elderly priest walking nearby. I approached him and asked him about Claire. Yes, he had known her—quite well in fact. He invited me into his residence. We sat and talked in a wood paneled room outfitted with display cases and framed artifacts. It was a room that doubled as a museum and monument to Claire. I soon realized that I was in the presence of a "true believer"—someone who had known Claire and had dedicated the remainder of his life to her memory and her cause. I'm not sure what he saw in me, this American professor who had come all the way from Seattle to ask about Claire, but I had the impression that he thought that in my role as historian I might be useful.

As we sat and talked, I could see through the window behind him to the garden beyond. There, a life-size statue of Joan of Arc was perfectly framed by the window. After he answered my questions about Claire, he turned the conversation toward the similarities linking Joan and Claire and the tragic outcomes of their respective careers. "Yes," he offered in a tone both bitter and mournful, "they burned Joan, but they sequestered Claire."

Would I like to see her house? Of course, I answered. I offered to drive and we made our way out of Loublande, heading west on D171 no more than a kilometer before turning off the highway onto the gravel road that led toward the Ferchaud farm at Rinfillières. He opened the farmhouse and gave me a tour of the interior, pointing out Claire's bedroom, including the bed beside which she had prayed, lovingly preserved as she had left it. We examined some of her writings and personal effects—books and prayer cards—some of which had been reproduced and made available as objects for sale. He recounted his memories of Claire, and he read aloud to me from her writings, reading emphatically and for effect by the dim light of the farmhouse.

At the end of my visit, we drove back to his residence. The mood in the car was somber. By then it was evident that although we shared a fascination with Claire, our motives were not the same. He believed deeply in the message of Claire—indeed, he was "keeper of the flame"—while my interest in Claire was historical and, for that reason, guarded and detached. His disappointment was palpable. I stopped the car in front of his residence. He asked me my name. "Jonas," I told him. "Like the man in the story of the whale." It was a biblical reference I had used many times in France to clarify the spelling of my name, so often confused with Jones.

"Ah, non, Monsieur," he corrected, opening the door and stepping out. "C'est plutôt l'homme qui ne voulait pas aller là où Dieu le voulait." "He's the man who didn't want to go where God wanted him." He closed the car door. I drove off into a light spring rain with the priest's words ringing in my ears.

NOTES

THE WAR IN THE EUROPEAN IMAGINATION

1. "Le futurisme," *Le Figaro,* 20 February 1909, quoted in Richard Humphreys, *Futurism* (Cambridge, 1999), 11. On futurist concepts and the Italian military, see Günter Berghaus, *Futurism and Politics: Between Anarchist Rebellion and Fascist Reaction, 1909–1944* (Providence, R.I., 1996), 101–3. On artistic and political aspects of futurism, see RoseLee Goldberg, *Performance Art: From Futurism to the Present* (New York, 1998); Simonetta Fraquelli and Christopher Green, *Gino Severini: From Futurism to Classicism* (London, 1999); Humphreys, *Futurism*; and Giovanni Lista, *Futurism and Photography* (London, 2001).

2. On Boine, see Mario Isnenghi, *Il mito della grande guerra da Marinetti a Malaparte* (Bari, 1970), esp. 75. Mary Lou Roberts's *Civilization without Sexes* (Chicago, 1994) traces the implications of the First World War's human devastation for gender constructs in Europe during the interwar period.

3. V.I. Lenin, *Imperialism: The Highest Stage of Capitalism* (first published in 1916 as *Imperializm, kak noveishii etap kapitalizm*).

4. On these themes, see especially Fritz Fischer, *Germany's Aims in the First World War* (New York, 1967), and Jay Winter's judicious remarks in *The Experience of World War I* (New York, 1989), 27–38. It was said that Kaiser Wilhelm II's strategic thinking was informed by Alfred Thayer Mahan's *Influence of Sea Power upon History* (New York, 1890). On the culture of state growth and expansion, see Stephen Kern, *The Culture of Time and Space, 1880–1918* (Cambridge, Mass., 1983), esp. 223–26, 233–34. See also Robert

Tombs, *Nationhood and Nationalism: From Boulanger to the Great War* (London, 1991); James Joll, *The Origins of the First World War* (London, 1992); Leonard V. Smith, *Between Mutiny and Obedience: The Case of the French Fifth Infantry Division during World War I* (Princeton, 1994); and Warren Zimmerman, *First Great Triumph: How Five Americans Made Their Country a World Power* (New York, 2002).

MIRACLE OR "MIRACLE"?

1. Jean-Baptiste Duroselle, *La grande guerre des Français, 1914–1918* (Paris, 1994), 76–77.

2. Marcel Le Clère, *Paris de la préhistoire à nos jours* (Paris, 1985), 586.

3. On the Western front during the first weeks of the war, see Georges Blond, *La Marne* (Paris, 1980), 159–95; Pierre Miquel, *La grand guerre* (Paris, 1983), 140–79; Duroselle, *La grande guerre des Français,* 68–91; and Martin Gilbert, *The First World War* (New York, 1994), 55–77. For concise summaries, see James F. McMillan, *Dreyfus to De Gaulle: Politics and Society in France, 1898–1969* (London, 1985), 63–64; Jean-Jacques Becker and Serge Berstein, *Victoire et frustrations, 1914–1929* (Paris, 1990), 29–39; and Alistair Horne, *Seven Ages of Paris* (London, 2002), 312–14.

4. Gabriel Perreux, *La vie quotidienne des civils en France pendant la grande guerre* (Paris, 1966), 19.

5. André Ducasse, Jacques Meyer, and Gabriel Perreux, *Vie et mort des Français, 1914–1918* (Paris, 1962), 42.

6. Becker and Berstein, *Victoire et frustrations,* 54.

7. Édouard Poulain, *Pour le drapeau du Sacré-Coeur! Pour le salut de la France!* (Beauchene, 1918), 16; Henri-Louis Odelin, Mgr, *Le Cardinal Amette, 1850–1920: Souvenirs* (Paris, 1926), 105; Jean Delumeau and Yves Lequin, *Les malheurs des temps: Histoire des fléaux et des calamités en France* (Paris, 1987), 386; and Jacques Benoist, *Le Sacré-Coeur des femmes de 1870 à 1960* (Paris, 2000), 1353.

8. Robert Gildea, *The Past in French History* (New Haven, 1994), 125.

9. Duroselle, *La grande guerre des Français,* 49.

10. Abbé Servant, curé-doyen de Saint-Gervais, "Mes impressions au courant de la plume pendant la guerre de 1914," manuscript journal in eight bound tablets, vol. 3, p. 20, in Archives départementales de la Vienne (Poitiers), série R: Guerre et affaires militaires, 7R: Guerre de 1914–18, 82.

11. See, for example, "La Guerre est une Croix qui nous rachète du Péché de la Volonté," 28 March 1915, in Gabriel Blanc, abbé, aumônier du Sacré-Coeur, à Digne, *France éprouvée, France triomphante! Quatre conférences sur la guerre données à la cathédrale de Digne en 1915* (Lyon, 1915), 32.

12. "A nos gouvernants," *La Croix,* 8 April 1915.

13. Saint-Étienne du Mont became the parish church on Mont Sainte-Geneviève after the Church of Sainte-Geneviève was pantheonized. See Henri-Louis Odelin, vicaire général du diocèse de Paris, "Les interventions du ciel en faveur de la France," *Le Pèlerin,* 11 April 1915.

CARNAL VISION AND SAINTLY AMBITION

1. On the ownership of Rinfillières, see Claire Ferchaud, *Notes autobiographiques,* 2 vols. (Paris, 1974), 2:131.

2. Ferchaud, *Notes autobiographiques,* 1:44–45.

3. Ferchaud, *Notes autobiographiques,* 1:45.

4. Ferchaud, *Notes autobiographiques,* 1:46.

5. See his preface to *Saint Joan* (Baltimore, 1972), 7.

6. On Margery Kempe, see *The Book of Margery Kempe,* translated by B. A. Windeatt (Harmondsworth, 1985). On Joan, in addition to Marina Warner's scholarly account (*Joan of Arc: The Image of Female Heroism* [New York, 1981]), see W. S. Scott, *Jeanne d'Arc* (London, 1974); Gerd Krumeich, *Jeanne d'Arc à travers l'histoire* (Paris, 1993); and Karen Sullivan, *The Interrogation of Joan of Arc* (Minneapolis, 1999). Also useful are Bernard Shaw's play *Saint Joan,* including his lengthy preface, and Mark Twain's readable historical fiction *Joan of Arc* (San Francisco, 1989). On Joan in contemporary French speech and print, see "Discours prononcé le 10 avril 1877 dans l'église provisoire du Sacré-Cœur de Montmartre par Mgr. Mermillod, évêque d'Hebron," *Bulletin de l'Oeuvre du Vœu National,* 10 June 1877, 637; "Les interventions du ciel en faveur de la France," *Bulletin de l'Oeuvre du Vœu National,* 11 April 1915, 2; and "A nos gouvernants," *La Croix,* 8 April 1915. On Marguerite-Marie Alacoque, see Louis-Victor-Emile Bougaud (bishop of Laval), *Life of the Blessed Margaret Mary Alacoque: Revelations of the Sacred Heart to Blessed Margaret Mary,* translated by "a Visitandine of Baltimore" (Baltimore, 1890); *Vie et oeuvres de Sainte Marguerite-Marie Alacoque,* 2 vols. (Paris and Fribourg, 1991); and Raymond Jonas, *France and the Cult of the Sacred Heart: An Epic Tale for Modern Times* (Berkeley and Los Angeles, 2000). For the resonances of

both Joan and Marguerite-Marie, see Jean-Baptiste Lemius, *Les grands desseins du Sacré-Coeur de Jésus et la France* (Fecamp, 1915), 6.

7. *La Revue du Bas-Poitou* 49 (1937): 202.

8. On the history of the Vendée, see Claude Petitfrère, *La Vendée et les Vendéens* (Paris, 1981); Jean-Clément Martin, *Blancs et bleus dans la Vendée déchirée* (Paris, 1987); and Jean-Clément Martin, *La Vendée et la France* (Paris, 1987). See also Jonas, *France and the Cult of the Sacred Heart,* 54–117. On the origins of religious dissent in the French Revolution, see Suzanne Desan, *Reclaiming the Sacred: Lay Religion and Popular Politics in Revolutionary France* (Ithaca, N.Y., 1990); and Timothy Tackett, *Becoming a Revolutionary* (Princeton, 1996). For an accessible historical fiction, see Anthony Trollope, *La Vendée* (Oxford, 1994).

9. Sophie Barat, the order's founder, had given it the name "Les Dames de la Foi" (the Women of the Faith) at its founding in 1800 because, although the Sacred Heart of Jesus was at the center of her plans for the order, the Sacré-Coeur was widely regarded as a seditious emblem. With the defeat of Napoleon and the return of the monarchy in 1814, Sophie Barat could at last reconcile her order's name with its devotional center. She renamed it "Les Soeurs du Sacré-Coeur" (the Sisters of the Sacred Heart). Louis Baunard, *Histoire de la vénérable mère Madeleine-Sophie Barat, Fondatrice de la Société du Sacré-Coeur de Jésus,* 2 vols. (Paris, 1892), 1:65. See also Jonas, *France and the Cult of the Sacred Heart,* 131–34, 137.

10. Ferchaud, *Notes autobiographiques,* 1:92.

11. Ferchaud, *Notes autobiographiques,* 1:114.

12. Ferchaud, *Notes autobiographiques,* 2:67.

13. Protocollo 34619, in Archivio Segreto Vaticano, Segreteria di Stato, Epocha moderna, Guerra 1914–18, rubrica 244 M 4C, fasc. 403.2.

14. Letter of 16 July 1916, in Claude Mouton, *Au plus fort de la tourmente: Claire Ferchaud* (Montsûrs, 1983), 149.

SPIRITUAL PATRONAGE

1. Claire Ferchaud, *Notes autobiographiques,* 2 vols. (Paris, 1974), 1:118.

2. In urging Claire to write, Bourget was likely following the lead of Monsignor Saudreau, to whom Audebert had first gone for advice regarding his

young parishioner. See the recent compilation *Autour des notes autobiographiques, 3: Claire des Rinfillières: Témoignages et documents inédits* (Paris, 1998), 99.

3. Thomas Kselman, *Miracles and Prophecies in Nineteenth-Century France* (New Brunswick, N.J., 1983).

4. Claude Mouton, *Au plus fort de la tourmente: Claire Ferchaud* (Montsûrs, 1983), 154.

5. *Claire des Rinfillières: Témoignages,* 33.

6. Ferchaud, *Notes autobiographiques,* 1:119. On such issues in the context of the bicentenary, see Steven Kaplan, *Farewell, Revolution: Disputed Legacies, France, 1789/1989* (Ithaca, N.Y., 1995), esp. 84–111, 374–95.

7. Jean-Baptiste Lemius, *Les grands desseins du Sacré-Coeur de Jésus et la France* (Fecamp, 1915). Many works on similar themes followed Lemius's pamphlet, some inspired in part by Claire's story. See, for example, Louis Perroy, *Le drapeau de la France: Une grande idée en marche* (Lyon, 1917); René Guerin, *La question du drapeau du Sacré-Coeur* (Angers, 1918); Ernest Jouin, *Le drapeau national du Sacré-Coeur: Historique, doctrine, ennemis* (Tours, 1918); Henry Perroy, *Le message d'éspoir, 1689: Un temple, une consécration, un drapeau* (Lyon, 1918); and Édouard Poulain, *Pour le drapeau du Sacré-Coeur! Pour le salut de la France!* (Beauchene, 1918). See also Jacques Benoist, *Le Sacré-Coeur des femmes de 1870 à 1960* (Paris, 2000), esp. 1558.

8. Protocollo 34619, in Archivio Segreto Vaticano, Segreteria di Stato, Epocha moderna, Guerra 1914–18, rubrica 244 M 4C, fasc. 403.2.

9. On Bourget's "orthographic corrections," see Abbé Servant, curé-doyen de Saint-Gervais, "Mes impressions au courant de la plume pendant la guerre de 1914," manuscript journal in eight bound tablets, vol. 6, p. 7, and vol. 7, p. 110, in Archives départementales de la Vienne (Poitiers), série R: Guerre et affaires militaires, 7R: Guerre de 1914–18, 82.

10. The literature, popular and scholarly, on nineteenth-century apparitions is vast. For an overview, see Kselman, *Miracles and Prophecies*. See also the anonymous *Pèlerinage breton à La Salette, à Tours, à La Chartreuse, à Fourvière, à Ars, et à Paray-le-Monial du 12 au 23 juin 1883* (Nantes, 1883).

11. Mouton, *Au plus fort de la tourmente,* 154.

12. *Le Courrier de la Vienne,* 7 June 1917.

13. Protocollo 34619, in Archivio Segreto Vaticano, Segreteria di Stato, Epocha moderna, Guerra 1914–18, rubrica 244 M 4C, fasc. 403.2. See also Mouton, *Au plus fort de la tourmente,* 154.

SILENT ERUPTIONS

1. Abbé Servant, curé-doyen de Saint-Gervais, "Mes impressions au courant de la plume pendant la guerre de 1914," manuscript journal in eight bound tablets, vol. 6, p. 7, in Archives départementales de la Vienne (Poitiers), série R: Guerre et affaires militaires, 7R: Guerre de 1914–18, 82.

2. Claude Mouton, *Au plus fort de la tourmente: Claire Ferchaud* (Montsûrs, 1983), 171.

3. On Bernadette Soubirous, see Ruth Harris, *Lourdes: Body and Spirit in the Secular Age* (London, 1999).

4. Mouton, *Au plus fort de la tourmente,* 95.

5. Mouton, *Au plus fort de la tourmente,* 52. A more restrained version can be found in Protocollo 34619, in Archivio Segreto Vaticano, Segreteria di Stato, Epocha moderna, Guerra 1914–18, rubrica 244 M 4C, fasc. 403.2.

6. *Le Courrier de la Vienne,* 11 June 1917.

7. Details taken from a notice posted at the site.

8. Claire Ferchaud, *Notes autobiographiques,* 2 vols. (Paris, 1974), 1:121.

9. Mouton, *Au plus fort de la tourmente,* 169.

10. Mouton, *Au plus fort de la tourmente,* 169.

11. Mouton, *Au plus fort de la tourmente,* 170–71.

12. Mouton, *Au plus fort de la tourmente,* 170.

13. See, for example, Christian Mange, "Bernard Benezet et l'iconographie du Sacré-Coeur au XIXe siècle," *Histoire de l'Art* 20 (1992): 79–87; Jacques Bainvel, "Dévotion au coeur-sacré de Jésus," in *Dictionnaire de théologie catholique*, vol. 3 (Paris, 1938), 271–351; and Louis Charbonneau-Lassay, *La mysterieuse emblematique de Jésus-Christ: Le bestiaire du Christ; Mille cent cinquante-sept figures gravées sur bois par l'auteur* (Paris, 1940).

14. Ferchaud, *Notes autobiographiques,* 1:119.

15. Ferchaud, *Notes autobiographiques,* 1:119.

16. On eroticism of the Sacred Heart devotion, see Raymond Jonas, *France and the Cult of the Sacred Heart: An Epic Tale for Modern Times* (Berkeley and Los Angeles, 2000), 16–22.

17. See Claude Langlois, "Féminisation du catholicisme," in *L'histoire de la France religieuse* (Paris, 1991), 3:292–310; *Le catholicisme au féminin: Les congrégations françaises à supérieure générale au XIXe siècle* (Paris, 1984); and Ralph Gibson, *A Social History of French Catholicism, 1789–1914* (London, 1989). See also Odile Arnold, *Le corps et l'âme: La vie des religieuses au XIXe siècle* (Paris, 1984). On the appeal for women of the Sacred Heart devotion, see the letter

dated 20 November 1866 to Père Drevon, in Victor Drevon, S. J., *Le coeur de Jésus consolé dans la Sainte-Eucharistie: Recueil de différentes publications concernant l'oeuvre de la communion réparatrice,* 2 vols. (Avignon, 1866–68), 2:120–21.

18. Caroline Walker Bynum, *Jesus as Mother: Studies in the Spirituality of the High Middle Ages* (Berkeley and Los Angeles, 1982); Leo Steinberg, *The Sexuality of Christ in Renaissance Art and in Modern Oblivion* (New York, 1983); and Caroline Walker Bynum, "The Body of Christ in the Later Middle Ages: A Reply to Leo Steinberg," *Renaissance Quarterly* 39 (1986): 399–439.

19. On the emotional attributes of the divine, see Raymond Jonas, "Anxiety, Identity, and the Displacement of Violence during the *Année Terrible*: The Sacred Heart and the Diocese of Nantes, 1870–1871," *French Historical Studies* 21 (1998): 55–75.

20. Ferchaud, *Notes autobiographiques,* 1:119.

IN THE FOOTSTEPS OF JOAN

1. Claude Mouton, *Au plus fort de la tourmente: Claire Ferchaud* (Montsûrs, 1983), 95.

2. Mouton, *Au plus fort de la tourmente,* 96–97.

3. "Rapport au préfet, le 30 mars 1873," in Archives départementales de la Loire Atlantique (Nantes), série V: Cultes, 2V3: Police générale du culte, faits divers, rapports, 1870–79.

4. "Rapport de la gendarmerie, le 29 avril 1873," in Archives départementales de la Loire Atlantique (Nantes), série V: Cultes, 2V3: Police générale du culte, faits divers, rapports, 1870–79. For contemporary political and medical debate on the subject of hysteria, see Georges Didi-Huberman, *Invention de l'hysterie: Charcot et l'iconographie photographique de la Salpêtrière* (Paris, 1982); Claude Langlois, "La photographie comme preuve entre médecine et religion," *Actes du colloque Charcot* 28 (1994), 325–36. See also Ruth Harris, *Lourdes: Body and Spirit in the Secular Age* (London, 1999), 318–19, 327–29, 356.

5. "Rapport de la gendarmerie, le 27 april 1873," in Archives départementales de la Loire Atlantique (Nantes), série V: Cultes, 2V3: Police générale du culte, faits divers, rapports, 1870–79.

6. "Rapport de la gendarmerie, le 12 avril 1873," in Archives départementales de la Loire Atlantique (Nantes), série V: Cultes, 2V3: Police générale du culte, faits divers, rapports, 1870–79.

7. *Le Pèlerin,* 28 November 1874, 570.

8. *Le Pèlerin,* 28 November 1874, 570.

9. On the status of *Le Pèlerin,* see Claude Bellanger, Jacques Godechot, Pierre Guiral, and Fernand Terrou, *Histoire générale de la presse française,* 5 vols. (Paris, 1969–76), 3:333–34.

10. Perhaps the challenge that Marie posed derived from her message, because her ideas about France and divine punishment surely did not originate with her. Since 1789, Catholic clergy had developed and embellished a view that the Revolution marked France's departure from its Christian tradition. France's subsequent relative decline, for some dramatically displayed in its shattering defeat in the Franco-Prussian War, had to be linked to the Revolution and French apostasy. The complaint of Marie Gagueny's pained Jesus—"they will not convert; they don't want my grace; they will be punished"— expressed commonplace sentiments and themes to which Marie had certainly been exposed. This was a post-1789 lament. It was sheer genius to combine such familiar ideas with a reenactment of the Passion of Jesus because, as Jesus's lament shows, the power in the image derives from the tension between divine love and France's indifference. Marie's tableau was compelling and *ravissant* because it situated the Passion of Jesus in the late nineteenth-century context of French de-Christianization, which became a kind of new crucifixion. As such, it also placed a divine imprimatur on what the Catholic clergy had been telling the faithful for decades.

11. Abbé Servant, curé-doyen de Saint-Gervais, "Mes impressions au courant de la plume pendant la guerre de 1914," manuscript journal in eight bound tablets, vol. 3, p. 183 (entry for 11 August 1915), in Archives départementales de la Vienne (Poitiers), série R: Guerre et affaires militaires, 7R: Guerre de 1914–18, 82.

12. Protocollo 34619, in Archivio Segreto Vaticano, Segreteria di Stato, Epocha moderna, Guerra 1914–18, rubrica 244 M 4C, fasc. 403.2.

13. Claire Ferchaud, *Notes autobiographiques,* 2 vols. (Paris, 1974), 1:121.

14. *Autour des notes autobiographiques,* 3: *Claire des Rinfillières: Témoignages et documents inédits* (Paris, 1998), 21.

15. Édouard Poulain, *Pour le drapeau du Sacré-Coeur! Pour le salut de la France!* (Beauchene, 1918), 46.

16. What was said of the commission charged to interrogate Joan of Arc— "a gathering of the finest clergy in non-occupied France"—could not be said of Humbrecht's commission. See Deborah A. Fraioli, *Joan of Arc: The Early Debate* (Woodbridge, Suffolk), 2000, 47.

17. *Claire des Rinfillières: Témoignages,* 19.

18. "Les événements de Loublande," *Le Courrier de la Vienne,* 9 May 1917.

19. The transcripts of the Poitiers Commission are held at the Archives diocésaines de Poitiers. According to the diocesan archivist, they are not available for consultation. A transcript is published in *Claire des Rinfillières: Témoignages,* but it impossible to know whether this transcript is complete without access to the original transcripts in the archives.

20. *Claire des Rinfillières: Témoignages,* 23.

21. *Claire des Rinfillières: Témoignages,* 24.

22. *Claire des Rinfillières: Témoignages,* 25.

23. *Claire des Rinfillières: Témoignages,* 29.

24. *Claire des Rinfillières: Témoignages,* 26.

25. The press made this point repeatedly. See, for example, "Les événements de Loublande," *Le Courrier de la Vienne,* 9 May 1917.

26. See "Partie officielle: Note de Monseigneur l'évêque," *La Semaine Liturgique du Diocèse de Poitiers,* 25 March 1917, 115.

27. Régine Pernoud, *The Retrial of Joan of Arc: The Evidence at the Trial for Her Rehabilitation, 1450–1456,* translated by J. M. Cohen (New York, 1955), 101.

A KIND OF APOTHEOSIS

1. See Leonard V. Smith, *Between Mutiny and Obedience: The Case of the French Fifth Infantry Division during World War I* (Princeton, 1994).

2. Leonard V. Smith, Stéphane Audoin-Rouzeau, and Annette Becker, *France and the Great War, 1914–1918* (Cambridge, 2003), 132.

3. Claire Ferchaud, *Notes autobiographiques,* 2 vols. (Paris, 1998), 2:14–16.

4. Ferchaud, *Notes autobiographiques,* 2:12.

5. Claire Ferchaud, "Première lettre au Président Poincaré," in *Notes autobiographiques,* 2:15.

6. See Raymond Jonas, *France and the Cult of the Sacred Heart: An Epic Tale for Modern Times* (Berkeley and Los Angeles, 2000), esp. 30–33.

7. By her reference to Poincaré as "chief *[chef]*" rather than president, Claire's language elided the distinction between president and king. Annette Becker, *La guerre et la foi: De la mort à la mémoire, 1914–1930* (Paris, 1994), 83.

8. Ferchaud, *Notes autobiographiques,* 2:76.

9. In this sense, Claire's experience was similar to that of hundreds of thousands of mobilized soldiers, for whom mobilization began with a train ride.

Given the centralized nature of the rail network, many trains to the front went by way of Paris.

10. Many provincials across Europe had feelings ranging from ambivalence to hostility about large cities, especially capital cities. See Jay Winter and Jean-Louis Robert, *Capital Cities at War: Paris, London, Berlin, 1914–1919* (Cambridge, 1997), 52–53.

11. Ferchaud, *Notes autobiographiques,* 2:78.

12. On this theme, see Pierre Darmon, *Vivre à Paris pendant la grande guerre* (Paris, 2002).

13. Gabriel Perreux, *La vie quotidienne des civils en France pendant la grande guerre* (Paris, 1966), 20.

14. Marcel Le Clère, *Paris de la préhistoire à nos jours* (Paris, 1985), 581; J. M. Winter, *The Experience of World War I* (New York, 1989), 170–71; and Jean Favier, *Paris: Deux mille ans d'histoire* (Paris, 1997), 912–15.

15. Ferchaud, *Notes autobiographiques,* 2:79.

16. Ferchaud, *Notes autobiographiques,* 2:86.

17. On Pontmain, see René Laurentin and A. Durand, *Pontmain: Histoire authentique,* 3 vols. (Paris, 1970); and Thomas Kselman, *Miracles and Prophecies in Nineteenth-Century France* (New Brunswick, N.J., 1983). See also Association de Notre-Dame de Salut, *Pèlerinage à Notre-Dame de Pontmain* (Paris 1916).

18. On Les Hommes de France au Sacré-Coeur, see Jacques Benoist, *Le Sacré-Coeur de Montmartre de 1870 à nos jours,* 2 vols. (Paris, 1992), 530–33; and A. Denizot, *Le Sacré-Coeur et la grande guerre* (Paris, 1994), 57.

19. On Lemius's ardent temperament and prodigious energy, see François Veuillot, "Le Père Jean-Baptiste Lemius," *Montmartre* (1938), 8–14.

20. Ferchaud, *Notes autobiographiques,* 2:89.

21. Ferchaud, *Notes autobiographiques,* 2:105–6.

22. Jean-Baptiste Lemius, *Les grands desseins du Sacré-Coeur de Jésus et la France* (Fecamp, 1915), 123, 127.

23. "Il faudra s'habituer à marcher sans lui . . . car j'entends bien ne pas m'occuper d'une petite fille de quatre sous." Ferchaud, *Notes autobiographiques,* 2:107.

24. Ferchaud, *Notes autobiographiques,* 2:99, 109.

25. Ferchaud, *Notes autobiographiques,* 2:110.

26. Ferchaud, *Notes autobiographiques,* 2:110–11.

27. Ferchaud, *Notes autobiographiques,* 2:114.

28. On the identity of Pierre l'Ermite, see Jacques Benoist, *Le Sacré-Coeur des femmes de 1870 à 1960* (Paris, 2000), 1559.

29. See "Le drapeau du Sacré-Cœur," *Le Siècle,* 2 June 1901, in Archives nationales, série F19: Cultes, 5636: Police, 3ème République: Agissements politiques sous forme religieuse.

30. Ferchaud, *Notes autobiographiques,* 2:120–21.

31. Ferchaud, *Notes autobiographiques,* 2:123–25.

32. On Lemius and the founding of Les Femmes de France, see Benoist, *Le Sacré-Coeur des femmes,* 1474–79.

33. Lemius campaigned on behalf of Claire and her message after he left Paris. In June of 1918, he visited Loublande to conduct a kind of "mission" before the thousands who gathered to see Claire and to celebrate the feast of the Sacré-Cœur. See *Le mémorial des Pyrénées,* 11 June 1918, reproduced in Claude Mouton, *Au plus fort de la tourmente: Claire Ferchaud* (Montsûrs, 1983), 132.

34. Ferchaud, *Notes autobiographiques,* 2:142.

35. In *Souvenirs sur notre bien-aimée Mère Fondatrice par le RP Jean-Baptiste Lemius OMI* (1924), 9–10, reproduced in Benoist, *Le Sacré-Cœur des femmes,* 1685.

36. Ferchaud, *Notes autobiographiques,* 2:139. The Baudry d'Asson family was a fixture of Vendéen politics during much of the Third Republic. The seat in the second electoral district of the arrondissement of Sables d'Olonne was passed from father to son just before the outbreak of war in 1914. For an incident in the career of Baudry d'Asson the elder, see Archives départementales de la Vendée (La Roche-sur-Yon), série 1M: Administration générale, 474: Censures de Baudry d'Asson, député, Affichage, 1879–80.

37. The text of the letter is in Ferchaud, *Notes autobiographiques,* 2:17–18.

38. It is not clear on what grounds Baudry d'Asson was able to persuade Poincaré to see Claire. Poincaré, like any good politician, was surely aware of the importance of humoring members of the legislature and of cultivating religious interests, or he (or his government) may have had a political debt outstanding to Baudry d'Asson. On political debts that Poincaré incurred during his presidency, see Gordon Wright, *Raymond Poincaré and the French Presidency* (Stanford, 1942), 55–56; and Benjamin Martin, *Count Albert de Mun, Paladin of the Third Republic* (Chapel Hill, N.C., 1978), 258.

39. The story of the encounter is adapted from Ferchaud, *Notes autobiographiques,* 2:170–72 and 2:28–31. Since we have only Claire's version of the

conversation, this reconstruction must be regarded as without independent corroboration.

40. Claire's after-the-fact recollections, apparently drafted during the Occupation in the early 1940s, can be found in Ferchaud, *Notes autobiographiques,* 2:170–72. Her detailed account of the dialogue, written shortly thereafter, begins on page 28 of the same volume.

41. This is also the conclusion of Annette Becker in *La guerre et la foi,* 83.

THE SACRED HEART AND
THE *UNION SACRÉE*

1. Georges Wormser, *Le septennat de Poincaré* (Paris, 1977), 248.

2. For a readable account of Poincaré's youth, see Gordon Wright's *Raymond Poincaré and the French Presidency* (Stanford, 1942).

3. After the war, Poincaré was the target of several critics who blamed him for precipitating the conflict. The title of Gustave Dupin's book *M. Poincaré et la guerre de 1914: Études sur les responsabilités* (Paris, 1931) suggests well enough the drift, as does Victor Margueritte's pithier *Les Criminels* (Paris, 1925), whose eponymous targets include not only Poincaré but also emperors, kings . . . and President Wilson. A less vehement statement, but also tending to inculpate Poincaré, can be found in Freiherr von Schoen, *The Memoirs of an Ambassador,* translated by Constance Vesey (London, 1922), esp. 161–69, 174–75. Léon Daudet would accuse Poincaré of losing the peace in *La pluie de sang* (Paris, 1932), esp. 319–21.

4. Jean-Jacques Becker and Serge Berstein, *Victoire et frustrations, 1914–1919* (Paris, 1990), 26–27; Jean-Baptiste Duroselle, *La grande guerre des français, 1914–1918* (Paris, 1994), 48–50; Michel Leymarie, *De la belle-époque à la grande guerre, 1893–1918: Le triomphe de la République* (Paris, 1999), 276.

5. Louis Barthou, another political leader, defined *union sacrée* this way: "There are no more political distinctions, no more religious differences, no more class struggle." Quoted in Becker and Berstein, *Victoire et frustrations,* 97. For women, *union sacrée* implied a more specific sacrifice: the sacrifice of sons. See Margaret H. Darrow, *French Women and the First World War* (New York, 2000), 58–60.

6. Jean-Jacques Becker, *1914: Comment les Français sont entrés dans la guerre* (Paris, 1977), 379–400; Jean-Jacques Becker, *La France en guerre, 1914–1918: La grande mutation* (Paris, 1988), 28–29; Becker and Berstein, *Victoire et*

frustrations, 15, 27; and Jean-Baptiste Duroselle, *La grande guerre des Français, 1914–1918* (Paris, 1994), 52–57. On indiscipline, the Left, and the army, see Douglas Porch, *The March to the Marne: French Army, 1871–1914* (Cambridge, 1981), 105–21.

7. Becker and Berstein, *Victoire et frustrations,* 27.

8. See *Le Pèlerin,* 29 November 1914, 10–11.

9. Raymond Poincaré, *L'invasion, 1914,* volume 5 of *Au service de la France: Neuf années de souvenirs* (Paris, 1928), 205.

10. See, for example, "Le drapeau du Sacré-Coeur: Protecteur des poilus de France," *Le Messager du Sacré-Coeur de Jésus,* July 1916, 442; and Charles Marcault, *Réalisons le message du Sacré-Coeur* (Paris, 1934), 76.

11. The subprefect of Charolles to the prefect of the Saône et Loire, 6 June 1915, in Archives départmentales de la Saône et Loire (Mâcon), série 4M: Police, 311: Affaires religieuses; agitations religieuses, congrès, pèlerinages, pétitions en faveur de la reprise des relations avec le Saint-Siège, 1906–17.

12. Louis Baunard, Mgr., *Le Général de Sonis d'après ses papiers et sa correspondance* (Paris, 1890), 318–25; Georges Cerbelaud-Salagnac, *Les Zouaves pontificaux* (Paris, 1963), 237. See also Raymond Jonas, "L'Année Terrible, 1870–1871," in *Le Sacré-Coeur de Montmartre: Un voeu national,* edited by Jacques Benoist, 31–41 (Paris, 1995); and Raymond Jonas, *France and the Cult of the Sacred Heart: An Epic Tale for Modern Times* (Berkeley and Los Angeles, 2000).

13. Marcault, *Réalisons le message du Sacré-Coeur,* 76.

14. Marcault, *Réalisons le message du Sacré-Coeur,* 76–77.

15. "Commissariat spécial, rapport du 12 juillet 1917," in Archives départementales du Rhône (Lyon), série 1M: Administration générale, 149: Rapports du commissariat special, mai–décembre 1917.

16. Joseph Burnichon, S. J., *Histoire d'un siècle, 1814–1914: La Compagnie de Jésus en France,* 4 vols. (Paris, 1914–22), 4:622–23.

17. "Commissariat spécial, rapport du 12 juillet 1917," in Archives départementales du Rhône (Lyon), série 1M: Administration générale, 149: Rapports du commissariat special, mai–décembre 1917.

18. See "Oeuvre de l'insigne du Sacré-Cœur," *Le Messager du Sacré-Coeur de Jésus,* March 1916, 126–27.

19. *Le Messager du Sacré-Coeur de Jésus,* March 1916, 126–27; "La foi de nos soldats: La protection du Sacré Cœur," *Le Pèlerin,* 2 July 1916, 10; *La Semaine Religieuse du Diocèse d'Angers,* 22 April 1917, 311; and *Bulletin de l'Oeuvre du Voeu National au Sacré-Coeur de Jésus,* 21 June 1917, 104.

20. See *Le Prêtre aux Armées: Bulletin bimensuel des prêtres et des religieux mobilisés,* no. 46, 1 January 1917, in Archives de l'armée de la terre, 1 K284, K104: Archives Veuillot, 1914–19.

21. Marcault, *Réalisons le message du Sacré-Coeur,* 76–77.

22. "Le Drapeau," *Le Messager du Sacré-Coeur de Jésus,* July 1916, 442.

23. "Le Drapeau," *Le Messager,* July 1916, 443.

24. "Le Drapeau," *Le Messager,* July 1916, 444.

25. "Vive le Sacré-Coeur!" *Le Pèlerin,* 10 June 1917.

26. André Boutrolle, "Nécrologie," *En Famille,* October 1917, 68–74, in Archives de l'armée de la terre, 1 K284, K104: Archives Veuillot, 1914–19.

CONSECRATION BY PROXY

1. On these themes, see Jay Winter, *Sites of Memory, Sites of Mourning: The Great War in European Cultural History* (Cambridge, 1995), 54ff.

2. See, for example, *Un catéchisme bref sur la guerre,* lettre pastorale (Orléans), 2 February 1915, cited in Jacques Fontana, *Les catholiques français pendant la grande guerre* (Paris, 1990), 224; *"La rançon par le sacrifice": Discours prononcé en l'église de Loigny le 2 décembre 1915 pour le 45e aniversaire de la bataille par M. l'abbé Augis, curé-doyen de Terminiers* (Chartres, 1915), 7, in Archives diocésaines de Chartres, Loigny-la-Bataille, fonds Provost, dossier 12, Correspondance 1915–18; and *La nécessité sociale de la religion,* lettre pastorale, 25 January 1917, cited in Fontana, *Les catholiques français,* 224.

3. Joseph Calot, S.J., "La guerre," in *Le Messager du Sacré-Coeur de Jésus,* September 1914, 513–18.

4. Calot, "La guerre," 514.

5. Calot, "La guerre," 518.

6. The French Catholic weekly, *Le Pèlerin,* 11 April 1915, 2, in an article entitled "Les interventions du ciel en faveur de la France," offered a summary of the Catholic version of the miracle of the Marne:

> Le vendredi 4, premier vendredi du mois, consacré au Sacré Coeur, tandis que la foule des adorateurs se presse dans la basilique du Voeu National, l'armée de von Kluck, qui n'était plus qu'à une journée ou deux de Paris, s'en éloigne et oblique vers l'Est. . . . Ne peut-on pas dire que le Sacré Coeur a sauvé Paris et la France, le vendredi 4 septembre, par l'éloignement imprévu de l'armée allemande . . . ?

See also François Veuillot, *La dévotion française de la guerre— Montmartre* (Paris, 1916), 29.

7. "La dévotion au Sacré Coeur de Jésus et la guerre," *Le Pèlerin,* 13 June 1915, 2.

8. "Commissariat spécial de Mâcon, rapport du 25 octobre 1915," in Archives départementales de la Saône-et-Loire (Mâcon), série 4M: Police, 310: Affaires religieuses; agitations religieuses, congrès, pèlerinages, pétitions en faveur de la reprise des relations avec le Saint-Siège, 1906–17.

9. On the Marne and the First Friday, see "Chronique religieuse de la basilique du Voeu Nationale au Sacré-Coeur," in *Bulletin du Voeu National au Sacré-Coeur de Jésus,* 20 February 1919, 31:

> Les débuts de septembre viennent comme chaque année nous rappeler les journées tragiques et glorieuses de la victoire dont nous vivons. Les Parisiens sous la présidence de leur Archevêque viennent en foule à Montmartre pour en commémorer pieusement le souvenir dans un acte de gratitude populaire envers Dieu. C'était justice! car le premier vendredi de septembre 1914, l'armée allemande s'était détournée soudain de la capitale pour aller se faire battre sur les bords de la Marne. Il nous est permis de dire que ce jour-là notre Basilique apparut selon l'espérance formulée dans le Voeu National comme la "citadelle inexpugnable qui protège Paris et notre patrie."

10. Catholic memory of the war was organized around such formative moments. In the closing weeks of the war, *La Semaine Catholique* of the diocese of Luçon described the victory of the Marne as one of the great signs in what it called "the triumph of the Sacré-Coeur": "Oui, c'est sur, dans ces premiers jours de septembre 1914, le Coeur Sacré de Jésus, en réponse à tant de supplications, en considération du sacrifice de tant de généreuses victimes, s'est vraiment penché sur la France. Il l'a sauvée!" "Le triomphe du Sacré-Coeur," *La Semaine Catholique de Luçon,* 13 April 1918, 236–37.

11. Lettres 67 (April 1687) and 81 (1688), in *Vie et oeuvres de sainte Marguerite-Marie Alacoque,* 2 vols. (Paris and Fribourg, 1991), 2:255 and 287.

12. See Raymond Jonas, *France and the Cult of the Sacred Heart: An Epic Tale for Modern Times* (Berkeley and Los Angeles, 2000), 34–53.

13. For Amiens, see Jacques Bainvel, "Dévotion au Coeur-Sacré de Jésus" *Dictionnaire de théologie catholique,* vol. 3 (Paris, 1938), 344. For Poitiers, see Jean Nicolas Loriquet, *Le salut de la France* (Poitiers, 1816); and *Les archives religieuses du pays Poitevin* 6 (1902), 99–104; 7 (1903), 105–12.

14. See Archives nationales, série F19: Cultes, 5636: Police, 3ème République: Agissements politiques sous forme religieuse: Fêtes de Jeanne d'Arc, 1890–1904; Consécration des communes au Sacré-Coeur, 1901–1905. See also A. Denizot, *Le Sacré-Coeur et la grande guerre* (Paris, 1994), 57.

15. See Jonas, *France and the Cult of the Sacred Heart,* 54–117.

16. "Communication de Monseigneur l'évêque de Luçon relative à la consécration de la France au Sacré-Coeur de Jésus, le 26 mai 1915," 3, in Archives diocésaines de Luçon, 1E8: Lettres circulaires. See also "Amende honorable et consécration de la France au Sacré Coeur de Jésus pour le 11 juin," *Le Pèlerin,* 6 June 1915.

17. See "Amende Honorable et Consécration de la France au Sacré-Coeur de Jésus" and "Communication de Monseigneur l'évêque de Luçon relative à la consécration de la France au Sacré-Coeur de Jésus, le 26 mai 1915," 4, in Archives diocésaines de Luçon, 1E8: Actes des évêques.

18. "Dépêche télégraphique, le 27 mai 1915," in Archives de l'armée de la terre, 5N14: Correspondance, ministre de la guerre.

19. "Communication de Monseigneur l'évêque de Luçon relative à la consécration de la France au Sacré-Coeur de Jésus, le 26 mai 1915," in Archives diocésaines de Luçon, 1E8: Actes des évêques.

20. Supplément au *Croix* de 23 mai 1915, "Lettre de S.E. le cardinal Amette proposant une consécration nationale au Sacré-Coeur le 11 juin 1915." The text, dated 17 May 1915, reads in part "Je joins à cette lettre la formule d'amende honorable et de consécration acceptée par Leurs Éminences."

21. "Traduction d'un télégramme chiffré parvenu le 29 mai 1915 de Montauban," in Archives de l'armée de la terre, 5N67: Correspondance, ministre de la guerre.

22. *Semaine Religieuse du Diocèse de Lyon,* 11 June 1915, 35, in Archives de l'armée de la terre, 1K284, K104: Archives Veuillot, 1914–19.

23. See *Semaine Religieuse du Diocèse de Nantes,* 1 October 1870, no. 40 (mandement du 22 septembre), 482: "Ce grand acte de consécration au Coeur de Jésus, qui se fera dans toutes nos églises, je voudrais, N.T.-C.F., le voir se répéter dans toutes les familles de mon vaste diocèse. Oui, je voudrais que . . . dans toutes les maisons chrétiennes, le père de famille, prosterné au pied du crucifix, avec son épouse, ses enfants, ses serviteurs, se donnât, lui et les siens, à ce Coeur adorable qui a connu toutes les douleurs et toutes les joies du foyer domestique. . . ."

24. "Archevêché de Paris, le 30 juin 1912," in Archives historiques du diocèse de Paris, basilique du Sacré Coeur, carton 5.

25. The accusation links to one of the earliest conspiracy theories of the French Revolution, that elaborated and popularized by the Jesuit Augustin Barruel in his *Mémoires pour servir à l'histoire du jacobinisme* (Vouillé, 1974), originally published in 1797.

26. Rapport: "Le Congrès de la Fédération Jeanne d'Arc," in Archives nationales, F7: Police générale, 13213: Police, mouvement catholique. This scenario recapitulates the claim of prewar anticlericals to the effect that Catholic priests used their influence among women to persuade those women, as wives, to influence the political choices of their husbands. See Judith Stone, *Sons of the Revolution: Radical Democrats in France, 1862–1914* (Baton Rouge, La., 1996), 330–33.

27. Rapport: "Paris, le 24 juin 1915," in Archives nationales, F7: Police générale, 13213: Police, mouvement catholique.

28. "Au Drapeau du Sacré-Cœur" (1915), in Archives diocésaines de Chartres, fonds Provost, dossier 12.

29. "Note pour les armées" (confidentiel) de Paul Painlevé, le 6 avril 1917," in Archives historiques du diocèse de Paris, Basilique du Sacré-Coeur, carton 5.

30. Gabriel Perreux, *La vie quotidienne des civils en France pendant la grande guerre* (Paris, 1966), 34–42.

31. Antoine Redier, *Méditations dans la tranchée* (Paris, 1918), 142.

32. Redier, *Méditations,* 145.

33. On religious practice in nineteenth-century France, see Gabriel Le Bras, *L'église et le village* (Paris, 1976); and Ralph Gibson, *A Social History of French Catholicism, 1789–1914* (London, 1989).

34. Geoffroy de Grandmaison, *Les aumôniers militaires* (Paris, 1915), 24.

35. For details, see Geoffroy de Grandmaison and François Veuillot, *L'aumônerie militaire pendant la guerre, 1914–1918* (Paris, 1923), which describes the chaplaincy efforts in considerable detail. See also Benjamin Martin, *Count Albert de Mun: Paladin of the Third Republic* (Chapel Hill, 1978), 290–91.

36. Nadine-Josette Chaline, "Les aumôniers catholiques dans l'armée française," in her *Chrétiens dans la première guerre mondiale* (Paris, 1993), 98. See also Jean-Baptiste Duroselle, *La grande guerre des Français, 1914–1918* (Paris 1994), 65.

37. See Douglas Porch, *The March to the Marne: The French Army, 1871–1914* (Cambridge, 1981), 125.

38. Grandmaison had published a statement about the chaplaincy project six years earlier. See his *Les aumôniers militaires.*

39. Grandmaison, *Les aumôniers militaires,* 34.

40. Grandmaison, *Les aumôniers militaires,* 24.

41. Grandmaison, *Les aumôniers militaires,* 8–9.

42. See "Lettre du 10 décembre 1914 de l'abbé G. Pouch, aumônier militaire, 5ème corps d'armée, 10ème division, ambulance no. 11," in Archives de l'armée de la terre, 1K284, K104: Fonds de l'association diocésaine du Vicariat aux armées françaises, Archives Veuillot, 1914–19.

43. "Lettre de l'abbé Guéguen, 21 décembre [1914]," in Archives de l'armée de la terre, 1K284, K104: Fonds de l'association diocésaine du Vicariat aux armées françaises, Archives Veuillot, 1914–19.

44. Grandmaison and Veuillot, *L'aumônerie militaire,* 286–87. For Gothic trees and more, see Simon Schama, *Landscape and Memory* (New York, 1995), 226–39.

45. Grandmaison and Veuillot, *L'aumônerie militaire,* 286–87.

46. "Lettre de M. Pangaud, aumônier militaire, 27ème division, 17 décembre 1915," in Archives de l'armée de la terre, 1K284, K104: Fonds de l'association diocésaine du vicariat aux armées françaises, Archives Veuillot, 1914–19.

THE UNRAVELING

1. "Lettre du 25 juin 1917 du P. de la Devezy, aumônier," in Archives de l'armée de la terre, 1K284: Archives Veuillot, 1914–19.

2. See, for example, Mathieu Tabaraud, *Essai historique et critique sur l'état des Jésuites en France depuis leur arrivée dans le royaume jusqu'au temps présent,* (Paris, 1828); Joseph de Guibert, S. J. *The Jesuits: Their Spiritual Doctrine and Practice* (Chicago, 1964); Malachi Martin, *The Jesuits: The Society of Jesus and the Betrayal of the Roman Catholic Church* (New York, 1987); Jean Lacouture, *Jésuites: Une multibiographie,* 2 vols. (Paris, 1992); Michel Leroy, *Le mythe jésuite de Béranger à Michelet* (Paris, 1992). For Jesuits serving as chaplains in the wartime military, see Georges Guitton, *Louis Lenoir: Jésuite, aumônier militaire (1914–1918)* (Paris, 1926).

3. Part of what Devezy's commanding officer feared had been openly expressed as a goal from the earliest stages of the war. See the pastoral letter, dated 24 May 1915, of the archbishop of Besançon and its confident prediction: "The image of the Sacred Heart has conquered a place on our battle front. When the Sacred Heart is attached to our flags, they will fly all the more quickly toward decisive victory." Quoted in Jacques Fontana, *Les catholiques français pendant la grande guerre* (Paris, 1990), 340.

4. Charles Marcault, *Réalisons le message du Sacré-Coeur* (Paris, 1934), 78.

5. See, for example, "Pétition pour le Drapeau du Sacré-Coeur," in *La Semaine Liturgique du Diocèse de Poitiers,* 54ème année (1917), 195.

6. On Amette, see Henri-Louis Odelin, Mgr., *Le Cardinal Amette, 1850–1920: Souvenirs* (Paris 1926), 105.

7. Letter to Cardinal Amette dated 6 March 1917, in Claire Ferchaud, *Notes autobiographiques,* 2 vols. (Paris, 1974), 2:19.

8. Letter from Cardinal Amette to Monsieur le Chanoine Crépin dated 12 March 1917, in Ferchaud, *Notes autobiographiques,* 2:22.

9. Ferchaud, *Notes autobiographiques,* 2:122.

10. Ferchaud, *Notes autobiographiques,* 2:31.

11. Ferchaud, *Notes autobiographiques,* 2:33.

12. *Le Pèlerin,* 13 May 1917.

13. These seconded calls in many dioceses since the beginning of the war for a national consecration and a new Sacred Heart tricolor flag. "[L]'archevêque de Besançon pouvait écrire en 1915: présentement, 'l'image du Sacré-Coeur a conquis une place sur notre front de bataille. Quand elle sera fixée à tous nos drapeaux, ils voleront plus vite à la victoire décisive.'" Fontana, *Les catholiques français,* 340, quoting lettre pastorale (Besançon), 24 May 1915 .

14. *La Semaine Liturgique du Diocèse de Poitiers*, 54ème année (1917), 195.

15. "Lettre du 17 mai 1917 au préfet de la Vienne du maire de Vouneil," in Archives départmentales de la Vienne (Poitiers), 4M: Police, 540: Enquête relative à l'apposition du Sacré-Cœur sur le drapeau national en 1917.

16. Ferchaud, *Notes autobiographiques,* 2:39–41; the text of the letter to Poincaré can be found on pp. 36–38.

17. Some soldier-poets also imagined Jesus intervening in the war. Wilfred Owen's "Soldier's Dream" imagines Jesus jamming rifles and rusting artillery pieces. See J.M. Winter, *Sites of Memory, Sites of Mourning: The Great War in European Cultural History* (Cambridge, 1995), 219.

18. See letter dated 30 May 1917 from the mayor of Nieuil-l'Espoir to the prefect of la Vienne, in Archives départmentales de la Vienne (Poitiers), 4M: Police, 540: Enquête relative à l'apposition du Sacré-Cœur sur le drapeau national en 1917.

19. See letter dated 15 June 1917 from the subprefect of Châtellerault to the prefect of la Vienne, in Archives départmentales de la Vienne (Poitiers), 4M: Police, 540: Enquête relative à l'apposition du Sacré-Cœur sur le drapeau national en 1917.

20. Marcault, *Réalisons le message du Sacré-Coeur,* 78–79.

21. See letter dated 20 June 1917 from the subprefect of Montmorillon to the prefect of la Vienne, in Archives départmentales de la Vienne (Poitiers), 4M: Police, 540: Enquête relative à l'apposition du Sacré-Cœur sur le drapeau national en 1917.

22. "'Note pour les armées' (confidentiel) de Paul Painlevé, le 6 avril 1917," in Archives historiques du diocèse de Paris, Basilique du Sacré-Coeur, carton 5.

23. Abbé Servant, curé-doyen de Saint-Gervais, "Mes impressions au courant de la plume pendant la guerre de 1914," manuscript journal in eight bound tablets, vol. 7, p. 8 (entry for 17 February 1918), in Archives départementales de la Vienne (Poitiers), série R: Guerre et affaires militaires, 7: Guerre de 1914–18, 82.

24. Humbrecht, the bishop of Poitiers, was apparently among those who put faith in this prediction. See Confidential letter from Humbrecht to Cardinal Amette, dated 29 March 1918, in Archives historiques du diocèse de Paris, Basilique du Sacré-Coeur, carton 5.

25. *La Croix des Deux-Sèvres,* 14 April 1918.

26. Fontana, *Les catholiques français,* 237.

27. Charles Marcault, *Le Message de 1689 a-t-il été réellement abandonné?* (Chinon, 1918), 72.

28. See Raymond Jonas, *France and the Cult of the Sacred Heart: An Epic Tale for Modern Times* (Berkeley and Los Angeles, 2000), 124–29; and Sheryl Kroen, *Politics and Theater: The Crisis of Legitimacy in Restoration France, 1815–1830* (Berkeley and Los Angeles, 2000).

29. *La Croix des Deux-Sèvres,* 26 May 1918.

30. "Le Sacré-Cœur," *La Croix,* 9 June 1917.

31. Undated document, apparently a summary of Crawley-Boevey's 1918 visit to Loublande, in Archives historiques du diocèse de Paris, Basilique du Sacré-Coeur, carton 5.

32. *La Croix des Deux-Sèvres,* 2 June 1918.

33. *La Croix des Deux-Sèvres,* 19 May 1918.

THE UNMAKING OF A SAINT

1. "On danse partout la Vendée, au grand dam de la piété." Abbé Servant, curé-doyen de Saint-Gervais, "Mes impressions au courant de la plume pendant la guerre de 1914," manuscript journal in eight bound tablets, vol. 8,

p. 372 (entry for 18 July 1919), in Archives départementales de la Vienne (Poitiers), série R: Guerre et affaires militaires, 7: Guerre de 1914–18, 82.

2. For a more positive account of the reception of African-American soldiers in France, see Jean-Yves Le Naour, *Misères et tourments de la chair durant la grande guerre: Les moeurs sexuelles des Français, 1914–1918* (Paris, 2002), 249–52. For contemporary African-American commentary on military service in the war, see Ida B. Wells-Barnett, *Crusade for Justice: The Autobiography of Ida B. Wells* (Chicago, 1970), 367–74. On the biblical curse of Ham, see George M. Frederickson, *Racism: A Short History* (Princeton, 2002), 39, 45.

3. Servant, "Mes impressions," 8:32.

4. Servant, "Mes impressions," 6:49.

5. Servant, "Mes impressions," 7:103.

6. Servant, "Mes impressions," 7:151.

7. Letter of 15 June 1917, in Archives départementales de la Vienne (Poitiers), série 4M: Police, 540: Enquête relative à l'apposition du Sacré-Coeur sur le drapeau national en 1917.

8. Protocolli 35374 (Périgueux) and 34073 (Nice), in Archivio Segreto Vaticano, Segreteria di Stato, Epocha moderna, Guerra 1914–18, rubrica 244 M 4C, fasc. 403.2.

9. Julien de Narfon, "Le cardinal Billot et la question du drapeau," *Le Figaro,* 4 May 1918.

10. Quoted in *Le Messager du Sacré-Coeur de Jésus* 93 (June 1918), 356. See also Jacques Maître, *Mystique et fémininité* (Paris, 1997), 415–16.

11. See, for example, Bernard Gaudeau, "Les deux étandards: Quelques réflexions au sujet de l'article qui précède," *La Foi Catholique* 22 (1er semestre, 1918), 194; "Les manoeuvres maçonniques contre le règne social du Sacré-Coeur,"*La Foi Catholique* 22 (1er semestre, 1918), 280; "Revue des intérêts du coeur de Jésus," *Le Messager du Sacré-Coeur de Jésus* 93 (June 1918), 356–59; and Édouard Poulain, *Pour le drapeau du Sacré-Coeur! Pour le salut de la France!* (Beauchene, 1918). A copy of Billot's letter, dated 23 March 1916, can also be found in the Archives historiques du diocèse de Paris, Basilique du Sacré-Cœur, carton 5.

12. See Gaudeau, in *La Foi Catholique* 22 (1er semestre, 1918), 278.

13. Letter of H. Densellier, 18 June 1918, in Archives diocésaines de Poitiers, M71: Militaires.

14. On Humbrecht and the Action Française, see Jacques Prévotat, *Les catholiques et l'Action Française: Histoire d'une condamnation, 1899–1939* (Paris, 2001), 128–29, 137, 388–91. On the Action Française itself, see Eugen Weber,

Action Française: Royalism and Reaction in Twentieth-Century France (Stanford, 1962).

15. For example, Monsignor Jouin, pastor of Saint-Augustin parish and probably Claire's most ardent supporter in Paris, challenged the attempts of his archbishop, Cardinal Amette, to control his activities in a letter in which he repeatedly cited the words and gestures of Humbrecht in favor of Claire and her mission. See Letter from Jouin to Amette, 2 July 1918, in Archives historiques du diocèse de Paris, Basilique du Sacré-Cœur, carton 5.

16. For the story of the painting based on Claire's visions, see "Les événements de Loublande," *Le Courrier de la Vienne,* 26 May 1917.

17. Claire Ferchaud, *Notes autobiographiques,* 2 vols. (Paris, 1974), 2:90.

18. Servant, "Mes impressions," 6:78.

19. Letter from Sr. M. Louise de l'Eucharistie to Amette, 7 June 1917, in Archives historiques du diocèse de Paris, Basilique du Sacré-Cœur, carton 5.

20. *La Croix,* 7 May 1918.

21. Protocollo 34619, in Archivio Segreto Vaticano, Segreteria di Stato, Epocha moderna, Guerra 1914–18, rubrica 244 M 4C, fasc. 403.2.

22. Letter from Humbrecht to the Archbishop of Reims, 2 May 1918, cited in Claude Mouton, *Au plus fort de la tourmente: Claire Ferchaud* (Montsûrs, 1983), 139.

23. "Monsieur l'Évêque de Poitiers à Loublande," *La Croix des Deux-Sèvres,* 30 June 1918 (news item dated 12 June); Ferchaud, *Notes autobiographiques,* 2:11.

24. See *La Croix des Deux-Sèvres* for 15 and 22 September 1918.

25. Servant, "Mes impressions," 8:161.

26. See "L'acte sauveur du 18 juillet 1918," in *La Foi Catholique* 22 (2ème semestre, 1918), 345, which claims that the story was first published in *La Semaine Religieuse d'Autun,* the weekly bulletin of the diocese of Autun. The account, published in 1919, of the Foch consecration in *Da Paray-le-Monial a Loublande: Storia e dottrina del regno del S. Cuore sulle nazioni* (Milan, 1919) by Adriano Bernareggi, "Sac. Dottor, professore nel Seminario Arcivescovile di Milano," attests to the rapid diffusion of the story beyond France. The account of the Foch ex-voto in the Basilica of Saint-Martin was published in *La Croix,* 21 April 1926, which can be found, along with related material, in the Archives diocésaines de Chartres, Loigny-la-Bataille, Fonds Provost, dossier 12: Correspondance 1915–18, divers. The story is repeated by Charles Marcault in *Réalisons le message du Sacré-Cœur* (Paris, 1934), 95–96, and in the commemorative sermon given at Loigny in 1948: "Loigny-la-Bataille, 2 décembre 1948,

78ème anniversaire des combats de 1870: Allocution prononcée au cours de la cérémonie funèbre par Monsieur le Chanoine Danthon, supérieur de l'École Saint-Louis à Montargis," in Archives diocésaines de Chartres, dossier 12: Correspondance, 1915–18. The story of Foch's consecration may well be true; Foch's piety is not in doubt and was well known at the time. Both Marshall Pétain and Foch were invited to the consecration of the Basilica of the Sacré-Coeur in 1919, an event seen as marking not only the completion of the basilica but also an end to the war. Foch accepted the invitation; Pétain politely declined. Undated letters in the Archives historiques du diocèse de Paris, Basilique du Sacré-Cœur, carton 5.

27. Abbé Servant, who had terminated his journal at the conclusion of the war, nevertheless thought to clip the newspaper account of the Holy Office's ruling and insert it into his journal. See "Mes impressions," 6:78.

28. Ferchaud, *Notes autobiographiques,* 2:179.

29. Ferchaud, *Notes autobiographiques,* 2:128.

30. On the Hippocratic origin of the *globus hystericus,* see Cristina Mazzoni, *Saint Hysteria: Neurosis, Mysticism, and Gender in European Culture* (Ithaca, N.Y., 1996), 8; and Jan Goldstein, *Console and Classify: The French Psychiatric Profession in the Nineteenth Century* (Cambridge, 1987), 323.

31. See, for example, Janet Beizer, *Ventriloquized Bodies: Narratives of Hysteria in Nineteenth-Century France* (Ithaca, N.Y., 1993); Mazzoni, *Saint Hysteria,* esp. 17–53, 180–96; and Elisabeth Bronfen, *The Knotted Subject: Hysteria and Its Discontents* (Princeton, 1998), esp. 176–81. The classic statement of the psychosexual etiology of hysteria is Sigmund Freud's *Dora: An Analysis of a Case of Hysteria* (New York, 1963), esp. 97–98.

32. See Goldstein, *Console and Classify;* and Jann Matlock, *Scenes of Seduction: Prostitution, Hysteria, and Reading Difference in Nineteenth-Century France* (New York, 1994).

33. On hysteria and the pathology of the crowd, see Susanna Barrows, *Distorting Mirrors: Visions of the Crowd in Late Nineteenth-Century France* (New Haven, 1981).

34. On Parisian spectacle, see Vanessa Schwartz, *Spectacular Realities: Early Mass Culture in Fin-de-Siècle Paris* (Berkeley and Los Angeles, 1988); on hysteria and histrionics, see Phillip R. Slavney, *Perspectives on 'Hysteria'* (Baltimore, 1990), 120.

35. Goldstein, *Console and Classify.*

36. Ferchaud, *Notes autobiographiques,* 2:74.

37. Ferchaud, *Notes autobiographiques,* 2:134.

38. Ferchaud, *Notes autobiographiques,* 2:108, 127–28.

39. Ferchaud, *Notes autobiographiques,* 2:134.

40. On hysteria as a product of tensions within a surrounding culture, see the remarks of G.S. Rousseau, in Sander Gilman and others, *Hysteria Beyond Freud* (Berkeley and Los Angeles, 1993), esp. 102–3.

41. Servant, "Mes impressions," 7:110.

42. Servant, "Mes impressions," 7:110.

43. On the consecration of another département, Maine-et-Loire, see *La Croix,* 4 September 1917, 7.

44. Ferchaud, *Notes autobiographiques,* 2:72.

45. Personal communication.

46. The remark also flatters Claire in its implication that there was intense interest in her case. During a visit to Rome in May of 1917, as interest in Claire was peaking in France, Baudrillart discovered that "hardly anyone talks about her here." When he met with Cardinal Gasparri and recounted the story of Claire's audience with Poincaré, Gasparri was "amused" and judged that the French president's response made "perfectly good sense." Gasparri also offered the opinion that given the divided state of the French people, it made no sense to allow partisan symbols on military uniforms. Alfred Baudrillart, Mgr., *Les carnets du cardinal Alfred Baudrillart,* edited by Paul Christophe, 1:*1939–1941* (Paris, 1999), 557.

47. See especially Thomas Kselman, *Miracles and Prophecies in Nineteenth-Century France* (New Brunswick, N.J., 1983). See also Gilbert-Joseph-Emile Combe, *Le Grand Coup, avec sa date probable [. . .] Étude sur le secret de La Salette comparé aux prophéties de l'Écriture et à d'autres prophéties authentiques* (Vichy, 1894); A. Schmid, *Mélanie, bergère de La Salette et le cardinal Perraud: Procès civil et religieux* (Paris, 1898); Henry Mariavé [pseud. of Henri Ernest Grémillon], *La leçon de l'hôpital Notre-Dame d'Ypres: Exégèse du secret de La Salette* (Montpellier, 1915); Association de Notre-Dame de Salut, *Pèlerinage à Notre-Dame de Pontmain, 22–24 janvier 1916* (Paris, 1916); René Laurentin, ed., *Pontmain: Histoire authentique* (Paris, 1970); Jean Stern, ed., *La Salette. Documents authentiques: Dossier chronologique intégrale* (Paris, 1984); and Ruth Harris, *Lourdes: Body and Spirit in the Secular Age* (London, 1999).

48. Notice from Poitiers dated 9 February 1918, in Archives historiques du diocèse de Paris, Basilique du Sacré-Cœur, carton 5.

49. *Le Courrier de l'Ouest,* 3 February 1972.

50. Baudrillart, *Carnets,* 2: 487–88.

51. François Bédarida and Renée Bédarida, *La résistance spirituelle 1941–1944* (Paris, 2001), 63n.

52. Bédarida and Bédarida, *La résistance spirituelle,* 65.

53. Baudrillart, *Carnets,* 1:555n.

54. Alain Denizot, *Le Sacré-Coeur et la grande guerre* (Paris, 1994), 215.

55. *La Semaine Religieuse de Poitiers* (1972) 56.

56. *Le Courrier de l'Ouest,* 3 February 1972.

BIBLIOGRAPHY

NOTE ON SOURCES

The tale of Claire Ferchaud is a story that had to be constructed from fragmentary evidence held in a variety of archives. One of my first stops was Paris, where government documents dating from 1916 to 1918 in the Archives nationales revealed a deep suspicion of Claire and her supporters. It became strikingly clear that wartime political leaders regarded Claire's campaign as the scheme of a dreamer—a distraction at best and treason at worst. After reading dozens of letters in French army archives just outside Paris at Vincennes, I began to understand why. Some members of the clergy, serving in the army as chaplains and assisted by sympathetic officers, were promoting Claire's message and mission among the troops. Was it treason to promote the idea, three years into an interminable war, that peace could be had in mere days if political leadership would only listen to an inspired and courageous young woman?

In public archives in Poitiers, I discovered the wartime journal of a common parish priest: Abbé Servant. He started writing his diary entries on 4 August 1914, the first day of the war. Every day he confided his thoughts, fears, and impressions to his diary. He was not an impartial observer, but he was disinterested—he had no particular stake in the story of Claire—and in that regard he served as a useful guide to when her story began to circulate and what effect it had on those who heard it. His penchant for pasting newspaper

189

clippings into his diary alongside hearsay and his own reflections gave me insights into how Claire's story built upon a blend of gossip, rumor, and journalistic reporting.

Poitiers was also the scene of a significant research disappointment. Access to diocesan archives (the local administrative archives of the Catholic Church in France) is granted routinely, but when I sought to pursue Claire's story in the archived papers of the archbishops of Poitiers, I encountered resolute resistance. The priest who served as archivist refused access to the transcripts of Claire's appearance before the commission of inquiry. "Cela ne se communique pas au publique, Monsieur," was the phrase that told me, gently but firmly, that I would not be allowed to consult the transcripts. Disappointing as this setback was, it taught me a great deal about the lingering sensitivity of Claire's story. Meanwhile, what might have presented an insurmountable obstacle to writing Claire's story became quite surmountable when I discovered that the Téqui publishing house in Paris had not only somehow gained access to the transcripts I had been denied, but had published them, along with Claire's autobiography. My disappointment was then reduced to being unable to determine, through comparison with originals at the diocesan archives, whether the published transcripts are complete. This will be a task for some future scholar. In the meantime, the incident made clear that the diocese of Poitiers is as careful today about who tells Claire's story as it was at the height of her fame during the Great War.

Finally, I pursued Claire's story in the Vatican Archives. I knew that a story as powerful as Claire's, with its divine visions and promises of military triumph, would have to have been communicated to the hierarchy of the Catholic Church. It took some hunting around—Vatican documents tend to be organized by date and correspondents rather than topic—but I found her. On 30 March 1917, in a lengthy letter that begins with the words "Très Saint Père," Claire described her mission to the pope. An accompanying multipage memorandum, apparently drafted by Claire's supporters in Poitiers, summarized her life and attested to her sanctity. How had the Vatican reacted? The draft of a bland and laconic acknowledgement of Claire's letter spoke volumes about the ambivalence Claire inspired. By the time I left Rome, I knew that I had what I needed to tell a story about belief, ambition, and the making and unmaking of a saint. I was ready to tell the tale of Claire Ferchaud.

ARCHIVAL SOURCES
Archives nationales, Paris

Série F7, Police générale

13213	Mouvement catholique
13214	Mouvement catholique (suite)
13216	Notes et presse sur l'activité de la Ligue patriotique des Françaises, 1910–1927

Série F19, Cultes

2371	Église du Sacré-Cœur de Montmartre
5562	Pèlerinages; établissement "Cœur de Jésus"
5610	Police: 3ème République. Rapports et notes sur l'attitude du clergé et particulièrement de l'épiscopat, 1872–1906. Prières pour l'Assemblée (1871)
5636	Police: 3ème République. Agissements politiques sous forme religieuse: fêtes de Jeanne d'Arc, 1890–1904; consécration des communes au Sacré-Cœur, 1901–1905
5639	Police: 3ème République. Coupures de journaux, 1897–1907
6535	Activité politique du clergé (par diocèse, sous les noms de personne) 3ème République

Archives de l'armée de la terre, Paris

1K284, K104	Archives Veuillot, 1914–19; Fonds de l'Association diocésaine du Vicariat aux armées françaises
5N14	Correspondance, ministre de la guerre, dépêches télégraphiques
5N67	Correspondance, ministre de la guerre, préfets

Archives départementales
ARCHIVES DÉPARTEMENTALES DE LA LOIRE ATLANTIQUE (NANTES)

Série V, Cultes

2V1	Police générale du culte, faits divers, rapports, 1800–1814

ARCHIVES DÉPARTEMENTALES
DE LA MAINE ET LOIRE (ANGERS)

Série 1M, Administration générale, rapports sur l'état de l'opinion publique et la situation générale du département

58 Fêtes et manifestations publiques organisées par des royalistes, 1881–1914

65 Cérémonies et manifestations religieuses: Fête-Dieu, fêtes de Jeanne d'Arc, processions, pèlerinage, missions, visites pastorales, etc., 1873–1913

66 Propagande cléricale: Tracts, affiches, catéchisme, soirées, missions, prédication, 1880–1914

67 Questions de l'enseignement, 1872–1913

68 Question des congrégations: Conférences, manifestations, incidents divers, placards et affiches à l'occasion des lois sur les congrégations, 1896–1903

ARCHIVES DÉPARTEMENTALES DU RHÔNE (LYON)

Série 1M, Administration générale

149 Rapports du commissariat special, mai–décembre 1917

Série V, Cultes

2V1 Police générale du culte, faits divers, rapports, 1900–1914

ARCHIVES DÉPARTEMENTALES
DE LA SAÔNE ET LOIRE (MÂCON)

Série 4M, Police

310 Affaires religieuses: incidents divers, 1879–1905

311 Affaires religieuses; agitations religieuses, congrès, pèlerinages, pétitions en faveur de la reprise des relations avec le Saint-Siège, 1906–17

312 Pèlerinages, affaires religieuses, mouvements catholiques

ARCHIVES DÉPARTEMENTALES DE LA VENDÉE
(LA ROCHE-SUR-YON)

Série 1M, Administration générale

442	Correspondance, rapports, coupures de presse, tracts, 1871–80
474	Censures de Baudry d'Asson, député; affichage, 1879–80
478	Cultes, instructions, personnel ecclésiastique, enquêtes, correspondance, an X–1926

Série 4M, Police

150	Cultes. Réglementation des sonneries de cloches, bancs des églises, sépultures, processions, 1904–1913
165	Évêque de Luçon, 1902–1905
178	Royalistes, 1895–1915
405	Troisième République. Réunions, manifestations religieuses. Correspondance. Rapports, 1879–1939
408	Réunions, manifestation et propagande des parties et groupements politiques, 1881–1929

ARCHIVES DÉPARTEMENTALES DE LA
VIENNE (POITIERS)

Série 4M, Police

370	Demandes de renseignements confidentiels, 1914–17
493	Affaires diverses, 1814–1928
540	Enquête relative à l'apposition du Sacré-Cœur sur le drapeau national en 1917

Série R, Guerre et affaires militaires

7R	Guerre de 1914–18
32	Télégrammes; Arrêtés, instruction, photographies, censure
37	Circulaires diverses
38	Lettres, instructions, télégrammes divers
39	idem.
82	Abbé Servant, curé-doyen de Saint-Gervais ("Mes impressions au courant de la plume pendant la guerre de 1914," 8 tomes ms.)

Archives diocésaines
ARCHIVES DIOCÉSAINES D'ANGERS

Pèlerinages

| 2K32 | Pèlerinages angevins à Lourdes |

ARCHIVES DIOCÉSAINES DE CHARTRES

Loigny-la-Bataille, fonds Provost
 Dossier 12   Correspondance 1915–18, divers
 Dossier 14   Poésies et drames

ARCHIVES HISTORIQUES DU DIOCÈSE DE PARIS

Basilique du Sacré-Cœur
 Carton 5   Bénédiction, 1891; Croix lumineuse, 1892; 25ème
            anniversaire, 1897; consécration 1919, œuvres de dévotion,
            règlement des chapelains, oeuvres de dévotion; 1912,
            projet d'une Adoration Perpétuelle, 1918, Claire
            Ferchaud
 Carton 7   Plans divers, vues ariennes, pèlerinage d'action de grâces
            de l'action catholique à la basilique du Sacré-Cœur (3
            juin–24 septembre 1944)

ARCHIVES DIOCÉSAINES DE LUÇON

 1E8   Lettres circulaires, 1872–1919
 4L2   Correspondance après 1905, dossier, la basilique du Sacré-
        Cœur, la-Roche-sur-Yon

ARCHIVES DIOCÉSAINES DE POITIERS

 M71   Militaires
 M72   Relations avec l'armée
 S1 1   Franc-Maçonnerie
 G3 3   Liturgie, autel privilégiés, dévotions Sacré-Cœur, Notre-
        Dame de Boulogne

Archivio Segreto Vaticano

Segretario di Stato 1914–22, indice 1089 III
 242   Cose di Francia
 248   Cose di Francia
Segretario di Stato, Epocha moderna, Guerra, 1914–18
 244 M 4C, fasc. 403, 1917

PERIODICALS

Bulletin de l'Oeuvre du Voeu National au Sacré-Coeur de Jésus
Le Courrier de la Vienne, 1917
Le Courrier de l'Ouest, 1972
La Croix
La Croix Angevine (Revue hebdomadaire du département), 1914
La Croix des Deux-Sèvres, 1918
La Défense Sociale (Organe de propagande et de défense républicaines et socialistes), 1916
Echo de Saint-Philbert (bulletin paroissial)
Le Figaro, 1918
La Foi Catholique (Revue critique, anti-kantiste des questions qui touchent la notion de la foi), 1918
Le Messager du Sacré-Coeur de Jésus (Bulletin mensuel de l'Apostolat de la Prière)
Le Pèlerin (organe du Conseil général des pèlerinages)
Le Réveil Choletais, 1916
La Revue de Bas-Poitou
La Semaine Catholique de Luçon
La Semaine Liturgique du Diocèse de Poitiers
La Semaine Paroissiale de Montbert (Loire Atlantique)
La Semaine Religieuse de Paris
La Semaine Religieuse de Poitiers (1972)
La Semaine Religieuse du Diocèse d'Angers (Revue liturgique et historique)
La Semaine Religieuse du Diocèse de Lyon
La Semaine Religieuse du Diocèse de Nantes
La Victoire

ANONYMOUS OR UNSIGNED WORKS

La Congregation des filles de la charité du Sacré-Coeur de Jésus. Paris: Letouzey, 1923.
Faisons pénitence pour le salut de la France. Paris: Imp. de l'Oeuvre des pauvres du Sacré-Coeur, 1903.
Guide officiel du pèlerin au Sacré-Coeur de Montmartre. Paris: Imprimerie des Arts et Manufactures et Dubuisson, 1892.

La Mission à Saint-Mars-La-Jaille prêchée par les RR PP de Maistre, Jégo, de Lasteyrie du Saillant; consécrations solennelles de la paroisse et de la commune au Sacré-Coeur; M. Jean-Baptiste Bonnin, curé; M. de la Feronnays, Maire [ca. 1919].

Montmartre: La basilique du voeu national au Sacré-Coeur; Guide. Paris, n.d. [after 1918].

Notre-Dame de Pontmain. Abbeville: Paillart, 1896.

Pèlerinage à Notre-Dame de Pontmain, 22–24 janvier 1916. Paris: Feron, 1916.

Pèlerinage Breton à La Salette, à Tours, à La Chartreuse, à Fourvière, à Ars, et à Paray-Le-Monial du 12 au 23 juin 1883. Nantes: Imp. de l'Ouest, 1883.

Petit manuel des Adoratrices du Sacré-Coeur. Paris: Adoratrices du Sacré-Coeur, 1894.

BOOKS, PAMPHLETS, AND SECONDARY SOURCES

Abel, Felix-Marie, Père, *Mots d'ordre du Sacré-Coeur à ses apôtres.* Moulins: Imprimeries réunies, 1923.

Agulhon, Maurice. "Politics, Images, and Symbols in Post-Revolutionary France." In *Rites of Power: Symbolism, Ritual, and Politics since the Middle Ages,* edited by Sean Wilentz, 177–205. Philadelphia: University of Pennsylvania Press, 1985.

Aillery, Eugen-Louis, Abbé. *Archives du diocèse de Luçon: Chroniques paroissiales.* Luçon: Bideaux, 1908.

Alacoque, Marguerite-Marie. *Vie et oeuvres de Sainte Marguerite-Marie Alacoque,* 2 vols. Paris: Poussielgue, 1920.

———. *Vie et oeuvres de Sainte Marguerite-Marie Alacoque,* 2 vols. Paris-Fribourg: Éditions Saint-Paul, 1991.

Alet, Victor, and P. Lejeune, *La France et le Sacré-Coeur.* Paris: Lethielleux et Dumoulin, 1904.

Anizan, Felix, Abbé. *Les Hommes de France au Sacré-Coeur.* Verdun (Meuse): Bureaux de l'Oeuvre diocésaine du Sacré-Coeur, 1913.

———. *Qu'est-ce que le Sacré-Coeur?* Paris: Lethielleux, 1910.

Appolis, Emile. "En marge du catholicisme contemporain: Millénaristes, cordiphores, et naundorffistes autour du 'secret' de La Salette." *Archives de Sociologie des Religions* 14 (1962): 103–22.

Arnold, Odile. *Le corps et l'âme: La vie des religieuses au XIXe siècle.* Paris: Éditions du Seuil, 1983.

Arnoux, Jacques. *Paroles d'un revenant.* Paris: Plon, 1925.

Audoin-Rouzeau, Stéphane. *Men at War, 1914–1918: National Sentiment and Trench Journalism in France during the First World War,* translated by Helen McPhail (English edition of *14–18: Les combattants des tranchées: à travers leurs journaux*). Providence, R.I.: Berg, 1992.

Aulard, Alphonse. *Christianity and the French Revolution,* translated by Lady Frazer. London: Ernest Benn, 1927.

Babonneau, P. *La France et le XIXe siècle: Discours prononcé lors du triduum séculaire en la basilique Saint-Nicolas de Nantes, les 28, 29 et 30 Décembre 1900.* Nantes: Lanoe-Mazeau, 1901.

Bachelier, Alcime. *Un nantais, prêtre-soldat: P. Landais, 1887–1916.* Nantes: Lanoe-Mazeau, 1917.

Backman, François. "La 'journée chouanne' de Chiré-en-Montreuil 1970–1990." In *Les usages politiques des fêtes au XIXe–XXe siècles,* edited by Alain Corbin, Noelle Gérôme, and Danielle Tartakowsky, 349–59. Paris: Publications de la Sorbonne, 1994.

Bainvel, Jacques. "Dévotion au coeur-sacré de Jésus." In *Dictionnaire de théologie catholique*, vol. 3, 271–351. Paris: Letouzey, 1938.

Barkun, Michael. *Disaster and the Millennium.* New Haven: Yale University Press, 1974.

Barruel, Augustin. *Mémoires pour servir à l'histoire du jacobinisme.* Chiré-en-Montreuil: Diffusion de la pensée française, 1973.

Baudelaire, Charles. *Petit poèmes en prose.* Paris: Garnier, 1948.

Baudrillart, Alfred, Mgr. *Les carnets du cardinal Alfred Baudrillart.* 2 vols., 1: *1914–1918*; 2: *20 novembre 1935–11 avril 1939.* Edited by Paul Christophe. Paris: Cerf, 1994–99.

———. *Le coeur de Jésus, source de vie: Discours prononcé en la basilique du Voeu National, à Montmartre, dimanche, le 24 juin 1917 à l'occasion de la journée du commerce et de l'industrie.* Paris: Diéval, 1917.

———. *Dictionnaire d'histoire et de géographie ecclésiastiques.* Paris: Letouzey, 1930.

———. *Elogio de Garcia Moreno: Di scurso pronunciado el 22 de diciembre de 1921 en la iglesia de San Sulpicio.* Barcelona and Paris: Bloud y Gay, 1921.

———. *La France, les catholiques, et la guerre.* Paris: Bloud et Gay, 1917.

———. *Notre propagande.* Paris: Plon, 1916.

Baunard, Louis. *Histoire de la vénérable mère Madeleine-Sophie Barat, fondatrice de la société du Sacré-Coeur de Jésus.* 2 vols. Paris: Poussielgue, 1892.

Becker, Annette. *La guerre et la foi: De la mort à la mémoire, 1914–1930.* Paris: Colin, 1994.

Becker, Jean-Jacques. *1914: Comment les français sont entrés dans la guerre*. Paris: Presses de la Fondation nationale des sciences politiques, 1977.

———. *La France en guerre, 1914–1918: La grande mutation*. Paris: Éditions complexe, 1918.

Becker, Jean-Jacques, and Serge Berstein. *Victoire et frustrations, 1914–1929*. Paris: Seuil, 1990.

Beckwith, Sarah. *Christ's Body: Identity, Culture, and Society in Late Medieval Writings*. London: Routledge, 1993.

Beizer, Janet. *Ventriloquized Bodies: Narratives of Hysteria in Nineteenth-Century France*. Ithaca, N.Y.: Cornell University Press, 1993.

Bellanger, Claude, and others. *Histoire générale de la presse française*. 5 vols. Paris: Presses universitaires de France, 1969–76.

Benoist, Jacques. *Le Sacré-Coeur des femmes de 1870 à 1960*. 2 vols. Paris: Éditions ouvrières, 2000.

Bernareggi, Adriano. *Da Paray-le-Monial a Loublande: Storia e dottrina del regno del S. Cuore sulle nazioni*. Milan: Società editrice 'Vita e pensiero', 1919.

Berthe, A. *Garcia Moreno, le héros martyr*. Paris: Retaux-Bray, 1890.

Besson, André. *Confiance! La France sera sauvée par le Sacré-Coeur*. Paris: Tequi, 1916.

Bittard des Portes, René. *Histoire des zouaves pontificaux*. Paris: Bloud et Barral, 1894.

Blanc, Gabriel. *France éprouvée, France triomphante! Quatre conférences sur la guerre données à la cathédrale de Digne en 1915*. Lyon: Vitte, 1915.

Bliard, Joseph. *Le salut de la France: Considérations philosphiques sur l'histoire contemporaine*. Bordeaux: Feret, 1871.

Bloch, R. Howard. "Naturalism, Nationalism, Medievalism." *Romanic Review* 76 (1985): 341–60.

Boissard, Charles. *La vie et le message de Madame Royer, 1841–1924*. Paris: Lethielleux, 1960.

Boisseleau, E., abbé. *Le Sacré-Coeur et la France: L'étendard du Sacré-Coeur à Loigny*. Luçon: Bideaux, 1911.

Bottineau, J. *Les portraits des généraux vendéens*. Cholet: Musée d'histoire de Cholet, 1975.

Bouflet, Joachim. *Encyclopédie des phénomènes extraordinaires dans la vie mystique*. 3 vols. Paris: Guibert, 1992.

Bourneville, Désiré. *Iconographie photographique de la Salpêtrière*. Paris: V. Adrien Delahaye, 1876.

Bowie, Fiona, ed. *Beguine Spirituality: Mystical Writings of Mechthild of Magdeburg, Beatrijs of Nazareth, and Hadewijch of Brabant.* New York: Crossroad Books, 1989.

Bowman, Frank Paul. "Le 'Sacré Coeur' de Marat, 1793." In *Les fêtes de la Révolution*, edited by Jean Ehrard and Paul Viallaneix, 155–79. Paris: Société des études robespierrietes, 1977.

Bredin, Jean-Denis. *The Affair: The Case of Alfred Dreyfus.* New York: Braziller, 1986.

Bronfen, Elisabeth. *The Knotted Subject: Hysteria and Its Discontents.* Princeton: Princeton University Press, 1998.

Brown, Peter. *The Cult of the Saints: Its Rise and Function in Latin Christianity.* Chicago: University of Chicago Press, 1981.

Bucaille, Victor. *Lettres de prêtres aux armées.* Paris: Payot, 1916.

Bugnot, Paul. *Réponse aux attaques de la franc maçonnerie contre l'église.* Auxerre: Imprimerie Auxerroise, 1906.

Burnichon, Joseph, S. J. *Histoire d'un siècle, 1814–1914: La compagnie de Jésus en France.* 4 vols. Paris: Beauchesne, 1914–1922.

Burns, Michael. *Dreyfus: A Family Affair, 1789–1945.* New York: Harper-Collins, 1991.

Bynum, Caroline Walker. *Jesus as Mother.* Berkeley and Los Angeles: University of California Press, 1982.

Chaline, Nadine-Josette, ed. *Chrétiens dans la première guerre mondiale. Actes des journées tenues à Amiens et à Péronne, les 16 mai et 22 juillet 1992.* Paris: Cerf, 1993.

Charbonneau-Lassay, Louis. *La mystérieuse emblématique de Jésus-Christ: Le bestiaire du Christ. Mille cent cinquante-sept figures gravées sur bois par l'auteur.* Paris: Desclée, de Brouwer, 1940.

Chauveau, Jacqueline. *La conjuration de Satan: La persécution religieuse sous la révolution de 1789.* Paris: Nouvelles Éditions Latines, 1969.

Chirol, Pierre. "La Basilique du Sacré-Coeur de Dijon; Julien et Gérard Barbier, architectes." *La Construction Moderne* 54 (1939): 130–34.

Cholvy, Gérard, and Yves-Marie Hilaire. *Histoire religieuse de la France contemporaine,* 1: *1800–1880.* Paris: Privat, 1985.

Christian, William A. *Local Religion in Sixteenth-Century Spain.* Princeton: Princeton University Press, 1981.

Ciammitti, Luisa. "One Saint Less: The Story of Angela Mellini, a Bolognese Seamstress (1667–17??)." In *Sex and Gender in Historical Perspective,* edited by Edward Muir and Guido Ruggiero, 141–76. Baltimore: Johns Hopkins University Press, 1990.

Cochin, Denys. *La guerre, le blocus, l'union sacrée, 1914–1922.* Paris: Plon, 1918.

Combe, Gilbert-Joseph-Emile. *Le grand coup, avec sa date probable, c'est-à-dire le grand châtiment du monde et le triomphe universel de l'église: Étude sur le secret de La Salette comparé aux prophéties de l'écriture et à d'autres prophéties authentiques.* Vichy: Vexenat, 1894.

Corbin, Alain, Noelle Gérôme, and Danielle Tartakowsky. *Les usages politiques des fêtes au XIXe–XXe siècles.* Paris: Publications de la Sorbonne, 1994.

Cordonnier, Charles. *Le Cardinal Amette.* 2 vols. Mortain: Éd. du Mortinais, 1949.

Crawley-Boevey, Matéo. *Jésus, roi d'amour (recueil des prédications).* Braine-le-Comte: Zech, 1948.

Crétineau-Joly, Jacques. *Histoire de la compagnie de Jésus.* 6 vols. Paris: Lecoffre, 1859.

Croiset, John, S. J. *The Devotion to the Sacred Heart of Our Lord Jesus Christ* (1694), translated by Patrick O'Connell. Westminster, Md.: Newman Press, 1948.

Darmon, Pierre. *Vivre à Paris pendant la Grande Guerre.* Paris: Fayard, 2002.

Darricau, Raymond. "Poitiers." In *Catholicisme hier, aujourd'hui, demain,* edited by G. Mathon, G.-H. Baudry, P. Guilluy, and E. Thiery, vol. 11. Paris: Letouzey, 1988.

Darrow, Margaret H. *French Women and the First World War.* New York: Berg, 2000.

Davesnes, Jean-Clair. *L'agriculture assassinée: Mort de la civilisation rurale.* Chiré-en-Montreuil: Editions du Chiré, 1992.

Davis, Natalie Zemon. *Women on the Margins: Three Seventeenth-Century Lives.* Cambridge, Mass.: Harvard University Press, 1995.

de Falloux, Alfred Frédéric. *Mémoires d'un royaliste.* Paris: Perrin, 1888.

de Franciosi, Xavier, S. J. *La dévotion au Sacré-Coeur de Jésus et au Saint-Coeur de Marie.* Nancy: Chevalier Frères, 1885.

de Gobineau, Arthur. *La chronique rimée de Jean Chouan et de ses compagnons.* Paris: Fournier, 1846.

de Grandmaison, Geoffroy. *Les aumôniers militaires.* Paris: Bloud et Gay, 1915.

de Grandmaison, Geoffroy, and François Veuillot. *L'aumônerie militaire pendant la guerre, 1914–1918.* Paris: Bloud et Gay, 1923.

de Larochejaquelein, Marie-Louise. *Mémoires de madame la marquise de Larochejaquelein.* 2 vols. Paris: Michaud, 1815.

de Llobet, Archevêque d'Avignon. *Le Cardinal de Cabrières.* Paris: Bonne Presse, 1944.

Delumeau, Jean, and Yves Lequin. *Les malheurs des temps: Histoire des fléaux et des calamités en France.* Paris: Larousse, 1987.

de Mun, Albert. "Les dernières heures du drapeau blanc." *La Revue Hebdomadaire* 11 (1909): 141–63.

Denizot, A. *Le Sacré-Coeur et la grande guerre.* Paris: Nouvelles éditions latines, 1994.

de Quatrebarbes, Théodore. *Une paroisse vendéenne sous la Terreur.* Rennes: Salmon, 1837.

Descouvrement, Pierre. *Saint Thérèse de Lisieux: La vie en images.* Paris: Cerf, 1995.

des Mauges, Charles. *Vendée, souviens-toi!* Angers: Siraudeau, 1910.

d'Hulst, Maurice Lesage d'Hauteroche. *Religion et patrie: Discours prononcé à la consecration de l'église de Loigny le 18 Septembre 1893 par Mgr d'Hulst, recteur de l'Institut Catholique de Paris, député du Finistère.* Chartres: Garnier, 1893.

Didi-Huberman, Georges. *Invention de l'hystérie: Charcot et l'iconographie photographique de la Salpêtrière.* Paris: Macula, 1982.

Dorgelès, Roland. *Les croix de bois.* Paris: Albin Michel, 1919.

Drevon, Victor, S. J. *Le Coeur de Jésus consolé dans la sainte Eucharistie: Recueil de différentes publications concernant l'oeuvre de la communion réparatrice.* 2 vols. Avignon: Aubanel, 1866.

Driskel, Michael Paul. *Representing Belief: Religion, Art, and Society in Nineteenth-Century France.* University Park: Pennsylvania State University Press, 1992.

du Bouays de la Bégassière, René. *Le drapeau national du Sacré-Coeur.* Paris: Douniol 1898.

———. *Notre culte catholique et français du Sacré-Coeur: Simples aperçus.* Lyon: E. Vitte 1901.

Durand, Yves, Marius Faugeras, Jean Guéhenneuc, Marcel Launay, and Noel-Yves Tonnerre. *Le diocèse de Nantes.* Paris: Beauchesne, 1985.

Duroselle, Jean-Baptiste. *La grande guerre des français, 1914–1918.* Paris: Perrin, 1994.

Duroselle, Jean-Baptiste, and Jean-Marie Mayeur. *Histoire du catholicisme.* Paris: PUF, 1949.

Eliade, Mircea. *Images and Symbols: Studies in Religious Symbolism,* translated by Philip Mairet. New York: Sheed & Ward, 1961.

Ellis, John. *Eye-Deep in Hell: Trench Warfare in World War One.* New York: Pantheon, 1976.

Favreau, Robert. *Le diocèse de Poitiers.* Paris: Beauchesne, 1988.

Ferchaud, Claire. *Autour des notes autobiographiques. Claire des Rinfillières. Témoignages et documents inédits.* Paris: Téqui, 1998.

———. *Notes autobiographiques.* 2 vols. Paris: Téqui, 1974.

Fontana, Jacques. *Les catholiques français pendant la grande guerre.* Paris: Cerf, 1990.

Ford, Caroline. *Creating the Nation in Provincial France: Religion and Political Identity in Brittany.* Princeton: Princeton University Press, 1993.

Fraioli, Deborah A. *Joan of Arc: The Early Debate.* Woodbridge: Boydell, 2000.

Frémont, Georges. *La grande erreur politique des catholiques français.* Paris: Bloud, 1910.

Freppel, Charles-Emile. *Oeuvres polémiques de monseigneur Freppel,* 8 vols. Paris: Palmé, 1881.

Furet, François. *Revolutionary France, 1770–1880,* translated by Antonia Nevill. Oxford: Blackwell, 1992 (English edition of *La révolution de Turgot à Jules Ferry, 1770–1880*).

Gabory, Emile. *Les Bourbons et la Vendée.* Paris: Perrin, 1923.

———. "'L'Union Sacrée' au pays des chouans en 1815." *La Revue de Bas-Poitou* 29 (1916): 43–46.

Gadille, Jacques. *Guide des archives diocesaines françaises.* Lyon: Centre d'histoire du catholicisme, 1971.

———. *La pensée et l'action politiques des évêques français au début de la IIIe République, 1870–1883.* 2 vols. Paris: Hachette, 1967.

Gaétan de Wismes. *Les Loup de la Biliais: Martyrs du Sacré-Coeur d'après des documents inédits.* Vannes: Lafolye, 1898.

Garnier, François, and others. *L'église de Vendée fait mémoire.* Luçon: 1993.

Genet-Delacroix, Marie-Claude. "Esthétique officielle et art national sous la Troisième République." *Le Mouvement Social* 131 (1985): 105–20.

Gérard, Alain. *"Par principe d'humanité . . .": la Terreur et la Vendée.* Paris: Fayard, 1999.

———. *Pourquoi la Vendée.* Paris: Colin, 1990.

Germain, Elisabeth. *Parler du salut? Aux origines d'une mentalité religieuse. La catéchèse du salut dans la France de la Restauration.* Paris: Beauchesne, 1968.

Gibson, Ralph. *A Social History of French Catholicism, 1789–1914.* London: Routledge, 1989.

Gide, André. *Les caves du Vatican.* Paris: Gallimard, 1922.

Gildea, Robert. *The Past in French History.* New Haven: Yale, 1994.

Gilman, Sander, Helen King, Roy Porter, G.S. Rousseau, and Elaine Showalter. *Hysteria Beyond Freud.* Berkeley and Los Angeles: University of California Press, 1993.

Ginisty, Charles. *Verdun! Les souffrances et la grandeur d'âme de la glorieuse cité; ou, Le martyre et la gloire de Verdun.* Paris: Bloud et Gay, 1917.

Girard, René. *La violence et le sacré.* Paris: Bernard Grasset, 1972.

Girault de Coursac, Paul, and Pierrette Girault de Coursac. *Louis XVI et la question religieuse pendant la Révolution.* Paris: OEIL., 1988.

Godechot, Jacques. *La Contre-Révolution: Doctrine et action, 1789–1804.* Paris: PUF, 1961.

Goldstein, Jan. *Console and Classify: The French Psychiatric Profession in the Nineteenth Century.* Cambridge: Cambridge University Press, 1987.

Gordon, Mary. *Joan of Arc.* New York: Viking Penguin, 2000.

Goyau, Georges. *L'Église de France pendant la guerre, août 1914–décembre 1916.* Paris: Bloud et Gay, 1917.

———. "France: État religieux actuel." In *Dictionnaire de théologie catholique,* vol. 6, 630–57. Paris: Letouzey, 1924.

Grégoire, Pierre Marie, Abbé. *Les religieuses nantaises durant la persécution révolutionnaire.* Nantes: privately printed 1920.

Grémillon, Henri Ernest [as Henry Mariavé, pseud.]. *En l'Honneur de Dieu souffrant. Doctrine des apôtres des derniers temps. La grande nouvelle, le message de l'Ésprit, ou le troisième testament.* [n.p.] 1927.

———. *La leçon de l'hôpital Notre-Dame D'Ypres: Exégèse du secret de La Salette.* Montpellier: Firmin et Montane, 1915.

Grente, Joseph. *Les martyrs de septembre 1792 à Paris.* Paris: Téqui, 1926.

Grubb, Alan. *The Politics of Pessimism: Albert De Broglie and Conservative Politics in the Early Third Republic.* Newark: University of Delaware Press, 1996.

Guerin, René, Abbé. *La question du drapeau du Sacré-Coeur.* Angers: Siraudeau, 1918.

Guillon de Montléon, Aimé. *Les martyrs de la foi pendant la révolution française.* 4 vols. Paris: G. Mathiot, 1821.

Guitton, Georges. *Louis Lenoir, jésuite, aumônier militaire (1914–1918).* Paris: Action populaire, 1926.

Gury, Christian. *L'honneur flétri d'un évêque homosexuel en 1937.* Paris: Kimé, 2000.

Hacquet, Pierre-François. *Mémoire des missions des montfortains dans l'ouest, 1740–1779.* Fontenay-le-Comte: Lussaud, 1964.

Hamon, Auguste, S. J. *Histoire de la dévotion au sacré-coeur de Jésus,* 5 vols. Paris: Beauchesne, 1923–1939.

Hardy, Paul. *Discours prononcé à l'occasion de la bénédiction du drapeau du groupe Saint-Martin De Vertou.* Nantes: Bourgeois, 1906.

Harrison, J. F. C. *The Second Coming: Popular Millenarianism, 1780–1850.* New Brunswick, N.J.: Rutgers University Press, 1979.

Hilgers, Joseph. *Livre d'or du coeur de Jésus; pour les prêtres et pour les fidèles: Indulgences et privilèges de la dévotion au coeur de Jésus.* Paris: Lethielleux, 1911.

Horne, Alistair. *The Price of Glory, Verdun, 1916.* London: Macmillan, 1962.

———. *The Seven Ages of Paris: Portrait of a City.* London: Macmillan, 2002.

Huet, François. *Le règne social du christianisme.* Paris: Firmin-Didot, 1853.

Janet, Pierre. *De l'angoisse à l'extase: Études sur les croyances et les sentiments.* Paris: F. Alcan, 1926.

Johnson, Paul E., and Sean Wilentz. *The Kingdom of Matthias: A Story of Sex and Salvation in Nineteenth-Century America.* New York: Oxford, 1994.

Joll, James. *The Origins of the First World War.* London: Longman, 1992.

Jonas, Raymond. "L'Année Terrible, 1870–1871." In *Le Sacré-Coeur de Montmartre: Un voeu national,* edited by Jacques Benoist, 31–41. Paris: DAAVP, 1995.

———. "Anxiety, Identity, and the Displacement of Violence during the *Année Terrible:* The Sacred Heart and the Diocese of Nantes, 1870–1871." *French Historical Studies* 21 (1998): 55–75.

———. *France and the Cult of the Sacred Heart: An Epic Tale for Modern Times.* Berkeley and Los Angeles: University of California Press, 2000.

Joséfa, M. T. *Le général de Sonis, le héros de Patay.* Paris: Tolra et Simonet, 1904.

Jouin, Ernest. *Le drapeau national du Sacré-Coeur: Historique, doctrine, ennemis.* Tours: 1918.

———. *Le péril judéo-maçonnique.* Paris: Revue internationale des sociétés secrètes, 1925.

———. *Le Sacré-Coeur de Jésus et le coeur maçonnique: Les deux étendards.* Tours: 1918.

Kagan, Richard. *Lucrecia's Dreams: Politics and Prophecy in Sixteenth-Century Spain.* Berkeley and Los Angeles: University of California Press, 1995.

Keiger, John F. V. *Raymond Poincaré.* Cambridge: Cambridge University Press, 1997.

Kempe, Margery. *The Book of Margery Kempe,* translated by B. A. Windeatt. Harmondsworth: Penguin, 1985.

Kleeblatt, Norman, ed. *The Dreyfus Affair: Art, Truth, and Justice.* Berkeley and
    Los Angeles: University of California Press, 1987.

Kleinberg, Aviad M. *Prophets in Their Own Country; Living Saints and the
    Making of Sainthood in the Later Middle Ages.* Chicago: University of
    Chicago Press, 1992.

Krumeich, Gerd. *Jeanne d'Arc à travers l'histoire.* Paris: Albin Michel, 1993.

Kselman, Thomas. *Miracles and Prophecies in Nineteenth-Century France.* New
    Brunswick, N.J.: Rutgers University Press, 1983.

Lacouture, Jean. *Jésuites: Une multibiographie.* 2 vols. Paris: Seuil, 1992.

Lacroix, Lucien, Mgr. *Le clergé et la guerre de 1914.* Paris: Bloud et Gay, 1915.

Laligant, Pierre. *Montmartre: La basilique du voeu national du Sacré Coeur.*
    Grenoble: Arthaud, 1933.

[La Motte, Eugène-Louis-Marie Le Fer de]. *Lettre pastorale de Mgr l'évêque de
    Nantes sur la guerre et le retour à Dieu et mandement pour le carême de l'an de
    grâce 1916* [22 février]. Nantes: Mellinet, 1916.

Langlois, Claude. *Le catholicisme au féminin: Les congrégations françaises à la
    supérieure générale au XIXe siècle.* Paris: Cerf, 1984.

———. "La photographie comme preuve entre médecine et religion." *Actes
    du colloque Charcot* 28 (1994): 325–36.

———. "Photographier les saintes: De Bernadette Soubirous à Thérèse de
    Lisieux." In *Histoire, images, imaginaires (fin XVe siècle–début XXe siècle),*
    edited by M. Ménart and A. Duprat, 261–72. Le Mans: Université du
    Maine, 1998.

Laprie, Félix. *Dieu et le peuple nantais: Discours prononcé pour la bénédiction de
    la première pierre de la basilique de Saint-Donatien, le 12 septembre 1873.*
    Nantes: Mellinet, 1873.

Larignon, Gilberte, and Héliette Proust. *Édouard de Monti de Rezé.
    L'inébranlable certitude: Le mouvement légitimiste dans l'ouest.* Laval: Siloë, 1992.

Laurentin, René, ed. *Pontmain: Histoire authentique.* Paris: Lethielleux, 1970.

Le Bras, Gabriel. *L'église et le village.* Paris: Flammarion, 1976.

Lebrun, François. *Le diocèse d'Angers.* Paris: Beauchesne, 1981.

———, ed. *Histoire des catholiques en France du XVe siècle à nos jours.* Toulouse:
    Privat, 1980.

Le Brun, Jacques. "Politics and Spirituality: The Devotion to the Sacred
    Heart." In *The Concrete Christian Life,* edited by Christian Duquoc, 29–43.
    New York: Herder and Herder, 1917.

Lecanuet, Édouard. *L'Église de France sous la troisième république: Les dernières
    années du pontificat de Pie IX, 1870–1878.* Paris: Alcan, 1931.

Le Floch, Henri. *Le Cardinal Billot, lumière de la théologie.* Paris: Beauchesne, 1947.

Le Goff, Jacques, and René Rémond. *Histoire de la France religieuse.* 3 vols. Paris: Seuil, 1988.

Lelièvre, Henri. *Les Ursulines de Bordeaux pendant la Terreur et sous le Directoire.* Bordeaux: Feret, 1896.

Lemius, Jean-Baptiste. *Les grands desseins du Sacré-Coeur de Jésus et la France.* Fecamp: Durand, 1915.

Léniaud, Jean-Baptiste. *Jean-Baptiste Lassus, 1807–1857; ou, Le temps retrouvé des cathédrales.* Paris: 1980.

Lenoir, Louis. *L'Eucharistie au front.* Toulouse: Apostolat de la Prière, 1923.

Leroy, Michel. *Le mythe jésuite de Béranger à Michelet.* Paris: PUF, 1992.

Levillain, Philippe. *Albert de Mun: Catholicisme français et catholicisme romain du syllabus au ralliement.* Rome: École française de Rome, 1983.

Leymarie, Michel. *De la Belle-Époque à la grande guerre, 1893–1918: Le triomphe de la république.* Paris: Livre de poche, 1999.

Lucas de la Championnière, Pierre Suzanne. *Mémoires sur la guerre de Vendée, 1793–1796.* Paris: Plon, 1904.

Maingueneau, Dominique. *Les livres d'école de la république, 1870–1914 (Discours et idéologie).* Paris: Le Sycomore, 1979.

Maître, Jacques. *Mystique et féminité.* Paris: Cerf, 1997.

———. *"L'orpheline de la Bérésina." Thérèse de Lisieux, 1873–1897: Essai de psychanalyse socio-historique.* Paris: Cerf, 1995.

———. *Les stigmates de l'hystérique et la peau de son évêque: Laurentine Billoquet, 1862–1936.* Paris: Anthropos, 1993.

Malcolm, Janet. *The Silent Woman: Sylvia Plath and Ted Hughes.* New York: Vintage, 1995.

Mange, Christian. "Bernard Benezet et l'iconographie du Sacré-Coeur au XIXe siècle." *Histoire de l'Art* 20 (1992): 79–87.

Marcault, Charles. *Le message de 1689 a-t-il été réellement abandonné?* Chinon: Sou de la Presse, 1918.

———. *Cri d'alarme: Les déstructeurs de la France.* Paris: Desclée, De Brouwer, 1932.

———. *Réalisons le message du Sacré-Coeur.* Paris: Desclée de Brouwer, 1934.

Mariavé, Henry (pseud.). *See* Grémillon, Henri.

Martin, Benjamin. *Count Albert De Mun, Paladin of the Third Republic.* Chapel Hill: University of North Carolina Press, 1978.

Martin, Jean-Clément. *La Vendée et la France.* Paris: Seuil, 1987.

Martin, Malachi. *The Jesuits: The Society of Jesus and the Betrayal of the Roman Catholic Church.* New York: Simon and Schuster, 1987.

Martin, Thérèse [Sainte Thérèse de l'Enfant-Jésus]. *Histoire d'une âme, écrite par elle-meme.* Lisieux: Office central de Ste Thérèse, 1925.

————. *Une rose effeuillée: Soeur Thérèse de l'Enfant-Jésus et de la Sainte-Face.* Paris: Saint-Paul, 1911.

Martin, Xavier. *Sur les droits de l'homme et la Vendée.* Bouère: Dominique Martin Morin, 1995.

Matlock, Jann. *Scenes of Seduction: Prostitution, Hysteria, and Reading Difference in Nineteenth-Century France.* New York: Columbia University Press, 1994.

Mazzoni, Cristina. *Saint Hysteria: Neurosis, Mysticism, and Gender in European Culture.* Ithaca, N.Y.: Cornell University Press, 1996.

McManners, John. *Church and State in France, 1870–1914.* New York: Harper and Row, 1972.

McNamara, Jo Ann Kay. *Sisters in Arms: Catholic Nuns through Two Millennia.* Cambridge, Mass.: Harvard University Press, 1996.

Menozzi, Daniele. "Una devozione politica tra '800 e '900: L'intronizzazione del S. Cuore nelle Famiglie." *Rivista di storia e letteratura religiosa* 33 (1997): 29–65.

Michelet, Jules. *Du prêtre, de la femme, de la famille.* Paris: Atheneum, 1845.

Mouton, Claude. *Au plus fort de la tourmente: Claire Ferchaud.* Montsûrs: Editions Résiac, 1983.

Nora, Pierre, ed. *Les lieux de mémoire.* Paris: Gallimard, 1984.

Odelin, Henri-Louis, Mgr. *Le Cardinal Amette, 1850–1920: Souvenirs.* Paris: J. de Gigord, 1926.

Ozouf, Mona. *L'école, l'église et la république, 1871–1914.* Paris: Colin, 1963.

Parenteau, Fé[lix?]. *Médailles vendéens.* Nantes: Guéraud, 1857.

Pernoud, Régine. *Joan of Arc: Her Story,* translated by Jeremy Du Quesnay Adams. New York: St. Martin's Press, 1998.

————. *Joan of Arc by Herself and Her Witnesses,* translated by Edward Hyams. New York: Stein and Day, 1966.

————. *The Retrial of Joan of Arc: The Evidence at the Trial for Her Rehabilitation, 1450–1456,* translated by J. M. Cohen. New York: Harcourt, Brace, [1955].

Perreux, Gabriel, *La vie quotidienne des civils en France pendant la grande guerre.* Paris: Hachette, 1966.

Perroy, Henry. *Le message d'éspoir, 1689: Un temple, une consécration, un drapeau.* Lyon: Vitte, 1918.

Perroy, Louis. *Le drapeau de la France: Une grande idée en marche.* Lyon: Vitte, 1917.

Petroff, Elizabeth Alvilda. *Body and Soul: Essays on Medieval Women and Mysticism.* Oxford: Oxford University Press, 1994.

————, ed. *Medieval Women's Visionary Literature.* New York: Oxford University Press, 1986.

Pierrard, Pierre. *Juifs et catholiques français.* Paris: Fayard, 1970.

Poincaré, Raymond. *L'Invasion, 1914.* Vol. 5 of *Au service de la France: Neuf années de souvenirs.* Paris: Plon, 1928.

Porch, Douglas. *The March to the Marne: The French Army, 1871–1914.* Cambridge: Cambridge University Press, 1981.

Port, Célestin. *La Vendée angevine: Les origines, l'insurrection, janvier 1789–31 mars 1793.* 2 vols. Paris: Hachette, 1888.

Poulain, Édouard. *Pour le drapeau du Sacré-Coeur! Pour le salut de la France!* Beauchesne: Cerizay, 1918.

————. *Pourquoi et quand vaincrons nous?* Paris: Téqui, 1916.

————. *La royauté du Christ, la vocation de la France et le drapeau du Sacré Coeur.* Nantes: Unic, 1919.

————. *La trahison et le drapeau du Sacré-Coeur.* Nantes: Unic, 1918.

Poulat, Emile. *Intégrisme et catholicisme intégral.* Tournai: Casterman, 1969.

————. Les Semaines Religieuses*: Approche socio-historique et bibliographique des bulletins diocésains français.* Lyon: Centre d'histoire du catholicisme, 1973.

Prevotat, Jacques. *Les catholiques et l'action française: Histoire d'une condamnation, 1899–1939.* Paris: Fayard, 2001.

Prouteau, Gilbert. *Église des Lucs-sur-Boulogne: Ses vitraux.* Fontenay-le-Comte: Lussaud, 1946.

Provost [M. l'abbé Provost, chanoine de Chartres]. *Loigny-la-bataille de 1870 à 1912.* Lille: Ducoulombier, 1912.

Ramière, Henry. *L'Apostolat de la prière: Sainte Ligue des coeurs chrétiens unis au Coeur de Jésus. Pour obtenir le triomphe de l'Église et le salut des âmes.* Lyon: Perisse Frères, 1861.

Rapley, Elizabeth. *The* Dévotes*: Women and Church in Seventeenth-Century France.* Montreal and Kingston: McGill-Queen's University Press, 1990.

Ravitch, Norman. *The Catholic Church and the French Nation, 1685–1985.* London: Routledge, 1990.

Redier, Antoine. *Les aumôniers militaires français, 496–1939.* Paris: Flammarion, 1940.

———. *Méditations dans la Tranchée.* Paris: Payot, 1918.

Rémond, René. *L'anticléricalisme en France de 1815 à nos jours.* Paris: Fayard, 1976.

———. *The Right Wing in France from 1815 to De Gaulle.* Philadelphia: University of Pennsylvania Press, 1966.

Rosenbaum-Dondaine, Catherine. *L'image de la piété en France, 1814–1914.* Paris: Musée-Galérie de la Seita, 1984.

Rubin, Miri. *Corpus Christi: The Eucharist in Late Medieval Culture.* Cambridge: Cambridge University Press, 1991.

Sabean, David. *Power in the Blood: Popular Culture and Village Discourse in Early Modern Germany.* Cambridge: Cambridge University Press, 1984.

Sadoul, Georges. *Ce que lisent vos enfants: La presse enfantine en France, son histoire, son évolution, son influence.* Paris: Bureau d'éditions, 1946.

Schmid, A. *Mélanie, bergère de La Salette et le cardinal Perraud: Procès civil et religieux.* Paris: Chamuel, 1898.

Scott, W. S. *Jeanne d'Arc.* London: Harrap, 1974.

———, ed. and trans. *The Trial of Joan of Arc: Being the Verbatim Report of the Proceedings from the Orléans Manuscript.* London: Folio Society, 1956.

Shaw, Bernard. *Saint Joan.* Baltimore: Penguin, 1974.

Siegfried, Agnès. *L'abbé Frémont.* Paris: Alcan, 1932.

Sirinelli, Jean-François, ed. *Histoire des droites en France.* Paris: Gallimard, 1992.

Smith, Leonard V. *Between Mutiny and Obedience: The Case of the French Fifth Infantry Division during World War I.* Princeton: Princeton University Press, 1994.

Sorlin, Pierre. *La Croix et les juifs, 1880–1889: Contribution à l'histoire de l'antisémitisme contemporain.* Paris: Grasset, 1967.

Stern, Jean. *La Salette. Documents authentiques; dossier chronologique intégrale; le procès de l'apparition, fin mars 1847–avril 1849,* 2 vols. Paris: Cerf, 1984.

Sullivan, Karen. *The Interrogation of Joan of Arc.* Minneapolis: University of Minnesota Press, 1999.

Thellier de Poncheville. *Dix mois de Verdun.* Paris: Gigord, 1919.

Tilly, Charles. *The Vendée.* Cambridge, Mass.: Harvard University Press, 1964.

Tisserant, Pierre. *Lettres, 1914–1917.* [n.p.] 1922.

Tombs, Robert. *Nationhood and Nationalism: From Boulanger to the Great War.* London: Harper Collins, 1991.

Touchet, Stanislas-Xavier. *Oraison funèbre du général baron Athanase de Charette, prononcée dans la cathédrale de Nantes, le samedi 2 décembre 1911.* Paris: Lethielleux, 1911.

—————. *La sainte de la patrie* [Jeanne d'Arc]. Paris: Lethielleux, 1921.

Twain, Mark. *Joan of Arc.* San Francisco: Ignatius Press, 1989.

Verdet d'Adhemar, Marie Blanche Angeline. *La femme catholique et la démocratie française.* Paris: Perrin, 1900.

Veuillot, François. *Le Christ-Roi sur Paris.* Paris: Alsatia, 1941.

—————. *La dévotion française de la guerre—Montmartre.* Paris: Bloud et Gay, 1916.

—————. *L'heure de la penitence.* Paris: Editions de Montmartre, 1941.

—————. "Le Père Jean-Baptiste Lemius." *Montmartre* (1938): 8–14.

—————. *Le Sacré-Coeur et les Hommes de France.* Langres: Maitrier et Courtot, 1902.

Waquet, Françoise. *Les fêtes royales sous la restauration; ou, L'ancien régime retrouvé.* Geneva: Droz, 1981.

Warner, Marina. *Joan of Arc: The Image of Female Heroism.* New York: Knopf, 1981.

Weber, Eugen. *Action Française: Royalism and Reaction in Twentieth-Century France.* Stanford: Stanford University Press, 1962.

Weygand, Maxime. *Foch.* Paris: Flammarion, 1947.

Wheeler, Bonnie, and Charles T. Wood, eds. *Fresh Verdicts on Joan of Arc.* New York: Garland, 1996.

Wilson, Stephen, ed. *Saints and Their Cults: Studies in Religious Sociology, Folklore, and History.* Cambridge: Cambridge University Press, 1983.

Winter, J.M. *Sites of Memory, Sites of Mourning: The Great War in European Cultural History.* Cambridge: Cambridge University Press, 1995.

Wormser, Georges. *Le septennat de Poincaré.* Paris: Fayard, 1977.

Wright, Gordon. *Raymond Poincaré and the French Presidency.* Stanford: Stanford University Press, 1942.

Zola, Emile. *Lourdes.* Paris: Charpentier, 1922.

INDEX

Hypnosis, 51–52
Hysteria, 145–52; as entrapment, 146;
  and histrionics, 147

Immaculate Heart of Mary, 44
Immolation, 75
Imperialism, and World War I, 5
Institut Catholique (Catholic
  University, Paris), 107, 158
Islam, 138

Jehovah, 44
Jesuits: and accusations of Jesuit conspiracy, 119; as chaplains, 111; and
  Sacred Heart flag, 90, 138–39
Jesus, visions of, 17–19, 25, 26, 36–37,
  43–46, 48–51; and androgyny,
  78; and prayer card based on
  Claire's visions, 136, 140–41;
  and priests, 78
Jesus as Mother, 45
Joan of Arc, 1, 19–20, 35–36, 47–48,
  51–61, 161; canonization of, 155;
  compared to Claire, 1, 53–61, 63–64,
  153, 155, 158, 161; immolation at
  Rouen, 155; speaking to Claire,
  36–37, 48
Joffre, Jules, 9

Kaiser Wilhelm II, 5, 119
Kempe, Margery, 20

La Rochelle, 15
La Roche-sur-Yon, 154
La Salette, 28, 33, 38, 156
La Tessoualle, 38
Lemius, Jean-Baptiste, 31; as Claire's
  spiritual advisor and confessor, 70,
  73–74; leading novena at

Loublande, 131; personality and
  career, 71–72, 78–79
Lenin, Vladimir, 4–5
Lent, 66
Leo XIII (pope), 141
Lépine (vicar-general, Poitiers), 55, 57
Ligue des Femmes Françaises, 90
Little Flower. *See* Martin, Thérèse
Loire River, 15
Lorraine, 9, 85
Loublande, 33, 35–40, 49, 52, 56, 156;
  chapel opened for Claire in, 142, as
  "vestibule of heaven," 131
Louis XIV, 64, 101
Lourdes, 28, 33, 156, 158. *See also*
  Soubirous, Bernadette
Loutil, Édouard (Pierre l'Ermite),
  77–78, 101
Louvre, 67
Luçon, 103
Lyon, 87–91; and national consecra-
  tion, 106

Maison des Soeurs de la Sagesse (con-
  vent school), 67, 69–70, 149; as
  boarding school, 76
Malvy, Jean-Louis (minister of
  interior), 127
Marcault, Charles, 91
Marinetti, Filippo, 3
Marseille, 101
Martin, Thérèse, 33; compared to
  Claire, 155; in role of Joan of Arc,
  157
Mary (mother of Jesus), visions of, 28,
  36, 39, 48, 50–51
Masonic Order, 106, 159; accused of
  plot against France, 126

Compositor:	International Typesetting & Composition
Cartographer:	Bill Nelson
Text:	11/15 Granjon
Display:	Granjon
Printer and binder:	Thomson-Shore, Inc.